The Future of Marriage

The Future of Marriage

David Blankenhorn

ENCOUNTER BOOKS
NEW YORK

First edition published in 2007 by Encounter Books, an activity of Encounter for Culture and Education, Inc., a nonprofit, tax exempt corporation.

Encounter Books website address: www.encounterbooks.com

Manufactured in the United States and printed on acid-free paper.

The paper used in this publication meets the minimum requirements of ANSI/NISO Z39.48-1992 (R 1997)(Permanence of Paper).

Library of Congress Cataloging-in-Publication Data

Blankenhorn, David.
The future of marriage / by David Blankenhorn.
p. cm.
ISBN 1-59403-081-2 (alk. paper)
1. Marriage. 2. Marriage—History. 3. Same-sex marriage.
I. Title.
HQ503.B53 2007
306.84'8—dc22

2006025736

10 9 8 7 6 5 4 3 2 1

The Future of Marriage

David Blankenhorn

ENCOUNTER BOOKS
NEW YORK

First edition published in 2007 by Encounter Books, an activity of Encounter for Culture and Education, Inc., a nonprofit, tax exempt corporation.

Encounter Books website address: www.encounterbooks.com

Manufactured in the United States and printed on acid-free paper.

The paper used in this publication meets the minimum requirements of ANSI/NISO Z39.48-1992 (R 1997)(Permanence of Paper).

Library of Congress Cataloging-in-Publication Data

Blankenhorn, David.
The future of marriage / by David Blankenhorn.
p. cm.
ISBN 1-59403-081-2 (alk. paper)
1. Marriage. 2. Marriage—History. 3. Same-sex marriage.
I. Title.
HQ503.B53 2007
306.84'8—dc22

2006025736

10 9 8 7 6 5 4 3 2 1

Dedicated to John W. Miller

Married love between man and woman is bigger than oaths, guarded by right of nature.

—*Aeschylus,* The Furies *(458 BCE)*

Is not marriage an open question, when it is alleged, from the beginning of the world, that such as are in the institution wish to get out, and such as are out wish to get in?

—*Ralph Waldo Emerson,* Representative Men *(1850)*

But the love relationship between a man and a woman becomes a marriage when it is entered into in the recognition that the personal feelings of both partners—no matter how much they had based upon them—must be subordinate to, and serve, an idea that for both of them is higher than love itself, the kind of idea that as a rule exacts the lifetime of both, and whose demands may reach even further.

—*Karen Blixen,* On Modern Marriage *(1924)*

Contents

Introduction

In the summer of 2003, I had lunch with Evan Wolfson, the executive director of Freedom to Marry, a group advocating equal marriage rights for same-sex couples. He wanted me to speak out publicly in favor of expanding marriage to include gay and lesbian couples. I hemmed, hawed, and equivocated. He had anger and urgency. I had anguish and doubts.

Some of our discussion concerned moral values. With passion, Evan spoke about equal human dignity. With passion, I told him that every child deserves a mother and a father.

He also offered me hardheaded political analysis. Sooner or later, the movement for same-sex marriage is going to win, he said. People like me—people who for years have been writing and speaking about the importance of marriage—have a choice: We can influence the course of events by getting in front of the issue and welcoming same-sex couples to the institution of marriage. Or, through our silence and equivocation, we can guarantee our irrelevance while also being viewed publicly as providing, at least indirectly, aid and comfort to some very bigoted people.

This book stems in part from that conversation. For starters, I didn't like the fact that in talking to Evan I was troubled and a bit defensive, unsure of what I finally believed. Had I really thought the issue through? Maybe I hadn't. Maybe I should.

Second, while no one knows the future, and while no one should trim one's conscience to fit current odds, I also believe that Evan's political analysis of the same-sex marriage issue is probably accurate. The change may well happen. And if it does, the people who opposed it will likely be viewed essentially as bigots. That second likelihood stings me personally in ways that Evan could not know. I was born in 1955 in Jackson, Mississippi. The civil rights movement of the 1960s was the morally paradigmatic experience of my life. One result is that I am a lifelong Democrat. Although my work on family issues sometimes prompts those who disagree with me to call me a conservative, I have always thought of myself essentially as a liberal. The last thing I want—the last thing my guilty-southern-white-boy self-understanding could take—is to be viewed as a bigot.

Third, as a moral matter, Evan is surely right to insist upon the equal dignity of all persons. This still-revolutionary principle—"all men [persons] are created equal"—deeply informs the American experience and character and is increasingly viewed globally as the essential universal moral law. On the issue of same-sex marriage, is this profound principle of equal dignity the heart of the matter? After all, part of the reason why the principle is so revolutionary is that it can grow and deepen over time. Groups that had long been considered effectively outside of its moral reach—African Americans, women, people of certain colors or languages or religions—can over time, and often as a result of great struggle, enter into its protective sphere. I believe that today the principle of equal human dignity must apply to gay and lesbian persons. In that sense, insofar as we are a nation founded on this principle, we would be *more* American on the day we permitted same-sex marriage than we were the day before.

This argument is a powerful and challenging one. It demands our intellectual and moral attention.

In talking to Evan, I also realized that we disagreed fundamentally on the matter of children. Other than telling me that he thought children were "adaptable," he seemed hardly interested in the issue, as if he had never really thought about it. For example, when I told him that marriage as an institution is centrally concerned with procreation in all human societies, he rejected the idea out of hand, proposing instead that marriage as a natural human institution is largely about private property. In this book, I try to show in some detail that he and others are wrong on this point. I mention it now only to show that for Evan, insofar as I understand his argument, marriage is fundamentally about the rights of adults.

For me, marriage is fundamentally about the needs of children. And in thinking and writing about it for nearly two decades, I have come to believe one thing with more certainty than anything else: What children need most are mothers and fathers. Not caregivers. Not parent-like adults. Not even "parents." What a child wants and needs more than anything else are the mother and the father who together made the child, who love the child, and who love each other. As G. K. Chesterton once said in a similar context, "That I know is a good thing.... If other things are against it, other things must go down."[1]

In recent decades, of course, the marital conduct of heterosexuals in the United States has done much to erode both the ideal and the reality of the mother-father childrearing union. Many advocates of same-sex marriage are only too happy to highlight this fact, and in one respect their point is a fair one. Why draw the line at same-sex marriage when we as a society seem to be unwilling to draw the line anywhere else? At the same time, for anyone who wishes the institution well, the concern remains. Redefining marriage to include gay and lesbian couples would eliminate entirely in law, and weaken still further in culture, the basic idea of a mother and a father for every child. Once this proposed reform became law, even to say the words out loud in public—"Every child needs a father and a mother"—would probably be viewed as explicitly divisive and discriminatory, possibly even as hate speech. For card-carrying child advocates and marriage nuts like me and my colleagues, this possibility is disturbing.

Many thinkers, perhaps most notably Isaiah Berlin, the great twentieth-century philosopher of liberalism, have pointed out that many important choices we face do not involve choosing between good and bad, but between good and good. It is good to deter crime by punishing criminals; it is also good to forgive. But doing more punishing means doing less forgiving, because the two goods are, to some extent, mutually exclusive.

Berlin's concept of goods in conflict is central to my understanding of society's need to make choices regarding the definition of marriage.[2] One good is the equal dignity of all persons. Another good is a mother and a father as a child's birthright. These goods are at least partially in conflict. Resolving that conflict—making a morally responsible choice about the future of marriage that is faithful to the essential purposes of the institution while at least recognizing both of these goods—is a major aim of this book.

I also hope that this book will help us expand today's intense media and public policy focus on same-sex marriage to an equally intense focus on marriage itself. After all, the term "same-sex marriage," though I use it in deference to its popularity and as a shorthand, is in some respects misleading and even patronizing, as some of its strongest proponents have pointed out. What gay and lesbian leaders are demanding is not a special status, not marriage with an asterisk or with a qualifying adjective in front. What they demand is simply marriage. So the question of marriage itself—what it is and why it matters—is surely where this debate ultimately leads.

It is important to consider the issue of "freedom to marry," meaning access to the institution, since it dominates the current marriage debate. But focusing too narrowly on it is harmfully incomplete, even arbitrary. Freedom to marry . . . in order to do what? What exactly *is* this institution to which some of our fellow citizens are so keen to gain access? Why do we have it in the first place? Where did it come from? How is it changing? What do we want its future to be? Why, even as so many of us fail at it and sometimes even mock it, do we still seem to feel so strongly about it?

To me, these are the essential questions. Without confronting them, we can never resolve or even seriously discuss "same-sex marriage." But irrespective of the eventual legal status of same-sex couples, for anyone who cares about the well-being of children and the vitality of our society, these questions about marriage are the fundamental domestic issues facing the United States today.

Marriage is the first and most important of society's institutions. The emergence of marriage as a way of living is arguably the decisive turning point in our history as a species. The institutionalization of marriage likely occurred simultaneously with and helped to advance our transition from prehistory to history—from the original primate condition, or what political philosophers call the "state of nature," to civilization. For this reason, the seventeenth-century English political philosopher John Locke, whose writings deeply influenced the men and women who founded the United States, properly calls marriage the "first Society."[3]

Let us step back a moment and try to look with fresh eyes. Imagine that you are an anthropologist from Mars, sent to Earth.

Your mission is to report back on these creatures called humans. What do they look like? What do they do? How do they organize themselves? How are they currently faring?

If you've been trained, as anthropology field researchers typically are, to begin at the beginning—to start with the most fundamental issues—you will report a cluster of related facts: Humans are social; they live in groups. They strongly seek to reproduce themselves. They are sexually embodied. They carry out sexual (not asexual) reproduction. And they have devised an institution to bridge the sexual divide, facilitate group living, and carry out reproduction. All human societies have this institution. They call it "marriage."

Let's zoom in closer. You are in North America, in a place called the United States, looking for more detail. In part, marriage there looks like marriage everywhere else. But this society also has its own particular marriage culture and traditions, which change over time. How is the institution faring here?

The evidence is mixed, but the overall answer is "not well." Interestingly, in many respects the society as a whole appears to be doing swimmingly at the moment. But not so for marriage—especially when analyzed as a social institution rather than merely a bunch of private relationships, and especially when assessed from the perspective of the offspring.

Marriage is society's most pro-child institution. Yet in the United States, more than one of every three children born today is born to a never-married mother.[4] About 40 percent of all first-time births are to unmarried mothers.[5] The United States probably has the highest divorce rate in the world.[6] More than 40 percent of all first marriages here are likely to end in divorce.[7] The divorce rates for second and third marriages are higher than for first marriages.[8] More than half of all U.S. children will spend at least a significant part of their childhood living apart from their father.[9]

In a famous speech at Howard University in 1965, President Lyndon Johnson called for a "War on Poverty." While the underlying sources of poverty in the United States are multiple and overlapping, the president said, "perhaps the most important" is "the breakdown of the Negro family structure."[10] Today, the breakdown of *white* family structure—the disintegration of marriage among whites—almost exactly matches the level of marriage breakdown among African Americans in 1965, a level that was viewed at the time by the federal government as a national emergency and the main reason for a significant antipoverty mobilization!

Was President Johnson right to link marriage trends to poverty trends and to trends in overall child well-being? Yes, *definitively,* we now know. And therein hangs a scholarly and political tale of some consequence.

In the 1970s and well into the 1980s, most U.S. family scholars insisted that child well-being is *not* substantially or causally related to marriage and family structure. A few dissidents argued that it is. The disagreements were intense and passionately felt—quite a few of the participants used sharp elbows as well as data and sweet reason. The stakes seemed high. The Institute for American Values, the think tank that I founded with some colleagues in 1988 and currently direct, was created primarily as a place for scholarly dissidents on this issue to meet and collaborate.

Today, scholarly opinion has shifted dramatically. One of the main intellectual struggles of the past generation is now largely over, because one side has won. As new research findings poured in, especially during the late 1980s and the 1990s, and as the weight of evidence became increasingly obvious to most people, yesterday's fighting words gradually became the new scholarly conventional wisdom: *Marriage matters.* It significantly influences individual and societal well-being. Most importantly, the health of our children is strongly linked to the health of marriage.

Some scholars, especially those who dislike marriage, lament this change of view. Many of them cut their academic teeth by accusing others of being nostalgic for the 1950s, but today they themselves are more than a little nostalgic for the 1970s. They have become the new dissidents. But almost no one denies that the shift in scholarly opinion has occurred or that it has important consequences for policy and for the larger public debate.

In the mid to late 1990s, what many of us call a "marriage movement" emerged in the United States. Today that movement is led by a growing and promiscuously diverse group of educators, counselors, service providers, public officials, researchers, community organizers, religious and civic leaders, and others. It cuts across political, racial, gender, and class lines. The movement's core goal, as articulated by more than a hundred of its leaders in a joint statement in 2000 and reaffirmed in 2004, is "to turn the tide on marriage and reduce divorce and unwed child bearing, so that each year more children will grow up protected by their own two happily married parents, and so that each year more adults' marriage dreams will come true."[11]

For three decades, marriage advocates have been grumbling that everything is getting worse. We need to break this habit. Some things have stopped getting worse; a few are getting better. For the first time in decades, there is some mildly encouraging demographic news. Divorce rates are declining modestly.[12] Rates of unwed childbearing, after increasing sharply year after year for decades, leveled off considerably from about 1995 to 2003, although a troubling rise was reported for 2004.[13] Teen pregnancy rates have declined dramatically.[14] Rates of reported marital happiness, after declining steadily from the early 1970s through the early 1990s, have stabilized and may be rising.[15] By far the gladdest tiding is that from 1995 to 2000, the proportion of African American children living in married-couple homes rose by about 4 percent.[16] Among all U.S. children, the proportion living in married-couple homes has apparently stabilized and may have increased slightly in the late 1990s.[17] For the time being, at least, we may have the wind at our backs.

"On the heels of a fatherhood movement," wrote Alex Kotlowitz in late 2002 in the *New York Times*, more and more young couples in inner cities "are considering marriage."[18] Kotlowitz's *Frontline* documentary on PBS television, "Let's Get Married," focused on the "burgeoning marriage movement." As Kotlowitz reported, "Now, everyone from the government to intellectuals are pushing marriage."

There is a "growing consensus," wrote the syndicated columnist Jane Eisner in early 2003, that "the central question of American life" now is: "How do we strengthen marriage as the primary social institution to rear children?" Reflecting on the year 2002, she wrote:

> Liberals, in particular, heard the wake-up call this year. No longer confined to the outer reaches of the Religious Right, the "marriage movement" is moving center stage, as those on the political left are belatedly adding their voices to this necessary debate.[19]

We in the United States are currently in the midst of what might be called a marriage moment—a time of unusual, perhaps unprecedented, national preoccupation with the status and future of marriage. One reason for this is the growing public and scholarly concern over the weakness of the institution, and particularly the effects of this weakness on the well-being of children. This concern is broadly based and has been building steadily for at least a decade. A second reason, closely connected to the first, is the emergence of the marriage movement. A third reason, currently dominant, is the controversy over same-sex marriage, which erupted in full force in the United States in mid 2003, making the marriage debate much hotter and more political. A major task of the marriage movement today is to understand and deal with this new challenge.

Marriage enthusiasts like me tend to be anguished over this controversy. We fret: How long must the tail wag the dog? Will the entire marriage debate for the foreseeable future be subsumed under the question of how we feel about homosexuality? What about the encouraging trends of the past decade? Will they be threatened or even undone by a fundamental redefinition of marriage? Is all the hope and work that so many have invested in the project of strengthening marriage—I suppose one is now obligated to specify *heterosexual* marriage—going be overwhelmed and even negated by the current controversy?

More positively, is there a way for the marriage movement to sue for peace and tone down this culture war? Search for a compromise on the grounds that we all have to find a way to live together? Perhaps even, as Evan Wolfson suggested, try to get in front of the issue rather than trail behind it, breathing dust?

If our national debate on same-sex marriage is finally to be redemptive rather than divisive, it needs to meet two tests. First, it must not only accept but also deepen and advance the principle that all persons are equal in rights and dignity. Second, it must also help us rediscover and renew marriage as the main protector of our children and our primary social institution. My central aim in this book is to confront the issue of same-sex marriage by confronting the issue of marriage itself. I hope that doing so will give aid to the marriage movement, potentially the most important domestic initiative of our time.

An Overview

> *"What's your proposition?" I says. "Let's have a proposition."*
> *—John le Carré,* The Incongruous Spy[20]

The first five chapters of this book focus on one question: *What is marriage?* For most people active in today's marriage debate, the answer requires only a few words. Marriage, they say, is a commitment between two people. It is an intimate, caring relationship. It is an expression of love. Any questions before we move on?

But these answers are wildly inadequate. And the issue of definition is anything but an academic quibble; the real-world stakes are quite high. The puerile formulations that currently dominate our debate tend to prevent us—often, I sense, they are *designed* to prevent us—from seriously examining the meaning and possibility of same-sex marriage. More generally, I am convinced that such treacly, greeting-card definitions of marriage, avoiding any hint of its institutional weight and public authority, have become a barrier to understanding what marriage in our society actually is.

The chapters aiming at a definition of marriage do not pretend to be a comprehensive history of marriage. As an institution, marriage has been around for at least five thousand years and exists in all or nearly all known human societies. That extraordinarily thick history could hardly fit into one book. Faced with a topic of such dimensions, most scholars choose to examine marriage in one society or a related cluster of societies, and to concentrate on a specific period of time. These studies are invaluable, yet they also tend toward near-sightedness. In particular, such carefully targeted monographs can usually tell us little or nothing about marriage as a cross-cultural human institution.

Another possible approach is to attempt a grand synthesis—a sky-level overview of the entire world history of the institution, from the earliest hunter-gatherers to contemporary Indonesian marriage to the "marriage gap" in the 2004 U.S. presidential election. The historian Stephanie Coontz makes precisely this attempt in her recent book, *Marriage, a History.*[21] In my view, books of this type usually suffer from serious shortcomings. Even the best of them—such as George Elliot Howard's three-volume *A History of*

Matrimonial Institutions (1904), Willystine Goodsell's *A History of the Family As a Social and Educational Institution* (1915), and Edward Westermarck's deservedly famous three-volume *History of Human Marriage* (1922)—necessarily leave out a great deal of material while skimming too quickly over too much.[22] Coontz's *Marriage, a History,* though more current, is a clear example of glossing marriage's history in a way that is superficial and unsatisfying.[23]

So this book is not a history of marriage, but it does aim to capture the essence of marriage as a human institution. What is it? When and how did it emerge? What are its basic purposes? Why do all societies have it? What are its primary institutional features? What are its core public meanings?

To answer these questions, I use an approach that blends history with anthropology, combining a few case studies with systematic cross-cultural analysis. It details a few episodes and turning points in the story of marriage—the biological and evolutionary roots of this way of living; the earliest historical record of marriage as a social institution; and marriage's role in a matrilineal society with much sexual freedom and unusually egalitarian gender roles. At the same time, it draws conclusions about marriage as a universal or nearly universal human institution.

The final three chapters ask, *What is marriage's future?* A major theme in these chapters is today's controversy over same-sex marriage. How should we understand it? What are the goods at stake on both sides of the issue? How would adopting gay marriage be likely to affect the future of marriage? But these chapters are not finally about gay marriage or about public policy affecting same-sex couples. Rather, they examine the new demand for equal marriage rights for same-sex couples in order to reach conclusions about what marriage's future should and can be. Here I repeatedly employ two rather awkward terms: *deinstitutionalization* and *reinstitutionalization*. I could not think of adequate substitutes, and to me these ideas are extremely important. In fact, I believe that nearly everything about the future of marriage hinges on them.

1

What Is Marriage?

MARRIAGE IS A UNIVERSAL institution, present in all known human societies. But there is no single, universally accepted *definition* of marriage—partly because the institution is constantly evolving, and partly because many of its features vary across groups and cultures.

Many attempts to define marriage over the centuries have been intellectually serious; some have been less so. Many have aimed at comprehensiveness. Some have been ennobling; others have been more pedestrian. But in the long sweep of this history, and amidst all this variability, of this we may be fairly certain: For sheer cultural illiteracy and intellectual vacuity, nothing can top the debate over the meaning of marriage taking place in the United States of America in the early years of the twenty-first century.

"Marriage is, more than anything else, the expression of love," writes Gregg Easterbrook of the *New Republic*.[1] For David Brooks, a *New York Times* columnist, marriage is a "sacred bond" in which two people "make an exclusive commitment to one another."[2] For Richard Cohen, a *Washington Post* columnist, the "last, best" meaning of marriage is "love and commitment."[3] Barbara Risman, a sociology professor who writes frequently about families, says approvingly: "Now marriage is seen by most people as love, intimacy, happiness."[4]

The scholar and journalist E. J. Graff has written a book entitled *What Is Marriage For?* Her answer is that marriage is "a commitment to live up to the rigorous demands of love, to care for each other as best you humanly can."[5] Andrew Sullivan, a prominent advocate of same-sex marriage, writes that "the essence of a good marriage is not breeding or even the romantic love that can blind us while it overwhelms us," but instead "a unique and profound *friendship*."[6]

In a court brief, thirty U.S. professors of history and family law explain to the judges that "the history of marriage" is "a history of change." Fine, but what is the thing that is changing? The scholars say that marriages, in essence, are "committed, interdependent partnerships between consenting adults." Marriage is therefore the state's "formal mechanism for recognizing adult partnerships."[7]

Nathaniel Frank, who teaches history at New School University in New York, writes: "The main reason marriage is considered good for society is that committed relationships help settle individuals into stable homes and families." Marriage fosters these committed relationships through "collective rules" that "strengthen obligations."[8] For the editors of the *Economist*, "the real nature of marriage" is a commitment "between two people to take on special obligations to one another."[9]

Writing in the *Olympian*, the journalist Dawn Barron defines marriage as "a personal journey" and "a commitment of two consenting adults who choose to live their lives connected."[10] Writing in the *Cincinnati Enquirer*, the teacher and guest editorialist Rich Schmaltz announces, "Marriage is cohabitation." Anything else? No, not really. Beyond living together, he tells us, referring to himself and his wife, "We define our relationship."[11] In the *Philadelphia Inquirer*, the syndicated columnist Crispin Sartwell puts it this way:

> Marriage is sometimes referred to as an "institution," but that's an odd application of the term. The Department of Defense is an institution. The University of California is an institution. A marriage is a private arrangement between parties committed to love.[12]

Let's call in the lawyers. In 2002, after more than a decade of deliberation, the prestigious American Law Institute published a report calling for major changes in U.S. family law, including eliminating many of the legal distinctions between married and unmarried couples. For these family law professionals, marriage can hardly be defined at all. They see marriage as radically subjective and almost infinitely malleable—really nothing more than a collection of discrete relationships and private accommodations. At one point in the report we learn that marriage should be understood as "an emotional enterprise, filled with high returns and high risks." Beyond this, it turns out that each marriage is unique: "Different couples arrive at different accommodations in their relationships, and some depart from social conventions. Intimate relationships often involve complex emotional bargains that make no sense to third parties with different needs and perceptions."[13] All we can say for sure, it appears, is that marriage is an emotional enterprise.

In 2003, the Supreme Judicial Court of Massachusetts issued a ruling effectively requiring the state legislature to take steps to redefine marriage to include same-sex couples. The essence of marriage, the court said, is "the exclusive commitment of two individuals to each other." The purposes of this commitment are "love," "mutual support," and a way of living that brings "stability to our society." The justices also wrote that "marriage is at once a deeply personal commitment to another human being and a highly public celebration of the ideals of mutuality, companionship, intimacy, fidelity, and family."[14]

In 2004, a superior court judge in the state of Washington ruled that same-sex couples can marry under Washington State law. In his ruling, Judge William L. Downing offered this definition: "To 'marry' means to join together in a close and permanent way." Rephrased a bit, marriage is "a close personal commitment" that "is intended to be permanent." Judge Downing added that such close, intended-to-be-permanent commitments are "spiritually significant."[15]

In 2005, a judge on the Supreme Court of the State of New York ruled that a New York State law effectively limiting marriage to male-female couples was unconstitutional. In her ruling, Justice Doris Ling-Cohan defined marriage as "the utmost expression of a couple's commitment and love," and as "a unique expression of a private bond and profound love between a couple." It is "highly personal" and "the most intimate of relationships." People who marry "publicly commit to a lifetime partnership with the person of their choosing." In addition, marriage is a basic right; it "provides an extensive legal structure" of practical benefits and protections; and it is constantly evolving.[16]

Canadian lawyers are also busy redefining marriage—as something that can't really be defined. In 2001, the Law Commission of Canada published an influential report entitled *Beyond Conjugality: Recognizing and Supporting Close Personal Adult Relationships.* Their central recommendation, as the report's title suggests, was that Canadian law should end (or move "beyond") its focus on the *form* of interpersonal relationships and instead focus on the "substance." For the commission, an example of wrongly dwelling on *form* is when the law asks: Is this couple married? Another example is when the law inquires: Does this couple consist of a man and a woman living together in a sexual relationship? (That's what the commission means by "conjugal.") By contrast, *substance* questions are when the law asks: Do these individuals care for and support one another? Have they voluntarily chosen to enter into a close personal relationship?

You get the idea. If the Law Commission of Canada has its way, marriage is basically out, and legal close relationships are in. But along the way, the commission does take the time to define marriage. On the one hand, it is a "form" that the law needs to get "beyond"; but it also is "a means of facilitating in an orderly fashion the voluntary assumption of mutual rights and obligations by adults committed to each other's well-being." As for government's legitimate interest in this facilitation of interpersonal commitment, the report says: "The state's objectives underlying contemporary regulation of marriage relate essentially to the facilitation of private ordering: providing an orderly framework in which people can express their commitment to each other, receive public recognition and support, and voluntarily assume a range of legal rights and obligations."[17] In short, marriage is merely the public recognition of private ordering in which people express commitment to one another.

These definitions are typical of the current debate. They are also radically insubstantial. Some of the words are sweet enough and true enough, but one searches in vain for any recognition of the fact that marriage might be something more than a private close relationship between two people.

I am not an unusually gregarious person, but I have "expressed love" to quite a few people in my life. I have a number of profound friendships and some intense personal commitments, all of which seem to me to be emotional enterprises. I am involved in a number of mutually supportive relationships, many of which, I am sure, enhance social stability. But none of this information tells you to whom I am married or why.

Consider the same matter from a societal perspective. Why does society care about marriage at all? Why do we bother with marriage laws? Is it because society feels obliged to structure and guide lasting friendships and emotional enterprises? Is there a compelling state interest in regulating expressions of love? Of course not. In such formulations, we end up playing a version of the children's game "Where's Waldo?" We are trying on every page to find Waldo, but he is nearly impossible to locate in all the clutter and seemingly intentional confusion.

Mae West once reportedly deadpanned that "marriage is a great institution . . . but I'm not ready for an institution." Neither are these fluttery definitions. Yet defining marriage as essentially a private emotional relationship obscures a large piece of reality. Notwithstanding Crispin Sartwell's opinion and Mae West's personal choices, and notwithstanding the American Law Institute's ludicrous assertions, marriage *is* in fact what sociologists call a social institution—a socially structured way of living, intended largely to meet *social* needs. Childrearing is probably the single most important social need that marriage is designed to meet, but there are numerous others as well. We do not build social institutions around purely private emotional connections that no third party can understand. If marriage does not have a valid, comprehensible public dimension, then marriage for all intents and purposes does not exist.

Next, consider the fact that these highly abstract definitions, in what would appear to be a sudden attack of Victorian prudery, all conspicuously fail to utter the secret word. That secret word is "sex." Having sex. Being sexually jealous and sexually exclusive. Sweaty, needy, flesh-and-blood, behind-closed-doors sex. Marriage is about many things, but until about five minutes ago, among certain let's-don't-say-it commentators, hardly anyone in the world ever pretended that marriage is not fundamentally about socially approved sexual intercourse. Which is why, in law and cultures everywhere, to consummate a marriage is to have sexual intercourse; and why refusing to consummate a marriage with sexual intercourse is almost universally viewed as a negation of the marriage and therefore as grounds for divorce; and why everyone knows that the term "marriage bed" means the place where the spouses have sex.

After all, what one assumption does everyone make about married couples? That they are involved in an emotional enterprise? Of course not. *It's that the spouses are having sex with one another!* Yet today in the United States, as we debate the future of the most important sexual institution ever devised by our species, we seem quite determined to define it in strictly asexual terms. It's like defining General Motors without mentioning cars.

There is another word almost entirely missing from the currently prevailing definitions of marriage. It's a word closely related to matters of sexual embodiment and sexual intercourse. That word is "children"—or what Andrew Sullivan calls "breeding." Children rarely make an appearance in the thin descriptions of marriage as a personal commitment or an expression of love. Mostly, they are not seen and not heard.

In fact, the Supreme Judicial Court of Massachusetts in its 2002 opinion explicitly considers and then rejects as "inappropriate" the view that marriage is centrally concerned with bearing and raising children. The justices point out that people applying for marriage licenses in Massachusetts do not have to prove that they are fertile and intend to have children. Moreover, "the Commonwealth affirmatively facilitates bringing children into a family regardless of whether the intended parent is married or unmarried, whether the child is adopted or born into a family, whether assisted technology was used to conceive the child, and whether the parent or her partner is heterosexual, homosexual, or bisexual."[18] The justices make their case with admirable clarity. Marriage and procreation are hereby defined as separate and unconnected. Adult emotional ties are over here where it says "marriage." Children are over there.

Yet this way of understanding marriage presents a formidable intellectual problem. For many centuries and across human cultures, virtually all scholars, jurists, and other commentators on marriage have emphasized that marriage as a human institution is deeply connected to bearing and raising children. Surveying the cross-cultural evidence, the anthropologist Helen Fisher sums it up simply: "People wed primarily to reproduce."[19]

Bertrand Russell was no friend of conventional sexual morality. But he recognized clearly enough that "it is through children alone that sexual relations become of importance to society, and worthy to be taken cognizance of by a legal institution." Thus: "The main purpose of marriage is to replenish the human population of the globe."[20]

Fisher is right. Russell was right. Without children, marriage as institution makes little sense.

After all, why did we humans invent marriage in the first place? Why do we keep it around? Here is a proposition that cannot be empirically proven, but that is almost certainly true. If human beings did not reproduce sexually and did not start out in life as helpless infants—if, for example, new humans arrived on earth fully grown, brought to society by storks—our species would never have developed an institution called marriage. We would be doing many interesting things, but getting married would not be among them. Accordingly, to insist that we erase children from our formal understanding of marriage comes very close to insisting that marriage itself makes no formal sense.

Notice also the circularity of this argument. What purports to be a definition—marriage is not connected to children—is in fact a redefinition that ends up negating the very thing being defined. Before our very eyes, the task of understanding marriage becomes a going-out-of-business sale.

In fact, the justices in Massachusetts, with seeming equanimity, contemplate precisely this prospect: The concept of "marriage"—"civil unions" or other similar terms, the justices make clear, simply won't do—is so important that denying it to same-sex couples means that they are "excluded from the full range of human experience." But why is this particular concept so important? On this point, the justices are stunningly inarticulate. Marriage, they tell us, is two people making a commitment to one another. We get sugary pieties—marriage "fulfills yearnings for security, safe haven, and connection"—that have almost no concrete meaning.[21] Then we are informed bluntly that marriage is essentially unconnected to having sex or to bearing and raising children.

Where does this logic lead us? In a 2004 follow-up opinion on the same set of issues, the justices in a curious aside opine that one "rational and permissible" strategy of achieving equality under the law in Massachusetts might be for the legislature to "jettison the term 'marriage' altogether."[22] Let's sum up their argument: Marriage is a vitally important word. The word has no meaning that anyone can pin down. One possible answer is to jettison the word altogether.

Why such intellectual anemia over this word? Part of the reason is the intensity of the debate over same-sex marriage. Proponents of equal marriage rights for gays and lesbians seldom focus centrally or specifically on sex, childrearing, or other aspects of marriage suggestive of a multipurpose social institution. Even as they seek access for same-sex couples to whatever remains of marriage's larger communal meanings, these advocates typically insist that we define marriage itself basically as an intimate personal commitment and a private close relationship. But the same-sex marriage debate is not the only reason for our intellectual muddle, or even the main reason.

A much more important cause is the way that heterosexuals have treated heterosexual marriage in recent decades. Leave aside for now the explosive increases in divorce, unwed childbearing, and children growing up in one-parent homes. Leave aside as well the sustained intellectual assault on marriage from those who view it as a failed and even dangerous institution. (My colleagues and I have spent years pursuing those topics in some detail.) Instead, consider the underlying change in how many Americans—straight as well as gay, ordinary citizens as well as opinion leaders, people who dislike marriage as well as many who like it quite a bit—have come to regard the very meaning of marriage.

One view is that the vow is prior to the couple. The vow—the way of living together as wife and husband, the institution—exists on its own, exerting authority that is independent of the couple. In a sense, the vow helps to create the couple. On their wedding day, couples become accountable to an ideal of marriage that is outside of them and bigger than they are.

A newer view is that the couple is prior to the vow. The way of living, the institution, is less an external reality, like the weather, than a subjective projection that derives its meaning almost entirely from the particular couple. Instead of the vow creating the couple, the couple creates the vow—which is literally the case in many, probably most, weddings today, where couples compose their own, individualized vows. (My wife and I did this when we married in 1986; most couples we know did.) As a result, each marriage can be viewed as unique, like a painting or a snowflake.

These two views reflect strikingly divergent conceptions of marriage. One view seeks to make the couple fit marriage. The other seeks to make marriage fit the couple. In one view, society presents a socially composed norm to the couple. In the other, the couple presents a privately composed norm to society. In the former view, marriage defines me. In the latter view, I define marriage.

The most important trend affecting marriage in America—far more consequential in the long run than arguing about same-sex marriage, or even expanding our definition to include it—is the belief that marriage is exclusively a private relationship, created by and for the couple, essentially unconnected to larger social needs and public meanings. This view has deep roots in our society and has been growing for decades, propagated overwhelmingly by heterosexuals, focusing on heterosexual marriage.

For example, in the early 1960s a majority of Americans believed that spouses in a troubled marriage should stay together for the sake of the children. Today the great majority of Americans believe the opposite.[23] What has changed is not our love for our children, but our underlying conception of what marriage is.[24] The growing belief is that marriage is less about the vow and society than about the private needs and feelings of the spouses. To the degree that this belief informs the debate on same-sex marriage, we should understand it not as a novel idea, specifically connected to homosexuality, but instead as one manifestation of a broader conception of marriage in our society.

Accordingly, the great challenge of our time lies neither in defending nor in thwarting same-sex marriage. The challenge is to renew marriage as a powerful way of living that calls forth and reflects the best in us, that successfully meets important social needs, and that is worthy of strong social support. If we could move toward this goal by embracing same-sex marriage, I would gladly embrace it. If adopting same-sex marriage was likely to be part of a larger societal shift leading to better marriages, less divorce, and less unwed childbearing—or, more modestly, if it seemed likely that adopting same-sex marriage would not significantly *undermine* efforts to renew our wider marriage culture—I am confident that most marriage advocates would favor its adoption. I know that I would. But if adopting same-sex marriage is likely to impede that larger goal, I will be against it.

Those who disagree with me can charge that I am proposing a moral metric in which, regardless of the ultimate policy decision on same-sex marriage, the rights of gays and lesbians take second place to the needs of an existing social institution. The charge would be accurate. But for me the same moral metric applies to other marriage issues that have nothing to do with homosexuality. For example, I have testified before state legislatures in favor of reforms in marriage law—such as longer waiting periods, mandatory counseling, and in some cases a requirement to show fault—that would place restrictions on "no fault" divorce, or what amounts to the unilateral right to divorce. In short, I favor limiting certain adult freedoms in the name of child well-being and the health of marriage as an institution.

In the case of same-sex marriage, one priority is the particular rights and needs of same-sex couples—the right to equal respect, the right to form loving, stable partnerships and families, and the need for greater social acceptance. Another priority is the collective rights and needs of children—the right to know and be loved by a mother and a father, and the need for as many children as possible to grow up under a strong shelter of marriage, our society's most pro-child institution. To the degree that these two priorities can be in harmony, or at least exist together in peace, I want to embrace them both. To the degree that I must choose, with some anguish I will choose children's collective rights and needs—I will choose marriage as a public good—over the rights and needs of gay and lesbian adults and those same-sex couples who are raising children.

The central issue in the same-sex marriage debate is not homosexuality; it is marriage itself. In the next few chapters, we will seek with fresh eyes to uncover an adequate answer to what might seem to be the simplest of questions: What is marriage? First, we examine a few shards of evidence from the prehistory of our species, including some findings from brain scientists who study the biochemistry of human attachment. Next, a visit to ancient Mesopotamia and the Nile Valley, where marriage first emerged in recorded history. Then to the Trobriand Islands, where marriage today is quite unlike the pattern familiar to us. Then we can craft a working definition of marriage for our time.

2

Prehistory

What were the basic patterns of sexual behavior in our species before the emergence of marriage? How did these patterns lead to marriage? No one really knows, but the origins of marriage appear to coincide with the origins of human civilization. The time prior to that—a period representing about 99 percent of the total time that humans have lived on the earth[1]—is a time about which we can only speculate, based on sparse and fragmentary bits of evidence. Yet scholars have speculated on the subject for more than two millennia.

Aristotle (384–321 BCE) suggests that marriage, "an older and more fundamental thing than the state," grew from love between man and woman that "is evidently a natural feeling, for nature has made man even more of a pairing than a political animal."[2] Aristotle traces primordial "pairing" first and foremost to the man and woman's "natural impulse . . . to leave behind them something of the same nature as themselves."[3]

The Greek historian and moralist Plutarch (46–120), pointing out that among the "ancient parents" of "primitive mankind" there was "neither any law which bade them rear their children, nor any expectation of gratitude or receiving the wages of maintenance," similarly emphasizes "the affection for offspring implanted by Nature" as a foundation for the eventual emergence of the institution.[4]

Other writers stress quite different aspects of an imagined sexual prehistory. Writing in the first century BCE, the Roman poet and Epicurean philosopher Lucretius, in a work of admirable ambition entitled *The Nature of the Universe,* argues that early men and women "lived out their lives in the fashion of wild beasts roaming at large," each individual being "taught only to live and fend for himself" and having "no notion of the mutual restraint of morals and laws." Sexual intercourse, unconnected to any notion of marriage or of male care for offspring, occurred either through mutual consent, by rape, or in what we today would call prostitution: "Mutual desire brought them together, or the male's mastering might and overriding lust, or a payment of acorns or arbutus berries or choice pears." Lucretius continues his story: "As time went by," humans "began to mellow." They began to build huts, use skins and fire, and create conditions such that "male and female learnt to live together in a stable union and to watch over their joint progeny."[5] Much current scholarship, as we will see, tends to support Lucretius' views.

Lucretius is also instructive on another crucial issue regarding the emergence and meaning of marriage—namely, where children come from. Today we are confident that we know the answer to this question. But our ancestors had widely divergent and fluid theories on this subject, with no small amount of confusion mixed in, and these theories (I will argue) influenced the way marriage first emerged and took shape across human societies.

Lucretius himself can illustrate this phenomenon, although he was a Roman gentleman writing some fifty years prior to the birth of Jesus, well into the historical era. He argues that sexual intercourse can at times be a "shared delight," desired by the woman as well as the man. As "proof," and apparently following both Aristotle and Hippocrates, he explains that the child will more closely resemble either the mother or the father depending on which seed, female or male, "masters" the other during the passion of sexual intercourse. Perhaps it's best to let him explain:

> In the intermingling of seed it may happen that the woman by a sudden effort overmasters the power of the man and takes control of [the sex act]. The children are conceived of the maternal seed and take after their mother. Correspondingly children may be conceived of the paternal seed and take after their father. The children in whom you see a two-sided likeness, combining

> features of both parents, are products alike of their father's body and their mother's blood. At their making the seeds that course through the limbs under the impulse of Venus were dashed together by the collision of mutual passion in which neither party was master or mastered.[6]

This thesis is only one of many ancient attempts to pin down scientifically the question of how a baby is made, and Lucretius' thinking on the matter is relatively advanced.

The intellectual *prehistory* of this issue—what our precivilizational ancestors believed about the processes of procreation—is something about which scholars can offer only educated guesses. But these guesses add up to interesting probabilities. Suffice it for now to say that early beliefs regarding the role of the mother's "blood" and the question of "seed"—is the child fundamentally the "seed" of the mother, the father, both, or neither?—appear to have been crucial to the invention of marriage as a social institution.

In the seventeenth through the nineteenth centuries in Europe, speculation about the prehistory of marriage often accompanied speculation about the birth of civilization. Many political philosophers of this period wanted to explain how humans first came to live together in societies and under governments. Typically they offered theories of how early humans had lived in "the state of nature" before the establishment of states and governments.

In the seventeenth century, Thomas Hobbes presented a theory similar in some respects to that of Lucretius. His masterwork, *Leviathan,* famously describes the state of nature as a harsh condition of "no Society; and which is worst of all, continuall feare, and danger of violent death; And the life of man solitary, poore, nasty, brutish, and short." As for the rearing of children, Hobbes argues that when there was "no Contract" between the male and the female, all responsibility for children was "in the Mother."[7] In the state of nature, males impregnate females, then move on. Sexual life is guided largely by force. "Who is the Father" often "cannot be known." Fatherhood—understood as a social role obligating the male to care for his offspring—does not exist.

Only when humans develop "Matrimoniall lawes" do fathers join mothers in raising the children that are born to them. This development is a major turning point for the human species, coinciding with, and largely signifying, the transition from the state of nature to society, from barbarism to civilization.

John Locke's speculations about human sexual and procreative conduct during the period of prehistory are roughly consistent with those of Hobbes and Lucretius. In his *Two Treatises of Government* he argues that God "put strong desires of Copulation into the Constitution of Men, thereby to continue the race of Mankind, which he doth most commonly without the intention, and often against the Consent and Will of the Begetter." After all: "What Father of a Thousand, when he begets a Child, thinks farther than the satisfying of his present Appetite?"[8]

In addition, says Locke, "God planted in Men a strong desire also of propagating their Kind, and continuing themselves in their Posterity," second only to the desire for self-preservation. Human parents therefore seek "to preserve what they have begotten, as to preserve themselves."[9] Here Locke echoes Aristotle, Plutarch, and many others. What Aristotle called the "natural impulse" to "leave behind them something of the same nature as themselves" is a fundamental basis of what would become family life and a principal reason why our early ancestors departed the state of nature to go "into Society."

The "first Society," Locke believes, was "between Man and Wife," and this bond was the seedbed of all human society. He defines marriage as

> a voluntary Compact between Man and Woman: and tho' it consists chiefly in such a Communion and Right in one another's Bodies, as is necessary to its chief end, Procreation; yet it draws with it mutual Support, and Assistance, and a Community of Interest too, as necessary to unite not only their Care, and Affection, but also necessary to their common Off-spring, who have a right to be nourished and maintained by them, till they are able to provide for themselves.[10]

Locke says a great deal here. Marriage is voluntary. It consists chiefly of the right to sexual intercourse. The main social good stemming from marriage is the bearing and raising of children, who have a need and a right to be nurtured by both parents. Marriage also leads spouses to support and assist one another, as befits parents engaged in the task of raising their children together, and as befits spouses who enjoy and care tenderly for one another.

Locke's argument about the origins of marriage was offered primarily as an argument against a book called *Patriarcha* by Sir Robert Filmer, a seventeenth-century royalist who believed that the king had a divine and absolute right to rule the nation based on a father's divine and absolute right to rule the family. In his *Two Treatises of Government,* Locke vigorously contests both aspects of this patriarchal thesis.

Filmer defines a father simply as a male who begets a child. Locke disagrees. Yes, in the state of nature, where violence and predation are the norm, "the bare act of begetting" is how a male typically participates in procreation. But when humans go "into Society"—first and foremost through marriage, the "first Society"—mere insemination is no longer enough to justify "the Title he hath to the Name and Authority of a Father." Humans are born completely helpless. Compared with the young of other species, human children remain dependent for an unusually long period of time, and they require "the joynt care of Male and Female" parents. For this reason, what marriage demands of men is not "barely Procreation," but also fatherhood as a defined *social* role, or what Locke calls "the Office and Care of a Father."[11]

Locke also disagrees with Filmer's view that the father is the absolute ruler of the family. In some countries where "Matrimony" clearly exists, he points out, "the Husband is allowed no such Absolute authority." Therefore it cannot be true that "the ends of Matrimony" require "such Power in the Husband." Different societies may define and regulate marriage in different ways, so long as these definitions and regulations are consistent with "the ends" for which marriage is made: "Procreation and mutual Support and Assistance." In the same passage, Locke defines the "ends" of marriage as "Procreation and the bringing up of children till they could shift for themselves."[12]

During the nineteenth century and into the twentieth, broad theories about the prehistory of sex and procreation were frequently offered in support of even broader theories, such as Freudianism. In applying his powerful new psychoanalytic insights to the study of totems and taboos in human societies, Sigmund Freud agreed with Charles Darwin that our earliest ancestors probably lived in "primal hordes," each headed by "a violent and jealous father who keeps all the females for himself and drives away his sons as they grow up." Later, due to male violence, this way of living gave way to a "fatherless society" in which kinship was determined through mothers and in which religion likely focused on "the great mother-goddesses." Still later, Freud theorizes, as the authority of fathers was partly restored, "a fatherless society gradually changed into one organized on a patriarchal basis."[13]

In his larger body of clinical and theoretical work, Freud viewed what he called the "father complex"—including "ambivalent" feelings toward the father and "a powerful unconscious element of hostility"—as a major influence on individual lives and on society as a whole. One of his central ideas thus was rooted in an imagined prehistory of father-dominated primal hordes and fatherless societies.[14]

A number of theorists in the nineteenth century argued that humans in the earliest periods of group living were sexually promiscuous, egalitarian, and matriarchal. By far the most well-known and politically influential of these analyses is *The Origin of the Family, Private Property, and the State* (1884) by Frederick Engels. Drawing on the earlier work of Lewis H. Morgan, an American who studied Native American tribes, and on the theory of "mother right" developed by the Swiss scholar Johann Bachofen, Engels portrays the prehistory (what he calls the "original state") of sexual life and procreation as something of a golden age—lots of free sex for anyone who wanted it, little if any sexual jealousy ("every woman belonged equally to every man and, similarly, every man to every woman"), social harmony, equality between the sexes, kinship ties determined by and through women (in part because paternity was seldom clearly established), and women acting as strong and even dominant social leaders.[15]

Then a terrible thing happened: Private property and capitalism were born; the ancient "mother right" was overturned; and men both took over the family and created the state to protect their newly gained privileges. According to Engels, "The overthrow of the mother right was the *world-historic defeat of the female sex*. The man seized the reigns of the house also; the woman was degraded, enthralled, the slave of the man's lust, a mere instrument for breeding children." History had begun. In the new order, paternal authority was total and ruthless: "In order to guarantee the fidelity of the wife, that is, the paternity of the children, the woman is placed in the man's absolute power; if he kills her, he is but exercising his right."[16]

Marriage laws enforcing monogamy took hold during this transitional period, not because of "individual sex love," says Engels, but in order for males to appropriate wealth and transfer it to their sons. A "wife" in the new, marriage-based order is someone "who differs from the ordinary courtesan only in that she does not hire out her body, like a wageworker, on piecework, but sells it into slavery once and for all." Marriage thus makes its appearance in history not as "the reconciliation of man and woman," but instead as "the victory of private property" and as "the proclamation of a conflict between the sexes entirely unknown hitherto in prehistoric times."[17] Engels, quoting Marx, argues that marriage as it actually emerged in human history "contains within itself *in miniature* all the antagonisms which later develop on a wide scale within society and its state."[18] The evils of marriage thus prefigure the evils of capitalist society.

"A Biological Foundation"

Modern anthropological and brain research throw additional light on the prehistory of marriage and the reasons for its emergence. Let's begin with an observation by the anthropologist Claude Lévi-Strauss, who reminds us that the family is everywhere "based on a union, more or less durable, but socially approved, of two individuals of opposite sexes who establish a household and bear and raise children."[19] He describes this marriage-based family form as "a social institution with a biological foundation."[20]

Does the prehistory of our species suggest a biological endowment for marriage? If so, that endowment is fragile at best. What anthropologists call "pair-bonding"—establishing a stable, long-term relationship with a spouse—is found in only about 3 percent of all mammal species.[21] Even among the higher primates (anthropoid apes and monkeys) that are genetically most similar to humans, a few species, such as gibbons and siamangs, form monogamous unions, but most do not. As a result, parenting among primates mostly means mothering. Fatherhood as a social role is rare. Indeed, most male primates, although they may live near their children, are unable even to identify them. With the exception of humans, no male primates regularly provide food to weaned offspring.[22] Thus, what might be called the original primate condition on earth probably resembled some of the classic descriptions offered by Lucretius, Hobbes, Locke, and others: sexual promiscuity, casual to nonexistent pair-bonding, and a near-total absence of social fatherhood.

But several million years ago, hominoid primates apparently began to demonstrate an unusual social behavior: Females and males began to become attached to one another and stay together—to bundle sexual desire, the procreative impulse, and the needs for emotional closeness and practical cooperation into a new, quite complex, and (it turns out) very successful way of living.

It is hard to overstate the importance of this development as a turning point in the life of our species. Consider these two facts: The primary division in our species is between male and female. This new way of living bridged that divide. The primary relationship in our species is between mother and child. The new way of living created in one fell swoop the second and third most fundamental relationships—the bond between the spouses and, deriving from it, the bond between father and child. For the first time, children acquired fathers who know them and help care for them. In turn, the emergence of social fatherhood—the male's commitment to a child that is dependent upon his sexual bond with the mother—completely revolutionized our ability to define kinship, thus making possible what would become a fundamental organizing principle for all human societies.

How and where did this new way of living first take hold and then begin to spread? When did it become the dominant human way of living? Precise answers to these questions are not available. But many centuries later, when cities were first emerging and laws written down, we humans, in another momentous leap, took steps to formalize and keep records of this way of living. We called it "marriage."

For humans, monogamous pair-bonding is primarily a *social* fact and achievement. It is far from innate or instinctual. Indeed, as we've just seen, stable unions and social fatherhood contradict much of our primate inheritance. At the same time, Claude Lévi-Strauss and others, including modern brain researchers, teach us that this behavior does have biological roots. Despite its cultural fluidity and variability, marrying behavior among humans is partly biologically primed.

Let's begin with the most fun and important part: sex. As the anthropologist Peter J. Wilson puts it, contemplating the roots of human kinship: "The process begins with the copulation of two adults of opposite sex."[23]

Among most primates, the sexual act is no big deal. Most females are sexually active and excitable only during relatively brief periods of estrus, or heat, in which the female's body odor changes and her genitals swell and change color, signaling the onset of ovulation and thus the likelihood of successful insemination. For these species, copulation is typically a quick, perfunctory, and highly efficient act. Certainly it does little if anything to foster intimacy or to unite the male and female of these species in a common way of life. In fact, among most primates, most of the time, sexual differences function primarily to keep the two sexes apart.[24]

For humans, by contrast, the sexual act is a big deal. Copulation is the center point, the baseline act, of an entire way of living in which sexual differences function primarily to *keep the two sexes together*. Copulation plays this unusual role for humans because humans, compared with other species, are highly sexy beasts. Both males and females are generally intensely interested in, and open to, a lot of sexual activity, all the time—not only the sex act itself, but elaborate foreplay and complex sexual stimulation and game-playing that go far beyond the mechanics of coitus, including the tendency of the sex partners to become emotionally entangled and intensely attracted to one another over a long period of time.

Many scholars point to the loss of estrus among humans as the key to this remarkable phenomenon. At some distant point in our past, in what the anthropologist Claude Masset calls an enormously consequential "biological innovation," estrus among humans gradually disappeared. Or more precisely, estrus became diffused evenly through time. Human females thus began to conceal rather than advertise ovulation.[25]

This biological innovation had radical social consequences. For human females, what had previously been a signal that was either "on" or (most of the time) "off" became a signal that is always "on." The core message of concealed ovulation is that *any* act of copulation has an equally good (or equally small) chance of resulting in successful procreation. Come up and see me, any time. It might be our lucky day.

And how did the human male react to this new message? As one might expect. His interest in copulation gradually shifted from periodic to continuous. Moreover, as each act of copulation became much less efficient in purely reproductive terms, the sex act itself gradually became less purely instrumental, merely a means of achieving insemination, and more an act that is prized and enjoyed for its own sake and in relationship to the female.

In this new human world, as Peter J. Wilson sums it up, "all females are receptive and all males ready." All the time. Male and female are now "characterized by their intense, continuing, and mutual sexual interest in each other."[26]

With the loss of estrus came a range of other sexy biological innovations. Female orgasms, for example, which seems to be unique to humans. Enlarged and sensitive female breasts, for example—breasts that expand during intercourse, with nipples that harden to even the slightest touch, and that, when caressed, increase the desire for intercourse. Most evidence suggests that the primary and perhaps sole functions of bigger and more sensitive female breasts are sexual invitation and sexual stimulation.

Forward-tilting vaginal canals, for example, which seem to have evolved to encourage frontal, *personal*, face-to-face (rather than rear-entry) sexual intercourse. Unusually large male penises, for example. A gorilla has three times the body bulk of a man, but a typical man's penis, I'm proud to report, is much larger than a typical gorilla's. Why? Take a guess. Large penises seem to increase sexual pleasure for both males and (especially) females. Sexually sensitive lips and ear lobes, for example. Dilated eye pupils, for example. A person's pupils expand when she or he is sexually interested—a signaling device that is well known to artists, cartoonists, and advertisers the world over.[27]

What end do these sexy biological innovations serve? Human sexiness is not primarily about mere reproduction. If it were, we could be—our distant ancestors almost certainly were—much more efficient about it. A few minutes of mounting, insertion, and ejaculation could do the trick. Instead, human sexiness is fundamentally about *creating the couple that will raise the child.*

Probably the most revolutionary social consequence of human pair-bonding: it transforms the male from an inseminator into a father. The sexual bond with the woman recruits the adult male into family life and radically expands the basic structures of human kinship. John Locke was right. What the "first Society" of female and male requires of men is not "barely Procreation," but also "the Office and Care of a Father." Modern scholars tell us that the loss of estrus is fundamentally linked to the creation of fatherhood as a social role, because it encourages stable, monogamous male-female relationships.

Concealed ovulation means that in order to ensure successful reproduction, sexual relationships need to last longer and become more intensive. The concealment of ovulation also reduces, from the male's perspective, the reproductive pay-off from random copulation with numerous females, especially those already having intercourse with another male. Finally, in the absence of the female's signaling of her period of ovulation, monogamous pair-bonding dramatically increases what scholars call paternal certainty—the male's belief that the child that is born is in fact his own offspring.[28]

Let's summarize. The loss of estrus and numerous other biological innovations seem designed to make human sex much sexier. Much more alluring. More preoccupying. More omnipresent. More an end in itself. More personal. More intimate. More emotionally complex and entangling. All this, in turn, helps to establish a *particular family structure*— the closely bonded, long-lasting, male-female childrearing unit, which revolutionizes human kinship by bridging the sexual divide and creating fathers for children. Biologically primed sexual behavior promotes this family structure, which in turn reinforces the sexual behavior.[29]

But this conclusion only begs the deeper question: Why this *particular* family form? Why would this family structure matter so much? After all, most species, including those that most closely resemble humans, get along well enough without it. Why would our species literally alter its biology in order to lavish sex appeal on one special way of females and males living together?

Scholars have proposed a number of possible answers to this question, but for most scholars, the key to the puzzle is children. The determining fact is that the human infant is, in effect, born prematurely and remains immature and dependent for many years.

Humans have large brains that have gotten larger over the course of our evolution as a species—large enough, in fact, to present potential problems when the baby's head is passing through the mother's birth canal. Over time, our species has solved this problem by giving birth to our babies *before* their brains and skulls have finished growing. As a result, human infants are more helpless, and more dependent, than the offspring of any other primate.[30]

As all parents know only too well, the human child remains largely incapable of even physical self-care for many years. For lemur young, the time of virtually complete physical dependency—let's call it "infancy"—lasts about six months. For gibbons, two years. For chimpanzees, three years. For humans? Six years.[31]

But of course, tying shoelaces and brushing teeth are only the beginning. Up through and long past the age of six, the human child has a profound need for intimate care and connectedness to others, not only for physical survival but also for basic questions of personal identity and moral and spiritual formation. As the anthropologist Sarah Blaffer Hrdy puts it, human beings are "born to attach."[32] Notwithstanding some of our inspirational myths, none of us is self-made. We are deeply and inescapably interdependent. We talk only because others talk to us. As children, we are smiled into smiling and loved into loving. Only our capacity and need for enduring attachments to others, beginning with our mothers, make possible the crucial tasks of empathizing with others and regulating our emotions and behaviors—traits that in turn largely define what it means to be human.[33] Helping an infant grow over the years into a flourishing human being is the most difficult, time-consuming, and important work of our species.

The main reason for sexually based pair-bonding among humans is that mothers cannot and should not do this work alone. For the prematurely born, large-brained, slowly developing, psychologically needy human infant, a mother alone is not enough. She needs someone to help provide food. She and the child need protection from predators and other dangers. She needs someone to relieve, spell, and comfort her. She needs a companion that she can count on. She needs someone to be her partner in raising the child—someone who will love the child (almost) as much as she does and who is willing to sacrifice deeply and permanently for the child's sake.

In short, to increase the likelihood of survival and success, the human infant needs a father and the human mother needs a mate. That's the central reason, according to most anthropologists, for "biological innovations" such as the loss of estrus and for much sexier human sex—to bind together the man and the woman who make and raise the child. It's the central reason why our species developed the unusual way of living that we would eventually call marriage.

Here's the irony: A lot more sexual intercourse among the humans, not so as to make a baby, but to make a couple to raise the baby. A lot more sexual heat, desire, and intensity, not for the purpose of multiple partners and sexual freedom, but to reinforce that most middlebrow and unhip of institutions: Mom and Dad nagging the kids about finishing their homework. Such is the crooked path of human evolutionary adaptation. Mother Nature must have a sense of humor.

Anthropologists can tell us some important things. Neuroscientists, with their jazzy methods of brain research, can tell us others. In particular, they can now show that the mechanisms by which men and women become attached to one another are discernible in the basic structure of the brain.[34]

It turns out that our emotions and behaviors are strongly influenced by neurotransmitters, or substances that transmit nerve messages and impulses in the brain. Hormones such as testosterone, estrogen, and dopamine, which circulate in our body fluids, can also be neurotransmitters, regulated by receptors located deep in the brain. Researchers have concluded that neurotransmitters are deeply implicated in the sexually based male-female childrearing unit.

Consider the hormone oxytocin. Studies suggest that sexual intercourse causes oxytocin to enter a female's bloodstream. This change affects her brain and limbic system in ways that appear to promote emotional intimacy and feelings of love toward her partner. Both childbirth and lactation also trigger releases of oxytocin into the bloodstream, apparently stimulating the mother's attachment to her baby.[35] Another recent neurological study similarly finds that a mother's love for her baby and her love for her sexual partner not only are both stimulated by the release of oxytocin but also activate the same areas of the brain.[36]

Both mother love and romantic love facilitate one-on-one bonding. Both, it turns out, are biologically rooted, and *in the same way*—each linked to the same hormone and each lighting up the same areas of the brain. Both of these brain-and-hormone phenomena help to create and reinforce a *particular family structure,* which Claude Lévi-Strauss calls the "conjugal" family, involving a male and a female who are closely bonded over a long period of time to one another and to their offspring.[37]

Consider the steroid hormone testosterone, which is associated in males with both aggression and sexual desire. Studies suggest that marriage—sexually bonding with a spouse—reduces levels of testosterone in men. This hormonal change appears to incline men to less violence, less sexual promiscuity, and more nurturant fatherhood. Stay close to your wife. Wash the dishes, help your daughter draw a picture, take a rain check on drinking and tomcatting with the boys. Be a nicer guy. Interestingly, divorce seems to cause an increase in testosterone.[38] Notice again the biologically and chemically based similarities between spousal bonding and parent-child bonding. It's as if the two go together, not just in song lyrics or in someone's theory, but in the wiring of our brains and in our deepest physical selves. Notice again that we are discovering biochemical foundations of a social institution.

Dopamine. Vassopressin. Prolactin. Endogenous opioid peptides. Estrogen. Progesterone. These and other chemicals interact with one another, and with the rest of the human organism, in fantastically complex ways.[39] But think about them this way: Falling head over heels in love. Wanting to gaze into your lover's eyes. Feeling driven by the need for physical union with your lover. Feeling tenderly toward your beloved, wanting to take care of her or him. Feeling deeply, solidly connected with your beloved, and partly as a result of that bond, also deeply connected to the child that the two of you made in love and brought into the world. Feeling almost addicted to your spouse, and knowing that your spouse is addicted to you, as if the two of you had somehow been drugged by chemical substances.

In fact, you *have* been drugged. You *are,* almost literally, addicted. The chemicals that are addicting you to one another are dopamine, vasopressin, oxytocin, and the others. They are also addicting you to your child.

When did these biochemical processes first begin to influence human behavior? No one knows for sure. Do these bond-making, spouse-addicting traits constitute yet another prehistorical "biological innovation" aimed fundamentally at uniting the couple who make and raise the child? It seems possible. Today's brain researchers, in exciting and rapidly advancing scientific work, are mapping out the astonishing biochemistry of the pair-bonded, childrearing couple. In other words, they are mapping out the biochemistry of marriage.

Toward Marriage

The great Finnish sociologist, philosopher, and anthropologist Edward Westermarck, in many ways the father of modern marriage studies, wrote in 1936 that marriage as "a social institution sanctioned by custom or law" contains "a deep biological foundation" and likely "developed out of a primeval habit" in which, over time, the human male and female (or in some cases the male and several females) came to live together for sexual gratification, companionship and mutual economic aid, and procreation and the joint rearing of offspring.[40] More recent scholarship, as we have seen, tends to reinforce and elaborate this conclusion.

Yet emphasizing the distant origins and biological bases of the turn toward marriage among humans should not blind us to the radical nature of this behavioral innovation. It was a species-changing turn. It helps to explain, possibly as well as any other fact, the success and eventual dominance of human beings on this planet.

Nor should the institution's deep foundations blind us to its ultimate fragility. Marriage corresponds to certain core human desires—sexual desire, the desire to reproduce and to raise children, and the need to love and be loved—but marriage as an institution is a social construction. As a cultural creation it is both heavy-handed ("Thou shalt not commit adultery") and precarious. Marriage has natural roots, but being married is certainly not natural for humans in the same way that breathing and eating are natural. On the contrary. As Westermarck and many others have recognized, marriage is finally an imposition of law and custom upon individuals whose "natural" behavior at any given moment might easily go another way.

The institution's precariousness, as well as its radical implications for society, become clearer when we consider those long periods of our prehistory in which stable male-female pair-bonding and fatherhood as a social role appear to have been at best poorly established. For example, the earliest known art and symbols left behind by *Homo sapiens* date from the Upper Paleolithic era, which began about forty thousand years ago. These works show virtually no evidence suggesting the presence in these societies of bonded male-female couples or of fatherhood as a role for men. Nor do these works evince even a rudimentary knowledge of the biological processes of insemination and resulting pregnancy.[41]

The archeologist Marija Gimbutas for many years studied the peoples who inhabited Europe from about 7000 to about 3000 BCE. She reports little if any evidence of social fatherhood or durable marriage in these societies. She finds, for example, that "the father image is not known to Paleolithic or Neolithic art."[42] Most of the deities in these Old European cultures are female: "it was the sovereign mystery and creative power of the female as the source of life that developed into the earliest religious experiences."[43] Male deities are few and far between, and seem primarily to play the role of either consort or brother. This culture of the mother-goddess probably reflects the prevalence of matrilineal (mother-headed) kinship systems in which "paternity was considered unimportant or difficult to establish."[44]

Old European burial practices are particularly revealing. Genetically related women and children were often interred together under the floors of houses. But no fathers, and no other male family members, are present in many of these communal burial grounds. Gimbutas speculates that "it is very likely that their bodies were exposed for vultures and their disarticulated bones were later buried somewhere in or out of the village."[45] Thanks a lot, Dad! Other evidence of everyday living arrangements in Old Europe also suggests essentially mother-headed family systems in which pair-bonding was weak and in which men were only marginal participants in family life.

Gimbutas gushes with unabashed enthusiasm about such arrangements. She clearly views this period of Europe's prehistory as something of a golden age, when the gods were female; women established and dominated families; and men (before dying and being thrown to the vultures) knew their place, which seems basically to have been somewhere else.

Gimbutas is too careful to accept without qualification Frederick Engels' more dogmatic simplifications. Yet her notion of an almost Edenic prehistory (the *New York Times* calls her scholarship "a dramatic story of paradise lost and now rediscovered") clearly echoes Engels' portrait of women on top and of free-and-easy human mating prior to the Fall—that is, prior to the beginning of both private property and recorded history. Apparently it does not occur to Gimbutas, any more than to Engels, to ask whether children need fathers who love them. Or whether men need to connect to women and to the next generation. Or whether women want and perhaps even need men who are something other than consorts with privileges.

The feminist historian Gerda Lerner writes: "The case against the universality of prehistoric matriarchy seems quite clearly proven by the anthropological evidence."[46] At the same time, Gimbutas, Lerner, and other scholars do offer evidence suggesting that during much of the sexual prehistory of *Homo sapiens*—some of whose earliest art, symbols, and settlement patterns are known to us—marriage was weak or nonexistent and fathers typically did not help to raise, and often did not even know, their children.

So the turn toward marriage among humans was a very gradual and uneven affair, occurring over many centuries, and in different degrees in different areas—even as its ultimate reach was to be nearly universal and its consequences for society nothing short of revolutionary. As we've seen, much of the turn appears to have been prompted and then reinforced by a series of slowly emerging physiological and perhaps even biochemical changes—those sex-enhancing, bond-making "biological innovations"—in human males and females. But we must remember that these changes themselves did not create marriage. They only helped to create the *possibility* of marriage among humans. Or perhaps even better, they helped to make marriage a plausible way to confront—arguably our *best* way to confront—some fundamental human questions.

Is it good to be alone? What is the meaning of our sexual embodiment? Should men and women live apart or try to share a common life? Is lasting sexual love possible? What is a parent? What do children need? Who are our kin? Struggling with these problems is part of what makes us human. These questions are never finally solved, by marriage or by anything else. But the turn toward marriage made it possible for us as a species to wrestle with these problems in a new way.

So as we passed from prehistory into history, humans formally envisioned and constructed a social institution, sanctioned by law and custom, called marriage.

3

The River Valleys

Most historians believe that human civilization began about five thousand years ago in the Tigris-Euphrates River Valley, in what was historically called Mesopotamia and is now Iraq, and in the nearby Nile Valley in Egypt. It was in these two river valleys that humans first built cities; wrote literature and laws; developed the wheel, the sail, and the sixty-minute hour; created state bureaucracies and kingdoms. And here they first launched marriage as a fully formed social institution. Here, a certain way of men and women living together was established by law as well as molded by custom. The first recorded marriages do not usually make the scholars' lists of civilization-shaping human developments that appear to have originated in that time and place, but they ought to. And therein hangs a small but revealing tale.

I live in New York City and love to visit the Metropolitan Museum of Art, one of the world's great art museums. On a visit there with my wife and children in late 2003, looking at antiquities from the ancient Near East, I came across a pair of molded ceramic plaques, about four thousand years old, from lower Mesopotamia. Each plaque depicts a man and a woman. The display note from the museum curators reads as follows:

> *Molded plaques with couples:* Plaques depicting sexual acts were mass-produced in Mesopotamia during the early second millennium B.C. and may have been used as private fertility amulets.

Sexual acts also may have been performed as part of temple rituals.

Reading the note and looking again at the plaques, I was startled and confused. I went home and began to learn what I could about Mesopotamian ceramic plaques depicting couples. I made an appointment to see one of the curators of the museum's department of ancient Near Eastern art. But most of all, I thought about those two images, returning to the museum several times to stare at them for long periods of time. (I think the guards in the gallery concluded that I was a little nuts. Maybe they're a little right.) I asked myself: Do they *both* look like "plaques depicting sexual acts"? Do *both* of them look as if they might have been used as private fertility amulets? Do *both* of them refer in some way to sexual acts performed as part of temple rituals?

One of them certainly does, but the other just as clearly does not. One depicts a man and a woman engaged in sexual intercourse. Both are naked. He is standing. She is straddling him, with her legs wrapped around his thighs. Each of them is grasping the other. Their faces, which we see from only one side, are largely indiscernible. The image communicates lust and raw, heated sex.

The man and woman on the other plaque are fully dressed and standing side by side, with their heads slightly turned toward one another, so that their eyes can meet. They are about the same height. We see their faces; they appear calm and serene. Their bodies are not touching, except that each has an arm delicately placed around the upper waist of the other. She is holding something apparently ornamental or symbolic in her other hand, perhaps beads or flowers. The image overall communicates a sense of quiet and privacy. At the same time, there is a certain formality and dignity in their pose, along with the suggestion of tenderness.

What do these two very old representations signify? And what explains how the museum scholars chose to describe them? I want to argue that, at the time they were fashioned, these two images were showing something relatively new happening in the world.

Let's start with the easy one. Images of couples having sex were common enough in early Mesopotamian art and have been found by archeologists in houses, temples, and tombs. Many of these images appear to be almost pornographic, as if intended for entertainment and (primarily male) sexual arousal. Irrespective of one's view of whether such an amulet might produce or be a symbol of magic, it is not hard to imagine these representations being viewed by many practically minded persons as fertility aids, intended to improve male sexual performance and the likelihood of a woman becoming pregnant.

Especially if they were used as fertility amulets, these erotic images also signal what we can now recognize as a deeply consequential development in how human societies understand where babies come from. Many human beings in many places and over many centuries, especially during the prehistory of our species, appear to have been fairly confident that the female body is the fundamental point of origin for human offspring and the basic material from which—with some help from the gods and a man—the human child is formed. By the third millennium BCE in both Mesopotamia and Egypt, this view had been almost completely overturned.[1] Even more surprisingly, the new culturally accepted view was essentially the *exact opposite* of the older one. The people who invented civilization in these two river valleys had come firmly to believe that the *male* body, not the female, was the fundamental point of origin for the human infant. The newer idea was that the male's semen was deposited in the woman's womb—like a seed planted in soil—and there it slowly grew into a child.

This new cultural and scientific understanding was to have revolutionary implications for Mesopotamian and Egyptian society generally, and for the newly emerging institution of marriage in particular. But for now—back to our two ceramic plaques—let us simply note that, as fertility aids, representations of men and women having sex are quite different from most prehistoric fertility totems and amulets, which rarely included males or suggested sexual intercourse.

The erotic couple in ceramic also gives a glimpse into the sexual attitudes and practices of the larger society. The practice of temple prostitution—understood as men paying money to have sex with women in temples, without shame or stigma—was probably widespread in Mesopotamia at the time. Similar sexual practices, often described as sacred (as distinct from commercial) prostitution, were also widespread and appear to have been connected to the worship of fertility goddesses.[2] The Greek scholar Herodotus, writing in the fifth century BCE, describes such a ritual in vivid terms.[3] We also know that Jewish leaders in the region who viewed sacred prostitution as idolatrous struggled mightily for many generations to eradicate it in their own community.[4] As the display note from the Metropolitan Museum suggests, our erotic couple in sexual embrace may symbolize or be connected to one of these temple practices.

Prostitution without shame or stigma was also widespread outside the temple, in the public square and under the city wall, around the harbor, and in the taverns. In fact, our erotic couple may have served originally as a tavern decoration, since taproom walls in ancient Mesopotamia frequently displayed plaques depicting frank sexual images, as well as clay tablets on which were written ribald prayers to the gods, asking for carnal favors and exciting sexual adventures. ("May my lips be honey, my hands my charm!")[5] The apparently frequently used term "ale wives" refers to the women who ran these taverns and perhaps also to all the women working in them as prostitutes.[6]

The prevalence of socially acceptable and even socially approved prostitution during this period, as well as the highly sexualized art and lyrics, suggest a sexual code that still easily accommodated sex for its own sake and sex disconnected from commitment. (By the way, does any of this sound familiar?) The relatively new institution of marriage was strong and flourishing, but other and probably much older forms of sexual life, often focusing on sex itself more than the sexual bond, were still alive and apparently doing quite well.

This dawn-of-civilization sexual culture, partly based on marriage and partly based on its antecedents and alternatives, is clearly evident in *The Epic of Gilgamesh*. Estimated to be about four thousand years old, these famous Mesopotamian poems are the world's oldest epic and first great work of literature.[7]

Gilgamesh is the young king of "strong-walled" Uruk, located in lower Mesopotamia in the land of Sumer, on the eastern bank of the Euphrates. As the epic begins, we learn that Gilgamesh is "very strong," but "like a wild bull he lords it over men." He wreaks havoc in the city and his people fear him, especially his sexual behavior: "His lust leaves no virgin to her lover, neither the warrior's daughter nor the wife of the noble."

Gilgamesh's friend and truest comrade is Enkidu. Even more than Gilgamesh, Enkidu at the beginning of the epic is a "wild man." He is seduced by a harlot, "a wanton from the temple of love," who persuades him to go to Uruk to meet and challenge Gilgamesh. The two young men meet, fight, and become friends.

The epic relates Gilgamesh's adventures, many of them with Enkidu, as he struggles to gain the wisdom necessary to become a just king. His journey to maturity is anything but an easy one, in part because he and Enkidu are on their own. Gilgamesh's mother and primary parent is the goddess Ninsun, who is reputed to be wise, but offers him no real guidance. Gilgamesh's father, from whom he inherits mortality, is not an important figure in the epic and appears to play no role in guiding his son toward manhood.

More generally, the Gilgamesh epic describes a world in which marriage is only one, and perhaps not even the main, way of organizing sexual life. It is a world in which the fathers of the community are fundamentally unable to guide or even restrain the strong, wild sons who rise up to seek dominance and satisfy their appetites. The story, then, is not ultimately about husbands and wives, or about parents raising children, but about brothers—and about their sexual adventures and values. Sex separated from commitment, especially in the form of prostitution, looms large in the story. One can easily imagine Gilgamesh and Enkidu in a tavern or in a temple, heartily familiar with and drawn to our copulating couple in ceramic.

There are key moments in the story in which a marriage ethic is explicitly contrasted with its opposite and marriage arguably fares the worst. Ishtar, the queen of heaven, is the powerful goddess of love, fertility, and war (quite a combination). She has a temple in Uruk, and she is one of the goddesses around whom the practice of sacred prostitution is organized. But at one point in the story, Ishtar proposes marriage to Gilgamesh: "Come to me Gilgamesh, and be my bridegroom; grant me seed of your body, let me be your bride and you shall be my husband." Gilgamesh refuses. He rebukes her for having seduced and then abandoned many previous lovers. Is Gilgamesh, in the name of marriage, rejecting an ancient and even sacred sexual code that predates and competes with marriage? Perhaps.

In any case, Ishtar is enraged and sends the Bull of Heaven to destroy Gilgamesh. He and Enkidu kill the celestial bull, but their disrespect of the gods means that Enkidu must die. Bitter and remorseful, Enkidu curses the harlot who years earlier had seduced him and sent him to Uruk: "Let you be stripped of your purple dyes, for I too once in the wilderness with my wife had all the treasures I wished." For it turns out that Enkidu, in order to enjoy the harlot and go to Uruk, had left behind a wife and children. But Enkidu, on the advice of the god Shamash, has second thoughts and retracts the curse. In praise of the harlot he says, "On your account a wife, mother of seven, was forsaken."

Later Gilgamesh undertakes long travels through the wilderness in search of the secret to everlasting life. He comes across a garden of the gods, similar to the Bible's Garden of Eden, where he meets the goddess Siduri. She offers him two bits of wisdom. First, he cannot regain his youth or avoid death: "You will never find the life for which you are searching." And second, he should enjoy the days that he is given: "Let your clothes be fresh, bathe yourself in water, cherish the little child that holds your hand, and make your wife happy in your embrace; for this too is the lot of man."[8] Such wise advice about marriage and fatherhood is rare in the Gilgamesh epic, and more honored by its heroes in the breach than in the observance.

If we had to decide which of our two molded plaques is the best illustration of the sexual ethic conveyed in *The Epic of Gilgamesh*, we would probably choose the copulating couple, the image intended to arouse and excite, the bawdy image of sex as sex, perhaps intended for public display in the tavern or the temple.

But the second plaque is not about sex as sex; it is about sex as relationship. Eroticism is clearly present in the image. The way they look at and touch one another tells us that these two have sex together, perhaps at times in the same heated style that the copulating couple displays. But the sex in this second plaque also has been subsumed in something larger—something that we might describe as transcendent. It is something public and ceremonial as well as private and intimate. It suggests not only a particular act, not only a particular relationship, but also a certain way of living.

Let's call it marriage. In fact, with only a bit of poetic license, I think we can fairly view this plaque as one of the world's oldest marriage portraits. There are some earlier—not *much* earlier!—indications of kings and queens having been married, and of gods marrying one another. But when it comes to mortals and ordinary citizens tying the knot in public and leaving a record of it behind, our couple in ceramic appears to have been one of the first.

It is unlikely that this plaque portrays two gods; the man's head, if he were a god, would probably be shaped differently. Nor is it likely that the plaque came from a temple. In ancient Mesopotamia, many people who could afford to do so placed images of themselves in temples, as supplications to the gods. But these images typically show individuals, not couples or families.

The museum curator at the Metropolitan also told me that in general, apart from explicitly erotic images, representations of couples are quite rare in the art of this time and place. It seems that men and women posing with each other in this way—smiling in front of the camera, as it were, to signify and help commemorate an important personal, legal, and social act—was not common, or had not been happening for very long.

In our image, the woman is holding something ornamental or ceremonial. He has thick, curly hair, and scholars believe that many men in this period shaved their heads and wore wigs for festive occasions.[9] But those are only details and guesses. Consider the portrait as a whole: the entire mood of this image, especially its unusual combination of intimacy and formality, public and private, suggests to me something much like a wedding portrait—one that is not very different from my own.

Instituting Marriage

Creating civilization means, probably more than anything else, creating complex social institutions. The great contribution of the ancient Egyptians and Mesopotamians to marriage was institutionalization—turning a particular way of women and men living together into a multifaceted, legally regulated, and historically recorded social institution.

In the previous chapter, we learned that in Europe as recently as five thousand years ago, family burial plots may typically have included genetically related women and children, but no fathers. Such evidence clearly suggests an entrenched pattern of early human societies in which marriage as a social institution was either weak or nonexistent. In a remarkable achievement, the Egyptians and Mesopotamians broke with that pattern. Archeologists report that in Eridu—often called the world's first city, located in lower Mesopotamia near the western bank of the Euphrates River—family burial areas typically included mothers, children, *and* fathers.[10] These people had imagined and built a different social institution.

What does it mean to build a social institution? Listen to the words of Lipit-Ishtar, who ruled over the regions of Sumer and Akkad in the Tigris-Euphrates Valley in lower Mesopotamia (where we met Gilgamesh) around 1900 BCE. The Laws of Lipit-Ishtar constitute one of the world's first legal codes.

In the prologue to the laws, the king describes his closeness to the gods and declares that he has "established justice in the lands of Sumer and Akkad." Near the top of his list of proud achievements is this one:

> With a . . . [decree], I made the father support his children. I made the child support his father. I made the father stand by his children. I made the child stand by his father.[11]

This extraordinary statement proclaims that every child has a right to a father. All fathers must be responsible fathers. Children must honor their fathers as well as their mothers. Recall that European kinship systems at least as late as 3000 BCE were likely ones in which "paternity was considered unimportant or difficult to establish."[12]

Lipit-Ishtar, in the name of justice, sought to overturn that ancient pattern through new laws.

Scholars have recovered at least portions of thirty-eight laws from Lipit-Ishtar's code. About one-third concern marriage and procreation, and they are very specific. Scholars believe that many of them arose from actual, often difficult, cases. As a result, many of them address the tangled sexual situations in which we humans often find ourselves. Here is one of them:

> If a man's wife has not borne him children, but a harlot from the public square has borne him children, he shall provide grain, oil, and clothing for that harlot; the children which the harlot has borne him shall be his heirs, and as long as his wife lives the harlot shall not live in the house with his wife.[13]

I'm not sure that this is the best possible solution. But it is consistent with the principles that every child deserves a father and that a wife has rights that must be respected.

What does it mean to build a social institution? Listen to the words of Dadusha, who ruled a kingdom called Eshnunna, located northeast of Babylon (now Baghdad), about 1800 BCE:

> If a man took the daughter of a man without asking her father and mother, and has not held a feast and made a contract for her father and her mother—even if she lives in his house for a full year, she is not a wife. If he did hold a feast and make a contract for her mother and her father, and took her, she is a wife.[14]

Here Dadusha provides a clear definition of marriage. There must be consent—in this case, from the bride's parents. There must be a contract. There must be a public celebration. The bride and the groom must have sexual intercourse. If these conditions are met, there is a marriage. Sexual intercourse alone does not a marriage make. Nor does living together, even for a year. To marry is to do something that is also contractual, communal, and public.

This law suggests that some women at this time simply began living with a male suitor; this practice may have been fairly widespread. Some women were prostitutes in the public square or tavern; others were temple prostitutes. But this new law recognizes and recommends something different—arguably a comparatively new way of living together involving a contract.

What exactly was this "contract"? Some contracts may have been more oral than written, and they probably included, as today's wedding ceremonies do, vows and other symbolic actions taken by the couple. The simple declarations "You are my husband" and "You are my wife" may have been used. One literary text says: "I will fill your lap with silver and gold: You are my wife, and I am your husband."[15]

These contracts also included an elaborate series of gift exchanges over time. For example, after the betrothal or engagement, which were typically arranged by the parents, the groom's family would give gifts of food and silver to the bride's family. In exchange, the bride's family would give gifts of silver, jewelry, household goods, and other items both to the groom's family and to the couple.

Some historians and other commentators have seriously misunderstood the purpose of these exchanges. Some have suggested that the gifts to the bride's family, or what some scholars (I believe misleadingly) have called the "bride price," meant that the man and his family were literally *purchasing* a wife. (Recall Engels' harsh accusations about the alleged buying and selling of wives under capitalism.) Others have suggested that these exchanges meant that the marriage itself was primarily an economic transaction between the two families. I would be rich if I had a nickel for every time someone who knows almost nothing about marriage has told me that marriage historically has been all about "property."

That is nonsense. For example, scholars have shown that families frequently expected the economic value of the gifts to the bride's family to be essentially equal to the value of the return gifts to the groom's family and the gifts from the bride's family to the bride, called the dowry. In purely material terms, these gifts largely cancelled out one another. Their real meaning was social and familial, not economic.[16] They were intended to bind the two families together, to demonstrate good will and good faith, and perhaps most of all, in ways both material and symbolic, to help the bride and groom as they started their life together as a married couple. The same logic explains the "feasts," or public celebrations, many of which may have lasted from five to seven days.[17]

After resolving the issues of consent, contract, and feasting, the bride and groom at the center of this now fully articulated institution have sexual intercourse. This society was not shy about focusing directly on sexual intercourse as the culmination of a marriage: the legal inauguration and socially approved foundation of a new life to be lived together. Beds—large beds—feature prominently in dowry lists, and the art of the time makes the purpose of these beds unmistakably clear. Getting married was sometimes called "erecting the bed." One marriage document of the time describes the marriage as "when they lay on their bed."[18]

Another important law of Eshnunna concerns divorce:

> If a man divorces his wife after having made her bear children, and takes another wife, he shall be driven from his house and from whatever he owns and may go after the woman whom he loves.[19]

This law does not demonstrate equality between wife and husband, nor does it stipulate equal access to divorce. It suggests that the divorced wife's right to economic compensation (the house and "all that he owns") is at least partly dependent on the presence of children. But the law does not reveal a society in which a wife is without rights, or one in which marriage is fundamentally a means for men to obtain property. Regarding women's (or at least mothers') rights, this law almost certainly represents a major advance over the norms and practices that preceded it. Moreover, the solution devised by Dadusha for this particular problem nearly four thousand years ago—given a little wiggle room over the definition of "all that he owns"—is not very different from the solution that most U.S. and European courts would offer today.

What does it mean to build a social institution? Consider the accomplishments of Hammurabi, who ruled a great kingdom in Babylonia in about 1750 BCE. The famous Code of Hammurabi has about 275 law provisions, about 65 of which concern marriage and family life. Listen to the basic story they tell.

Cohabitation. The first provision says simply that if a man lives with a woman, but has not drawn up a marriage contract, "that woman is not a wife."

Wedding gifts. If an engaged man changes his mind on account of another woman, all of the presents given to his family during the engagement must be returned.... If the father of an engaged woman changes his mind about the marriage, he must pay back "double" the value of the gifts that were given to his family.... If an engaged man's friends disparage him to his prospective in-laws, such that his prospective father-in-law calls off the wedding, he must pay back double the value of the gifts given to him; but no one doing any of the disparaging may marry the woman in question.

Adultery. If a married woman commits adultery, she and the other man will be bound and "thrown into the water"—yet if her husband decides to spare her life, the king may also decide to spare the life of the other man.... If a man has sexual intercourse with a virgin living in her father's house who is betrothed to another man, the male violator will be put to death and the female violator will go free.... If a husband accuses his wife of adultery, but she was not caught in the act, she can swear her innocence by the gods and remain in her home as his wife. If a man accuses *another* man's wife of having committed adultery, but she was not caught in the act, she is to submit to a river ordeal as a divine judgment of her guilt or innocence.... If a wife having an affair with another man has her husband killed, she is to be impaled.

Sex. If a man has sex with the wife of his son, that man will be bound and thrown into the river. If a man has sex with the woman who is *engaged* to marry his son, he must pay an amount of money to the engaged woman and return her dowry; she is free to marry the husband of her choice.... A man who commits incest will be banished from the city.... If a widowed woman has sex with her son, both of them will be burned.... If a man's father dies, and that man has sex with his father's widow who is a foster mother or stepmother to him, that man will be disinherited.

Husband taken captive. If a husband is captured in war and leaves sufficient resources behind, his wife may not cohabit with another man—if she does so, she will be put to death. Yet if *insufficient* resources were left behind, she may "enter the house of another" while "incurring no blame at all." If a wife of a captive husband takes up blamelessly with another man and has children with him, only to have the husband finally return, she is to return to the first husband, but the children of the second marriage will stay with their father. (You think that exhausts the possibilities here? Think again.) If the absent husband is actually a runaway rather than a captive of war, and his wife has remarried, only to have the runaway husband return to the city and want her back, she remains the wife of the second husband.

Divorce. If a man wants to divorce a wife who has borne him no children, he may do so, but he must pay the full bride price stipulated by the marriage contract (some contracts said that the final installment of the bride price was not due until after the birth of the first child)[20] and give her back the dowry; if there was no bride price, he must give her an amount of money.... If a woman seeks to abandon her husband and disparages him, the husband may divorce her and does not have to pay her anything; if he decides *not* to divorce her, he may marry a second wife and have the original wife ("that woman") live in his house as a servant.... If a woman repudiates her husband and refuses to have sex with him, but is found by the courts to be blameless, while her husband is wayward and is disparaging her, she may leave her husband without incurring any blame and may take her dowry with her; but if she is found to be guilty, she will be thrown into the water.

In sickness and in health. If a man's wife becomes seriously ill, he may marry another woman, but the ill woman remains his wife and he must house and support her as long as she lives.... But if the ill woman refuses to live in the husband's house, he must return her dowry to her, and then she may leave.

For richer or poorer. A creditor may not seize a man's wife due to a debt the man incurred before his marriage. Nor may a creditor seize a woman's husband due to a debt the woman incurred before her marriage. In the case of debts incurred after the marriage, "both of them shall be answerable to the merchant."

In death and old age. If a husband who has died has left property to his wife, their children cannot bring a claim for the property against her; the widow can leave the estate to whichever of the children "she loves," but she cannot leave anything to an outsider.[21]

What does it mean to build a social institution? Laws aren't everything, so let's hear some poetry and proverbs about marriage from the Nile Valley. Egyptian law during this dawn-of-civilization period, including family law, was never codified into great law codes similar to those in Mesopotamia. And it was not until the first millennium BCE that we find Egyptian marriage contracts similar to those in Mesopotamia, even though indirect evidence suggests that such contracts probably did exist in earlier periods.[22] Yet the Egyptian contribution to a marriage culture is quite important. Some of this contribution predates the Mesopotamian accomplishment by a number of centuries, and what happened in Egypt probably influenced what happened somewhat later in Mesopotamia.

In about 2450 BCE, an old man named Ptah-Hotep, apparently an important advisor to the Egyptian pharaoh Izezi, compiled a set of wise sayings and instructions for good living intended for his son and for young Egyptians generally. The Egyptians clearly delighted in such "wisdom literature." Instructions such as those prepared by Ptah-Hotep were widely used, for example, in Egyptian schools.

Instructing a father on how to treat a dutiful son, Ptah-Hotep writes: "He is thy son, whom thy *ka* [guiding vital force] engendered for thee. Thou shouldst not cut thy heart off from him." And: "If a man converses with his children, then they will speak to their children. . . ." Here we see a clear affirmation of the importance of fatherhood. But if the son is rebellious and displeasing to the gods, "Thou shouldst cast him off: he is not thy son at all. He was not really born to thee." Here we see an apparent harshness—a trait that is more typical of fathers than of mothers, and one that would be explicitly warned against many centuries later in the Christian scriptures.[23]

But listen to Ptah-Hotep on the subject of marriage, or what the Egyptians frequently termed "founding a household." Ptah-Hotep tells his son: "found thy household and love thy wife at home as is fitting. Fill her belly; clothe her back. Ointment is the prescription for her body. Make her heart glad as long as thou livest." He has a thought or two about who wives are and how to win their affection: "Her eye is her stormwind. Let her heart be soothed through what may accrue to thee; it means keeping her long in thy house. . . ." As for paying attention to other women, Ptah-Hotep warns:

> beware of approaching the women. It does not go well. . . . He who has a wandering eye for the women cannot be keen. A thousand men may be distracted from their own advantage. One is made a fool. . . . Do not do it—it really is an abomination—and thou shall be free from sickness of heart every day.[24]

A later set of instructions from a father to a son, probably dating from somewhere between 1100 and 800 BCE, echoes this advice, saying, "Every man who is settled in a house should hold the hasty heart firm. Thou shouldst not pursue after a woman. Do not let her steal away thy heart." There are also some thoughts about treating a wife with respect:

> Thou shouldst not supervise too closely thy wife in her own house, when thou knowest that she is efficient. Do not say to her, "Where is it? Fetch it for us!" when she has put it in the most useful place. Let thy eye have regard, while thou art silent, that thou mayest recognize her abilities. How happy is it when thy hand is with her![25]

We moderns often seem to assume that couples long ago were not as emotionally aware as we are today. Perhaps their spousal feelings for, or against, one another simply didn't run as deep as ours do. Perhaps marriage in those days wasn't actually about sex-as-relationship and generativity after all, but instead "really" about, say, property or social status.

Nonsense. Except in some respects among that very small slice of humanity who are royalty or nobility—who at times *do* marry largely in order to strengthen political and economic alliances between groups—that has never been true. No one denies that property and social status (and many other big realities as well) affect all spheres of human social life, from education to medicine to, yes, marriage. But what affects something is different from the thing itself. For almost all of humanity, marriage has always and in all places been "really" about the male-female sexual bond and the children that result from that bond. That was certainly true in the two river valleys where this distinctive way of men and women living together became a vibrant public institution.

We can remind ourselves of the tender side of this fact by listening to some love songs from more than three thousand years ago. Egyptians apparently loved love songs. As in the case of the Song of Solomon (the "Song of Songs") in the Hebrew scriptures, one's beloved in these songs is often called "my sister" or "my brother." Here is one sung by a woman:

> I have found my brother in his bed,
> And my heart is still more glad,
> When he said to me:
> "I shall not go far off.
> My hand is in thy hand,
> I shall stroll about,
> And I shall be with thee in every pleasant place."
> He makes me the foremost of maidens.
> He injures not my heart.

For at least the past two decades in the United States, when it comes to mainstream popular music by and for teenagers and young adults, it is quite rare to hear a male singing a sincere love song. There is plenty of cynicism and sex-as-sex, but not much about the beloved. By contrast, here is an Egyptian man from long ago singing:

> To say to me, "Here she is!" is what will revive me.
> Her name is what will lift me up.
> The going in and out of her messengers is what will revive my heart.
> More beneficial to me is the sister than any remedies.
> She is more to me than the collected writings.
> My health is her coming in from the outside.
> When I see her, then I am well.
> If she opens her eye, my body is young again.
> If she speaks, then I am strong again.
> When I embrace her, she drives evil away from me—
> But she has gone forth from me for seven days![26]

The Two Cultures

One of the world's first recorded attempts at cultural analysis is the narrative tale "Enki and Inanna." This story of two gods comes from the land of Sumer in lower Mesopotamia—where we met Gilgamesh—and appears to date from roughly the same period as *The Epic of Gilgamesh.* In the story, the gods Enki and Inanna struggle over possession of a series of "divine decrees"—secret laws that govern all the essential traits and activities of human beings and operations of human society. What makes the story anthropologically significant is that the author provides a full list of these divine laws, and therefore a full list of what the author views as the most important experiences and institutions of human civilization. There are one hundred of them, of which about seventy are currently intelligible to scholars.

The list as a whole is fascinating—it includes "terror," "the troubled heart," "music," "kingship," "eldership," and "metalworking"—but I read it eager to learn whether marriage had made the list of civilization's core acts and institutions. It did not. (At least it is not present in the two-thirds of the list that is readable.) But here are two that *are* present: "sexual intercourse" and "prostitution."[27]

Is this finding a fluke? The result of an incomplete text or an imperfect translation? Perhaps; but I don't think so. Recall our ceramic plaque of the copulating couple, and recall one of the central themes of the Gilgamesh epic: the strong presence in Mesopotamian society of sex-as-sex and of prostitution as a socially accepted and even approved institution.

Think of it as the two sexual cultures, each vibrant, and each in some respects competing against the other for the allegiance and participation of ordinary men and women. One of these cultures was old even then; call it the traditional culture of prostitution, cohabitation, and males as inseminators-not-fathers. The other culture was more recent, just beginning to formalize its traditions and working out its procedures and legal codes. It was reform-minded, even at times idealistic. Call it the newer culture of marriage.

Over and over again in the river valleys, we see the two cultures in conflict. Even as Egyptian poetry and wisdom literature stressed the importance of "founding a household" based on lifelong marriage, Herodotus told several stories also suggesting that, at least among Egyptian elites, attractive prostitutes were highly prized and widely praised.[28]

In Mesopotamia, the goddess Ishtar, the "queen of heaven" who tried to seduce Gilgamesh, was the revered patron goddess of prostitution and of sexual libertinism. A Babylonian hymn to Ishtar, written as long ago as 2000 BCE, says in praise of the goddess:

> Sixty then sixty satisfy themselves in turn upon her nakedness.
> Young men have tired, Ishtar will not tire.[29]

Worshipped as the model of female sexuality and as the divine patron of both free love and fertility, Ishtar has a relationship to marriage that is ambiguous at best. We have already seen, in the Gilgamesh epic, how Ishtar seeks to use her sexual charms to win Gilgamesh, even pleading with him to marry her, only to have Gilgamesh rebuke her by asking, "Which of your lovers did you love for ever?"[30]

Here we glimpse the cultural context in which marriage became institutionalized. We can see the newer culture of marriage challenging the status quo. In a society that accepted and often celebrated prostitution, Lipit-Ishtar decreed that a married man who has a child with a prostitute must support the mother and child financially, and that the child is his heir, but that the prostitute is not a wife and cannot live in the same house as the wife. In a society that accepted cohabitation and sex-without-commitment as viable ways of life, Hammurabi decreed that if a man and a woman are living together, but there is no formal contract, they are not married. Those are confrontational, culture-changing decrees.

Humans are highly sexual creatures, and the marriage achievement in the two river valleys did not occur in a sexual vacuum. We can fully understand the emergence and meaning of marriage only by understanding the antecedents and available alternatives to marriage.

In Egypt and Mesopotamia, the clearest alternatives to marriage appear to have been prostitution and informal cohabitation. So here we can hazard a judgment call. In these ancient societies, in which people who could do so sometimes behaved badly, in which the powerful tended to have their way, and in which adult men tended to have the most power, which way of living—the sex-as-sex culture or the marriage culture—is likely to have been the most progressive, pro-child, and humane?

What Is Marriage?

Does this achievement from the ancient Near East in formalizing and recording a marriage culture give us an answer to our global question of what is marriage? The answer is no. Looking at the institutionalization of marriage in these two river valleys can tell us some things, but not others. Let's start with the things we have learned.

First, if we wish to understand the essential qualities and purposes of marriage, it is important to look at origins. In particular, looking at origins shows us that marriage, although built on deep natural and biological foundations, is ultimately a social invention. Pair-bonding appears to be natural to our species. Getting married is not. People getting married had a beginning, and that beginning demanded great vision and creative effort by specific people in specific times and places. We learn in particular from the river valley accomplishment that marriage is something that is consciously achieved by society.

Second, the basic marriage template that emerged from the ancient Near East has greatly influenced Western civilization and world history. After this template emerged in history—let's call it the river valley model—it did not stay put. For many centuries, this model had quite a run, the consequences of which are still very much with us.

The model first began migrating westward about three thousand years ago, through the people of Israel. Jewish history and culture are closely intertwined with both Mesopotamia and Egypt. For example, we learn in the Hebrew scriptures that Abraham and Sarah (through whom God first made his covenant with Israel) are from the land of Sumer in lower Mesopotamia and that Moses (through whom God revealed the Ten Commandments) was born and raised in Egypt. The marriage regulations contained in the three law codes in the Hebrew scriptures—in the book of Exodus (written in the eleventh century BCE) and in the books of Deuteronomy and Leviticus (both written in the seventh century BCE)—largely incorporate the earlier Mesopotamian codes and Egyptian teachings. The Hebrew scriptures as a whole, beginning with the Genesis story of the marital couple Adam and Eve, presuppose and build on marriage norms that appear to have been first delineated centuries earlier in the two river valleys.[31]

These same marriage norms were essentially embraced and built upon some 2,000 years ago by Jesus and his followers, and more than 1,300 years ago by Mohammed and his followers. So here is the result: Three of the world's great religions—not to mention several empires, including the Roman, the Ottoman, and the British—can trace their fundamental marriage norms directly back to the Egyptian and Mesopotamian accomplishment.

Third, the river valley accomplishment clearly shows us that marriage is more than a private relationship. As I tried to show in Chapter One, almost everyone speaking out in the current marriage debate in the United States either implicitly assumes or emphatically insists that marriages are essentially private relationships to be defined by the couples themselves, not by society. They are wrong. If looking at the emergence of marriage in human groups tells us anything, it tells us that marriage is not only a private relationship, but also a social institution.

A social institution[32] may be defined as a relatively stable pattern of rules and structures intended to meet basic social needs. It is bigger than an organization or a process. A baseball team is an organization. A baseball game, or a baseball season, is a process. But over and above these is something else that defines and guides baseball as a whole—the Baseball Rule Book and the codes, values, and traditions that determine how the players and other participants relate to one another and what the game means and is intended to do. That vital "something else" is the social institution of baseball.

Similarly, a husband and wife living together is an organization. A wedding is a process. But over and above them is something else that defines and guides the enterprise. That "something else" is the social institution of marriage: the laws, customs, values, and traditions that influence how the spouses relate to one another and that convey to them (and other couples) what marriage means and is intended to do.

How do you know if you are looking at a social institution? For starters, a social institution creates and maintains rules, including rules for who is, and is not, a part of the institution. (Remember Dadusha: Even if you've had sex and lived together for a year, if there is no contract and no public celebration, you are not married.) It maintains guidelines for behavior that are relatively binding for the people who participate in the institution. (Dadusha again: If you abandon your wife and children, you lose all that you own.)

More broadly, a social institution creates public meaning. For the people who are a part of it, and to a lesser but still important degree for the society as a whole, a social institution builds and expresses shared agreements about what is important and what is to be valued. (Lipit-Ishtar: The fathers must stand by their children. Hammurabi: A husband must support his seriously ill wife as long as she lives.) The philosopher Charles Frankel once wrote that "responsibility" is "the product of definite social arrangements."[33] Regarding any issue that we as a society deem to be truly important, we do not collectively fall silent or leave things to chance. We build social institutions to create authoritative public meaning.

Finally, and perhaps most importantly, social institutions exist in order to solve basic problems and meet core needs. Why does the institution of marriage exist? It emerged in the two river valleys, and exists everywhere, to address a fundamental human problem and meet a fundamental human need. The problem is that humans are divided into males and females and that they reproduce sexually. The need is for a shared life between the sexes and for the successful raising of children.

Where Do Babies Come From?

Let's now reflect briefly on what we don't know. We have not defined marriage yet, because the marriage achievement in the two river valleys, despite its enormous importance, was historically specific and culturally particular. Marriage is universal. The early and even seminal model from the river valleys helps aim us toward a global definition, but it does not get us all the way there. The main reason is that the river valley model is overtly patriarchal, and marriage need not imply patriarchy, or male dominance over women and children.

A couple of qualifications are in order. First, let's avoid for now the question of whether, and to what degree, *all* human societies to date have been dominated by men. Second, let's not allow the word "patriarchal" to become a scare-word that divides us as contemporary Americans from everyone who lived before us. I have tried to show in this chapter that the basic human problems confronting those who first institutionalized marriage are pretty much the same problems that we face today, and that the solutions they devised for those problems are fairly similar to those that we debate and implement today.

At the same time, there was clearly a patriarchal distortion at the center of those early societies, and it clearly influenced their institutionalization of marriage. What are the key indicators of male dominance in a society? The first is patrilineal descent, or naming and conceptualizing families primarily according to who is the father. The second is property laws guaranteeing the inheritance rights of sons over daughters. The third is male dominance in sexual relationships, including a sexual double standard in which female conduct is more strictly regulated than male conduct. And the fourth is male dominance in political, legal, military, and religious institutions.

On all four counts, the river valleys were male-dominated. Women had rights as persons, and the institutionalization of marriage significantly *increased* rights for married women. But the laws were codified and administered by men, and men had significantly more freedom than women to be independent and act for themselves. Take the example of divorce: As we've seen in the law codes, wives in Mesopotamia had a right to divorce in certain circumstances, and husbands could not divorce at will without paying a penalty, often a heavy one. Yet a wife's ability to divorce usually depended on her being blameless and her husband being blameworthy, whereas a husband's right to divorce was not restricted in a similar way.

I want to suggest that one key to explaining this patriarchal distortion concerns where babies come from. Or more precisely, where people *think* babies come from.

One of the oldest and most influential beliefs held by human beings on this matter was that the female body is the primary source of children. In this view, the female much more than the male participates directly with the divine in the mysteries of creation and procreation. (I once asked the psychiatrist and anthropologist David Gutmann why it is usually the old men of the tribe who lead the prayer. He smiled and said that perhaps men got the role of talking to the divine because everyone knew that women already had the divine in them.)

The great Mesopotamian creation story is "Enuma Elis" ("When on high," after the epic's opening words). In the story, the father-god Apsu (the "begetter" of all) and the mother-goddess Tiamat ("who bore them all") produce children. This happens as a result of "their [Apsu and Tiamat's] waters commingling as a single body." In turn, the children of Apsu and Tiamat—as a consequence of some high family drama over the course of several generations, including acts of cosmic patricide and matricide—end up creating the world.[34] This story is very old, but scholars believe there is an even older one, in which the font of creation is not the couple, but the female alone. Described simultaneously as a figure, as a place, and as matter (apparently watery, like the sea), she is female and self-generative, the source of the sources. She is "Nammu, the Lady of the Gods, the Mother who gave birth to the Universe."[35]

The Hebrew scriptures were created over the course of more than a millennium, from about 1200 to about 100 BCE, and they owe a great deal to Mesopotamian law and literature. They are also clearly patriarchal, strongly upholding patrilineal descent and therefore a model of marriage and society built largely on the principle of the father as the originator of families.[36] Here again, scholars believe there is an older idea behind this one. In a brilliant study, the psychologist and biblical scholar David Bakan shows that "the basic theme" of the Hebrew scriptures is the meaning of fatherhood and, in particular, the importance of transforming the male from a mere inseminator into a nurturing father and lifelong husband. According to Bakan, one reason for this preoccupation is that the fatherhood idea, compared with the motherhood idea, is so weak and fragile. It is also newer.

The earliest Hebrew clans, Bakan suggests, were organized on a *matrilineal* basis, just as, according to some anthropologists, the earliest European societies likely were organized without reference to, and perhaps without knowledge of, biological paternity. Bakan shows how the creators of the Hebrew scriptures struggled for many generations to erase the old mother-as-source idea from their sacred writings and replace it with a new and robust affirmation of patrilineal descent. He also examines repeated and still-remaining evidence in the scriptures, in the story of Abraham and Sarah and their son Isaac and elsewhere, of Jewish belief in the principle of divine impregnation. "The idea of God as father," he observes, "may well have been understood historically as more literal than metaphorical."[37]

One more example. In the second, historically most recent version of the creation story in Genesis, the first woman, Eve, is created from the rib of the first man, Adam (Genesis 2:21–22). The meaning of this claim is far from obvious, and the metaphor of the rib may in fact derive from an earlier Mesopotamian story.[38] But it effectively reverses the older implication of the female creator-goddess: Instead of the male coming from the female, it's now the other way around. Yet the first, historically oldest version of the Hebrew creation story puts it differently: "So God created man in his own image, in the image of God he created them; male and female he created them" (Genesis 1:27). Bakan suggests that the later version, with Eve formed from Adam's rib, is one part of a largely successful effort by the creators of the scriptures to produce a more unambiguously patrilineal narrative.

In the Hebrew scriptures, and more generally in Mesopotamia and Egypt, the effort was successful. As a result, what the historian Gerda Lerner calls "the supremacy of the Goddess" came gradually to an end, as cultural narratives of creation and procreation either ceased emphasizing the primacy of female creator-goddesses or eventually replaced them with images of the divine as father.[39] In the societies themselves, it appears that matrilineal descent was replaced by patrilineal descent. The idea that mothers are the basic originators of children was replaced by the idea that fathers are the basic originators of children.

The marriage scholar David Mace describes the new "idea of gestation" that organized this shift intellectually and drove it culturally: "The woman simply provides a receptacle for the protection and nourishment of the male 'seed,' from which the new life wholly derives its nature and being." And: "The woman provides nothing of her essential self to the new being. She merely provides in her womb the human incubator in which the man's seed becomes his child, the reproduction of his image."[40] A Mesopotamian commentary on the god Marduk puts it this way: "His sperm is gold."[41]

This idea, possibly born in the river valleys, has profoundly influenced Western and world culture, in particular our conception of marriage and our laws and customs regulating marriage. I believe that it lies at the heart of what I am calling the patriarchal distortion. Let's briefly consider how widespread and influential this idea eventually became.

In the Law Code of Manu, one of India's foundational legal and philosophical texts, probably written between 200 BCE and 100 CE, the lawgiver asks: If a married woman has a child by a man other than her husband, who is the child's father? Manu states that sacred opinion on this question is "divided," but in reviewing the case for the biological father, the lawgiver writes:

> Between the seed and the womb, the seed is considered dominant; for the offspring of all creatures is marked by the characteristics of the seed.... the seed, as it develops, does not manifest any of the qualities associated with the womb. Even when different kinds of seeds are sown by farmers in the very same plot at the right time, they are seen in the world to sprout differently, each according to its nature.[42]

In the eighth century, from the Qur'an, we learn that Allah, to create a new human being, "placed him as a drop of seed in a safe lodging [the womb]." The question is asked, "From what thing does Allah create man?" The answer is: "From a drop of seed he creates and proportions him." And we are told: "So let us consider from what he [man] is created. He is created from a gushing fluid that issues from between the loins and the ribs."[43]

Plato, writing in the fourth century BCE, argues that "seed" exists in both women and men.[44] But Plato's most famous student, Aristotle, describes at some length the male parent as the "generative parent" or "fashioning agent." Because the male seed is purer, hotter, more active and powerful, and more divine than the female's, it is the male seed alone that provides the child's essential "soul." Thus "the semen produced by the male is the cause of the offspring." A child is the joint issue of the male and female, Aristotle tells us, only in the way that a piece of furniture is the joint issue of the carpenter and the wood. Once conception has taken place, Aristotle tells us, the process operates like a seed sown in the ground.[45]

The Eumenides ("The Furies"), written by the Greek playwright Aeschylus in the fifth century BCE, explicitly features the conflict between the old principle of matrocentrism—the baby comes essentially from the mother—and the newly regnant principle of fathers as the essential originators of children. In this remarkable play, a wife kills her husband for the sake of her lover. The son avenges his father's murder by killing his mother. The Furies, the old and dethroned mother-goddesses, do not blame the mother for what she did, because she is not related by blood to the man she killed, but they do blame and pursue the son for killing his mother. Yet the son is protected by two younger gods, Apollo and Athena, the latter of whom emerged, not from a mother's womb, but from the head of Zeus. The Furies lash out at Apollo: "Robber is all you are." By overturning the "primeval" principles of matriarchy, Zeus has "ridden down powers gray with age" and has "blighted age-old distributions of power." He has "destroyed the orders of an elder time." But the playwright lets Apollo, the newly dominant patriarchal god, settle the dispute once and for all by declaring:

> The mother is no parent of that which is called
> her child, but only nurse of the new-planted seed
> that grows. The parent is he who mounts.[46]

Here in Greece is further evidence from ancient texts suggesting that an "age-old" idea of mother as originator existed prior to the idea of father as originator, and that a conflict between the two theories ultimately resulted in at least partial displacement of matrocentrism by patrocentrism in some societies.[47]

What does this shift tell us about the meaning and definition of marriage? I want to suggest three ideas.

First, the affirmation of patrilineal descent in the two river valleys clearly contributed to the rise of a high culture of fatherhood—a culture in which fathers were expected to, and largely did, stick with their families and care for their children. In the scale of things, this was no small achievement—especially from a child's point of view.

Second, and equally clearly, this affirmation of fathers as the originators of children contributed to a culture of male domination and to the continuation, and at times the deepening, of many abuses and gender inequalities in these societies. In the scale of things, this was no small problem—especially from a woman's point of view.

Finally, and most obviously, the affirmation was wrong! What I am calling the patriarchal distortion in these societies rested on a deeply flawed understanding of where babies come from. The word "patriarchy" literally means "father" (*pater*) at "the beginning or origin" (*arche*). But fathers are not the essential originators of children any more than mothers are. The fact that one erroneous idea seems to have replaced an equally erroneous and probably much more ancient idea, and also that it contributed in important ways to the rise of fatherhood as a social role for men, is ultimately not the heart of the matter, at least for us today. The heart of the matter is what is true, and this idea is simply untrue.

Regarding the definition of marriage, we are left with this question: Do marriage and male dominance go together naturally? Is the patriarchal distortion that we find in the river valley model a part of the definition of marriage itself? Alternatively, does marriage as a human institution transcend the issue of matrilineal versus patrilineal descent? To answer this question, let's go to the South Pacific.

4
Trobriand Islands

I AM AN OLD WOMAN, a grandmother. I live on the island of Boyowa. I can tell you what you want to know. I can explain why children here tend especially to look like their fathers.

Try an experiment. Put a ball of soft mash in your hand. Close your fingers around the ball and press gently. Then open your hand. You will see an imprint of your hand and fingers on the ball, won't you? That's how it is with a father and his child.

When his wife is pregnant, the husband frequently touches her. In this way he helps mold the developing child. The couple sits together often. Each night they sleep together. Often they have sexual intercourse, for it is well known that frequent intercourse during pregnancy contributes to the growth and vitality of the developing child. The husband's molding influence on the child's appearance begins with, and stems from, his closeness to his wife.

As soon as the child is born, it is "received in the arms of the father," so that he can hold and care for the child, continuing to mold the child, like the ball of mash. A father on this island seeks to smile his child into smiling, and his looks of affection help teach the child where to look, and how, so that the child's face begins even more to resemble her father's. It is beautiful to see. It is also well known that most fathers here are very devoted to their children and treat them tenderly, which further helps to explain why our children resemble their fathers.

Naming also plays a role. Of course, the child's official name comes from the mother. Our naming system is matrilineal because babies come from mothers. But the child's unofficial name, the intimate and familiar one used every day, is chosen by the husband's family and is given to the child as a gift from the father. Doesn't it make sense that the intimacy of the naming and the resemblance of the names would contribute to physical resemblances between father and child?

There are other special gifts. Soon after the birth, the father gives the baby earrings made of small, beautiful shells. Even very young children, boys as well as girls, wear them. The earrings demonstrate to everyone that the husband is a good provider and a strong presence in the child's life. For a child's ears to be unpierced and without these earrings is a sign of shame—it means that the child is fatherless, which is a terrible thing.

Some time after the gift of the earrings comes the gift of the necklace. This necklace is also made of beautiful shells and is even more expensive than the earrings. It shows that a man has status and wealth that he is making available to his child. With these gifts, the husband is giving something of himself, something of his intention and capacity, that helps to make the child physically beautiful. When mothers stop nursing, children typically start sleeping with their fathers—another opportunity for the father to mold the person that the child is becoming. How can these realities fail to affect the child's appearance?

The missionaries, trying to persuade us to worship their god, whom they call a father, tell us that human babies are made from the male semen. But common sense shows that what they say is preposterous! If male semen emitted during sexual intercourse were the actual source of babies, how could it be that some couples have sexual intercourse many times but no baby is ever made? There are also frequent examples on this island of pregnant women who say sincerely and believably that they have not had sexual intercourse. Maybe some are not telling the truth. But are all of them lying? It is not logical to think so.

No, it is well known that a baby spirit—a baby essence, waiting and wanting to be born—settles onto the head of the woman and, if the time is right, passes down through her body and into her womb. There the spirit mixes with her menstrual blood and becomes a human baby. For this reason, a woman can tell almost immediately when she is pregnant, because she stops menstruating. The menstrual blood no longer leaves her body, because the blood is busy inside, making the baby. The man's semen has nothing to do with it! Of course, it is well known that sexual intercourse opens up the woman's vagina, making it easier for the baby to exist in the womb and to come out during childbirth. But the baby itself is a true gift from Tuma, the spirit world that is unseen, coming to its parents through the mother and made of her body alone.

The child looks like her father because of the deep intimacy between the father and child, which comes from and is made possible by the marriage of the man and the woman.

Where Do Babies Come From?

The Trobriand Islands are twenty-two mostly low-lying coral islands located just below the equator in the South Pacific, near the eastern tip of Papua New Guinea. The largest and most densely populated of these islands is Kiriwina, formerly called Boyowa. The Trobrianders primarily speak Kilivila, one of the many Austronesian languages spoken by the peoples of Melanesia.

The Trobriands are about as far from the river valleys in Mesopotamia and ancient Egypt as it is possible to be, not just geographically and chronologically but also culturally. So if we wish to test the hypothesis that there is a core, cross-cultural *there* to marriage—that underneath all the astonishing diversity of custom, there is in fact a definable human universal called *marriage*—then comparing the marriage model born in the ancient river valleys with marriage in twentieth-century Melanesia is a worthwhile experiment.

Trobriand marriage is different in ways that should be intensely interesting to modern Western heirs to the river valley model who are curious to know whether *all* marriage, by definition, contains a patriarchal distortion, particularly sexually repressive norms and a double standard that privileges men and disempowers women. To explore this question, there is no better place to go than the Trobriand Islands. And the Trobrianders themselves, it turns out, are fascinating and extremely attractive people.

The Trobriand Islands are well known throughout the world among students of anthropology, in large measure due to the work of Bronislaw Malinowski in the early decades of the twentieth century. One of the founders of anthropology as a modern scientific discipline, Malinowski did his most important research in the Trobriand Islands, where he lived and did field work between 1915 and 1918. Since that time, important additional research has been conducted by a number of anthropologists, including H. A. Powell in the early 1950s and Annette B. Weiner in the 1970s and early 1980s.

As we learned through the old grandmother's voice, traditional Trobriand culture teaches that a father is biologically unrelated to his child. The classical view is that a woman becomes pregnant when the soul or spiritual essence of a baby enters her body, in some cases vaginally, but more often by settling on her head and descending through her body to the womb. Male-female sexual intercourse, while viewed as related to the pregnancy in some way, is not regarded as either the proximate cause or the fundamental explanation of the pregnancy. Specifically, male semen is viewed as materially unrelated to the presence of the baby in the mother's womb and to the physiological development and appearance of the child.

Trobriand religion teaches that when a Trobriander dies, his or her spirit travels to the island of Tuma, where it lives happily in a world inhabited by other spirits—a world that cannot normally be seen by living human beings. These spirits are called *baloma.* When a *baloma* grows old and wrinkled, it goes into the salt water to bathe, loses its skin, and regresses into a tiny spirit-baby, a kind of human embryo in spirit form. These spirit-babies are called *waiwaia.*

A *waiwaia* cannot remain among the spirits but must eventually return to the island on which it had previously lived as an embodied person. Upon its return, the *waiwaia* finds a woman who is from the same matrilineage as itself and enters her body, mixing with her blood in order to form a human baby.

There is heated debate among anthropologists as to how non-Trobrianders can best understand these traditional ideas. Some argue that most Trobrianders have believed literally that sexual intercourse does not cause pregnancy. Others argue that most Trobrianders have regarded these teachings less as a scientific explanation than as a broad metaphysical and religious doctrine and an important cultural myth.[1] In either case, the traditional Trobriand view of reproduction can tell us something about the meaning of marriage.

Let's begin with the most obvious point: The classical Trobriand theory is an almost *perfect inversion* of the Mesopotamian and Egyptian theory. The marriage culture that was born in the two river valleys contained, in its fundamental view of human reproduction, a clear patriarchal distortion. Just as clearly, classical Trobriand culture contains a matriarchal distortion. In the former, the fundamental originator of the human child is the father. In the latter, the fundamental originator of the child is the mother.

According to Malinowski, the Trobriand "theory of procreation" is the basis of that society's "whole doctrine of matrilineal identity in kinship."[2] The "idea that it is solely and exclusively the mother who builds up the child's body" emerges as a key organizing principle of Trobriand life and "the most important factor in the legal system of the Trobrianders."[3]

For example, consider the issue of adoption. It is considered extremely wrong and shameful for a Trobriand woman to have a child if she is not married. For this reason, children born outside of marriage are typically adopted by married couples. And since a Trobriand father is viewed as biologically unrelated to his child, therefore legally, and also to a large degree sociologically, a man's adopted child is regarded as no less "his" child than the child that is born of his wife![4]

In the Trobriands, the legal head of each family is not the husband, but the mother's brother, who is considered to be the closest male relative of his sister's children. The uncle is also the child's legal guardian and typically plays a major role in the child's life.[5] Part of his obligation involves the law of *urigubu,* which Malinowski describes as the "most sociologically sensational feature of Trobriand marriage" and "perhaps the most important factor in the whole social mechanism of Trobriand society."[6] The *urigubu* largely concerns gardens.

The Trobrianders are wonderful, prolific gardeners.[7] Garden produce, particularly yams, forms the basis of their diet and a foundation of their economy. But Trobriand gardens are also much more than a means of producing food. Well kept and aesthetically pleasing gardens are highly admired as markers of status and achievement. To say that a Trobriand man is a "good gardener" is to pay him one of the society's highest and most sought-after compliments. Garden magic—each village has a head garden magician—is one of the society's principal forms of magic. Like rice in Japan, yams in the Trobriands are more than food. They also contain many symbolic and ritual meanings—some of them related to marriage.

The main feature of the *urigubu* is a harvest gift of yams presented annually to the married couple by the woman's brother, the family's legal head. The gift is large and economically important, typically amounting to about half of all the yams that the couple and their children will consume during the year. The harvest gift from the uncle is also mandatory. It is a great shame for a Trobriand man to fail his sister and her family in this regard. If he cannot perform this obligation, usually one of his sons or his father or another of his kinsmen will.

Here's how the process typically works: Each year Kalogusa, a Trobriand husband and father, will keep about half of his yam harvest for himself, his wife, Isepuna, and their children, storing it in the yam house he has built. With much ceremony, he will give the other half—typically consisting of the better, more appealing produce—to his sister, Dabugera, her husband, To'uluwa, and their children. At the same time that Kalogusa is performing this obligation on behalf of To'uluwa and his family, however, To'uluwa is busily preparing the *urigubu* presentation for *his* sister, who lives with her husband and children in a nearby village. But Kalogusa's wife, Isepuna, *also* has a brother, who is preparing a harvest gift to present to Isepuna, Kalogusa, and their children. In fact, when we consider that most Trobrianders have a number of siblings, it gets considerably more complex.

What is the purpose of circulating the harvest in this way? In large part, the *urigubu* reflects the matriarchal distortion, the belief that children come from the mother only, so that the child's closest male relative and legal guardian is the mother's brother. His obligation regarding the *urigubu* is one of the clearest social and economic indicators of the fact that Trobrianders determine their bloodlines and their family responsibilities on a matrilineal basis.

At the same time, the *urigubu* helps to shape Trobriand marriage. Only a married woman can receive the harvest gift. The first presentation comes a few months after the couple is married, accompanied by special ceremony and display focusing on the newlyweds. It constitutes one of the final and most important of the many gift exchanges connected to Trobriand marriage.[8]

More broadly, the *urigubu* adds structure and stability to Trobriand marriage. The law guarantees that the fortunes and wishes of the married couple will be closely linked to the fortunes and wishes of both the husband's family and the wife's family. This linkage actually begins prior to marriage, during courtship. Trobriand young people enjoy considerable freedom in choosing their marriage partners, but far from complete freedom. A girl's brother (and father) can express disapproval of the match by threatening to withhold the *urigubu*.[9] In these and similar ways, the complex web of obligations, rules, and interdependent relationships surrounding the *urigubu* emerges as both an anchor and a building block of marriage as social institution in the Trobriands.[10]

For these reasons, we should understand the *urigubu* less as the simple result of the matriarchal distortion than as the result of a family system that *combines* matriarchal principles with marriage principles. The *urigubu* nicely unites both aspects of Trobriand family life: the importance of the mother's lineage and the special role of her brother, and the importance of marriage and fatherhood.

Let's be clear: The Trobriands are by no means a matriarchal *society*, if by matriarchy we mean social arrangements through which women as a group have political and decision-making power over men. For example, the office of chief in traditional Trobriand society is reserved for upper-status males. The village leader, the "head man," is by definition male. Similarly, village and tribal council meetings have traditionally been male-run affairs.

But at the same time, while Trobriand society is certainly not a matriarchy, it has some interesting features regarding the status women.

Malinowski was obviously impressed by the independence and high social standing of Trobriand women. Men and women in the Trobriands, he reports, are regarded as "being of equal value and importance." He pointedly remarks that the idea of female infanticide, so common in many societies, would be both "abhorrent" and "absurd" from a Trobriand perspective. Prostitution is foreign to Trobriand culture.

The Trobriand family household, Malinowski informs us, "is founded on the principles of equality and independence of function." Walking around a village, he observes "men and women mixing freely and on terms of equality." Listening to their conversations, he reports: "We can hear the women scold their husbands, usually in a very good-natured manner."[11] And further:

> The frank and friendly tone of intercourse, the obvious feeling of equality, the father's domestic helpfulness, especially with the children, would at once strike any observant visitor. The wife joins freely in the jokes and conversation; she does her work independently, not with the air of a slave or servant, but as one who manages her own department. She will order her husband about if she needs his help.[12]

The sexual double standard that we saw in Egypt and Mesopotamia, in which female conduct is more tightly regulated than male conduct, is mostly absent from Trobriand culture. Sexual faithfulness in marriage is valued, but no more for women than for men. And for the unmarried of both sexes, including children, an active sexual life, including intercourse with multiple partners over time, is permitted and even expected and encouraged. In general, when it comes to sexual expression, Malinowski reports that "the Trobriand woman does not consider herself man's inferior, nor does she lag behind him in initiative and self-assertion."[13]

In the two river valleys, as we have seen, men had easier access to divorce than did women. But in the Trobriands, men and women have traditionally had equal access to divorce. The most commonly stated cause of marital conflict and separation in the Trobriands is adultery. In cases of separation, the parents and relatives of the spouses often try to encourage reconciliation, and these family members do have economic and other means of persuasion at their disposal. But in the final analysis, either spouse who is determined to leave the marriage can do so on what we in the United States would call an essentially "no fault" basis.[14]

From the husband's vantage point, one practical reason to avoid divorce is that the annual *urigubu* presentation of yams to his family is dependent upon his remaining married to the woman whose brother is presenting the gift. This reality probably does not similarly constrain a Trobriand woman who may be considering divorce and remarriage. The *urigubu* means that a Trobriand woman brings an important (and usually portable) economic resource to her marriage, which may enable her to act with some autonomy. It seems likely that most Trobriand divorces are initiated by women. Malinowski reports that "there are many instances of a woman leaving her husband simply because she does not like him."[15]

The previous chapter specified the four main pillars of a patriarchal society: patrilineal descent; inheritance laws favoring males; male dominance in sexual life, including a sexual double standard; male dominance of political, legal, military, and religious institutions. Ancient Egypt and Mesopotamia were deeply patriarchal on all four counts.

By contrast, in the Trobriand Islands we find matrilineal descent, inheritance determined by female bloodlines, a high degree of equality in sexual life, and the general absence of a sexual double standard. Only in the fourth (admittedly quite important) area are the Trobriands unambiguously patriarchal. Overall, Trobriand women enjoy high status and considerable personal freedom and autonomy—not only in contrast to other Melanesian societies, but in contrast to just about anywhere. The matriarchal distortion in the classical Trobriand understanding of conception is closely tied to the unusual status of women in Trobriand society.

Instituting Marriage

Regarding sexual behavior and courtship, the historical Trobriand Islands remind me a great deal of the contemporary United States. Groups of older Trobriand boys, for example, typically live for a period of time prior to marriage in a *bukumatula,* or bachelors' house. Here, boys can and do, without social disapproval, regularly invite girlfriends to sleep over with them. It's not very different from what happens in a typical college dormitory today.[16]

When one of these *bukumatula*-based sexual relationships becomes romantically serious, the two lovers stop having sexual relationships with others and become a steady couple. They usually live together for a period of time. Then, if all goes well, they get married. Sound familiar?

But let's look at how Trobrianders *marry.* When a couple decides to marry, the first step is fairly simple. Typically the couple have been sleeping together each night, usually in the boy's parents' hut. But one morning, instead of leaving the hut before sunrise to go about her usual activities, the young woman remains. The sun comes up. The lovers sit together near the front of the hut and eat a meal together, cutting each yam into two pieces, so that each spouse eats one-half of the whole. It is the first time that they have eaten together. This first shared meal publicly declares the couple's decision, or at least their desire, to marry.

The next step is parental and family approval, which customarily is all but mandatory.[17] If the bride's parents and uncles approve of the match, on either the day of the marriage declaration or the day after, the bride's mother prepares several small baskets of cooked yams and the bride's father takes this gift over to the groom's parents' hut, ceremonially placing the baskets in front of the hut.

The second marriage gift closely follows the first and also comes from the bride's family. The third gift is a presentation of platters of uncooked vegetables, again given by the bride's family to the groom's family. Note that in each of these three ceremonies, the girl's *father,* by presenting gifts, must formally assent to his daughter's marriage.[18]

The fourth marriage gift comes from the groom's family. It consists of platters of cooked vegetables, intended to acknowledge and repay the gifts of vegetables that were recently received from the bride's family.

The fifth marriage gift is especially important. It comes from the boy's father and is presented to the bride's family. It consists of valuables such as polished axe blades of green stone, shell necklaces, and shell bracelets. At the next harvest, the bride's family will reciprocate by presenting a gift of yams to the groom's father and his family.

Annette Weiner, whose Trobriand research in the late 1970s and early 1980s focused particularly on women's roles, reports that soon after a couple declare their marriage by eating yams together,

> the young man's sister brings three long skirts to her new sister-in-law. First she ties each one around her brother's wife's waist, and then with a knife she cuts the fibers until the length is just below the knee. No longer can the woman wear the short, provocative miniskirts that adolescents wear. Her days of adolescent sexual freedom are gone. Both she and her husband take off their red shell necklaces, for to continue to wear them indicates that they are still looking for lovers.[19]

These initial gift exchanges signify that both families agree to and will support the marriage. They serve as the society's seal of approval for the couple. They also, as in the case of the skirts and necklaces, help convey to the young couple what marriage means, showing them how to make the transition from being single to being married. Finally, these gifts foreshadow the later, ongoing exchanges that will continue to influence and guide the couple in their life together. They are important components of marriage as an institution in the Trobriands.

After the last gift, there is a pause, usually until the next harvest. During this time, the newlyweds may continue to live in the boy's parents' hut while their own hut is being built, and each day the girl's mother cooks and brings them one bowl of yams and other food, which they eat together from the same plate.

When the harvest comes, they move into their own home. There, the wife for the first time assumes responsibility for preparing and cooking their meals. Moreover, once they are in their own home, the spouses no longer eat together. Sharing the meal, a profound and public sign of marital intimacy, is deemed appropriate only as a means of initially declaring the marriage and as an expression of the newlywed or honeymoon stage of the marriage.[20]

The getting-married process is complete—in a sense, the couple becomes finally and fully *married*—when the wife's uncle (or in some cases her father) makes the first harvest presentation to the newly formed household. The harvest gift is not the only *urigubu* obligation owed by the brother to his married sister and her husband. From now on, the husband can call upon the wife's brother and her other male relatives for a variety of services, such as helping him with projects that require communal labor, helping him transport his *urigubu* gift to *his* sister and her husband, watching over him when he is sick, protecting him against sorcery, coming to his aid in feuds, and, when he dies, performing rites of mourning. These gifts, too, must be reciprocated.[21]

Such exchanges thicken and strengthen Trobriand marriage. Through them, each marriage is embedded in a web of obligations and commitments extending to the community as a whole. They help to ensure that marriage in the Trobriands is an *institution* rather than merely a private relationship.

As a legal matter, divorce in the Trobriands is easy to obtain. But as a social institution, Trobriand marriage tends to resist divorce. As Annette Weiner writes, "Divorce is not easily effected, and relatives on both the girl's side and the boy's side are often instrumental in repairing a marital separation."[22] If you are unmarried, Trobriand sexual norms are remarkably permissive. But Malinowski observes that "the matrimonial knot, once tied, is firm and exclusive."[23]

This matrimonial tie extends beyond the end of a Trobriander's life. The death of a spouse initiates a long and intense period of mourning, including many rituals and gift exchanges, some involving valuables made by women. As Malinowski puts it, mourning the death of one's spouse in the Trobriands is "but a link in the life-long chain of reciprocities between husband and wife and between their respective families."[24]

When a husband dies, for example, traditionally his widow cuts her hair, blackens herself with soot and grease, and wears a mourning costume provided by her dead husband's sisters. She lives alone in a special hut for six months to two years. For several years after his death, she will carry her husband's jawbone with her wherever she goes. To compensate her for this suffering and repay her devotion, her dead husband's relatives will give her significant gifts over time.[25]

For Every Child, Two Parents

Although marriage on the Trobriand Islands has an unusual pattern, it does shed light on the universal form, particularly if we examine the Trobriand father.

There are many reasons to assume that Trobriand fatherhood might be pretty thin stuff. In the classic teaching, the father is not even biologically related to his child. Trobriand culture has comparatively few of the traditional patriarchal furnishings. There is a quite permissive and largely egalitarian code of sexual conduct, with little if any evidence of a double standard. There is equal access to legally no-fault divorce. Women have high status and a significant degree of independence. The father's power stemming from his breadwinning capacity is also diluted, since his wife's brother provides much of the family's economic support.

Yet the Trobriand father is not marginal. Most Trobriand fathers are emotionally quite close to their children. Malinowski reports that the Trobriand husband "fully shares in the care of the children. He will fondle and carry a baby, clean and wash it, and give it the mashed vegetable food which it receives in addition to the mother's milk from birth." The Trobrianders have a special word, *kopo'i,* that can mean breastfeeding but can also mean the tender care of a father for his child. Malinowski explains:

> The father performs his duties with genuine natural fondness: he will carry an infant about for hours, looking at it with eyes full of such love and pride as are seldom seen in those of a European father. Any praise of the baby goes directly to his heart....[26]

The anthropologist Stanley N. Kurtz concludes that "much of what we think of as 'mothering' is actually performed by the Trobriand father."[27] Malinowski repeatedly observed that Trobriand children are much more attached to their fathers than to the uncles who legally head their families.[28] When he asked Trobriand children about their fathers, the children often explained the importance of the *kopo'i* and stressed how much they owed to the man whose "hands have been soiled" with his child's urine and excrement.[29] When Annette B. Weiner asked young adults in the Trobriands about their fathers, they similarly framed their responses in the classic and quite beautiful Trobriand vocabulary of gifts given and of what is owed. This is what she would frequently hear:

> My father always worked hard for me; he always gave me everything for nothing. When I was a small girl [or boy], he cut firewood for me, he bought fish for me to eat, he gave me betel nuts to chew, and he always gave me yams to eat. Because he gave me all those things for nothing, I love that man very much.[30]

For a Trobriand woman, to bear a child outside of marriage—to have a child that the Trobrianders call "fatherless"—is dishonorable, even shameful.[31] Trobrianders often told Malinowski that bearing a child with "no father" is wrong because "there is no man to take the child in his arms."[32]

If you want to insult a Trobriander deeply—to show contempt and scorn and seek to humiliate—tell her that she physically resembles her mother (even if her mother is beautiful). Or tell him that he looks like his sister or his brother. Malinowski, trying to be friendly, made this mistake early on during his stay on Boyowa, and quickly learned that he had a committed a serious breach of custom and had injured the persons whom he was trying to flatter.

On the other hand, Trobrianders regularly point out, with obvious pleasure and pride, that Trobriand children look like their fathers. Trobriand belief regarding this particular resemblance is firm, clear, and public. After a man dies, for example, his relatives and friends customarily visit his children and give them gifts in order, as they put it, to "see his face in theirs."[33]

Why are Trobriand children, who everyone insists do *not* look like their own mothers or siblings, viewed as strongly resembling men to whom they are believed to be biologically unrelated? Our fictional grandmother at the beginning of this chapter gives the main reasons: A man's day-to-day physical closeness to his wife, including his sexual intercourse with her during pregnancy, helps to form the preborn child, especially the face. The *kopo'i*—the father's tender care and feeding of the newborn—also helps to orient and shape the child's features. When the mother stops nursing, the child sleeps with the father for a period of time, which contributes further to molding the child's appearance. The Trobriand father gives his newborn child its unofficial but usually more intimate name.

A bit later, the father will also give the child special gifts—colorful shell earrings and a valuable shell necklace—that make the child attractive and demonstrate to the community that this child has a father who loves and protects her.[34]

Clearly, the Trobriand belief about physical resemblance serves to reinforce the father-child bond. It says to the child, "look who you are like," and to the father, "look at *your* child." It bolsters fatherhood as a social role.

Combined with the virtual taboo against recognizing physical resemblances between mother and child or between siblings, the Trobrianders' insistence on father-child resemblance is a clear example of a largely *matrilineal* society embracing and acting on a *patrilineal* concept. More precisely, we are seeing that a generally matrilineal belief system (children come from mothers only) can at times be compromised and even overshadowed by an apparently patrilineal idea (children look like their fathers).

Some societies, including ancient Egypt and Mesopotamia, strongly privilege patrilineal descent and also what more generally might be called father-right. Other societies, including the Trobriand Islands, lean heavily in the direction of matriliny and mother-right. But these differences between mother-right and father-right, while obviously important, are almost always differences of emphasis or degree. They are almost never absolute or categorical divides. So it's not at all strange that a largely matrilineal society like that of the Trobriand Islands should also clearly recognize and repeatedly stress the importance of fatherhood, even occasionally doing so in a way that might appear to contradict their own deeply held beliefs about the origins of children.

Here we reach a key point in our inquiry into the meaning of marriage. In the study of kinship, a central finding of anthropology is that in the crucial area of filiation—defined as who the child affiliates with, emotionally, morally, practically, and legally—the overwhelming majority of human societies are bilateral. Almost *all* human societies strongly seek for the child to affiliate with *both* its mother and its father.[35]

Let's look at another Trobriand example of this phenomenon. It concerns male inheritance—in the Trobriands, women and men have their own possessions—and in particular a father's ability to give important gifts to his son. Since Trobrianders reckon kinship through maternal bloodlines only, a man's main possessions and special rights are properly inherited, when he dies, not by his son but instead by his sister's son, who stands as the nearest male heir in their matrilineage. These rights and possessions may include magic, garden plots, trees, special roles in dances and ceremonies, fishing and canoe rights, heirlooms, and tools. Moreover, the man in question is formally obligated to pass on some of these items to his nephew and legal heir *before* he dies, when and if the nephew presents him with a special payment for them, called a *pokala.* All this reflects the mother-right.

On the other hand, the Trobrianders have a saying: No man loves his sister's children as much as he loves his own children. As a result, accommodations to father-right are made. While they are still living, Trobriand fathers may give many of their goods directly to their sons, who unlike the nephews are not required to give the *pokala.* When the man dies, or when the nephew presents the *pokala,* the son is expected to relinquish what the nephew is owed. But for many years of their lives, most Trobriand fathers can effectively give much of what they possess to their sons. Moreover, in some cases, especially regarding the crucial use of magic, it appears that many Trobriand fathers actually do pass on the gift in perpetuity to their sons, notwithstanding the general principle of matrilineal inheritance.[36]

A final example of bilateral filiation: When a son reaches puberty, he is customarily expected to leave the home of his mother and father, who are living in the father's village, and live instead for the rest of his life in his mother's village, where his lineage is based—*unless* his father needs him to remain nearby in order to help fill the yam house! Not surprisingly, many Trobriand fathers discover that they need help with the yams, and thus they keep their sons nearby, often even after the sons marry. Malinowski calls this practice "a regular institution."[37]

So father-right manages to assume a place for itself in Trobriand law and custom, even in the overall context of mother-right. After a careful review of Malinowski's data on Trobriand fathers, including their central role in guiding the marriages of both daughters and sons, Marguerite S. Robinson concludes that "the Trobriand father is invested with important, and, in some respects, decisive jural, economic and ritual roles, rights and responsibilities."[38]

For every child, a mother *and* a father. That's the primary rule. Even for societies largely guided by mother-right. Even for societies with unusually permissive sexual codes. Even for societies in which the father is viewed as a biological stranger to his child.

Malinowski called it the "rule of legitimacy." This rule states in essence that "the group of mother and child is incomplete and the sociological position of the father is regarded universally as indispensable." Some of the specific features and expressions of this principle vary from society to society, depending upon a range of factors, but

> through all these variations there runs the rule that the father is indispensable for the full sociological status of the child as well as of its mother, that the group consisting of a woman and her offspring is sociologically incomplete and illegitimate. The father, in other words, is necessary for the full legal status of the family.[39]

Let's pause for a moment over that loaded word, "illegitimate." Some people today sharply criticize this word, and many people in recent years have stopped using it, primarily in order to make clear that they do not wish to blame or stigmatize the children in question. I share this concern, and I personally do not use the term "illegitimate," for precisely this reason.

But Malinowski was writing decades ago, not as a moralist and certainly not as someone who wished to stigmatize children. He wrote as a scientist, an anthropologist, seeking to discern the fundamental patterns of kinship through time and across human societies. He was looking for the essence of how human groups reproduce and how societies organize to protect children. And he became convinced of the key answer—in the Trobriand Islands, of all places! Now we can see more clearly why Malinowski became so deeply interested in Trobriand culture, and especially why he was fascinated by what happens to fathers when fatherhood has only a social and not a biological basis.

Malinowski enunciated his principle of legitimacy many times in his writings. No two iterations are exactly the same. Here from 1927 is a particularly clear and relevant version:

> In all human societies—however they might differ in the patterns of sexual morality, in the knowledge of embryology, and in their types of courtship—there is universally found what might be called the rule of legitimacy. By this I mean that in all human societies a girl is bidden to be married before she becomes pregnant. Pregnancy and childbirth on the part of an unmarried young woman are invariably regarded as a disgrace. Such is the case in the very free communities of Melanesia described in this essay. Such is the case in all human societies concerning which we have any information. I know of no single instance in the anthropological literature of a community where illegitimate children, that is children of unmarried girls, would enjoy the same social treatment and have the same social status as legitimate ones.
>
> The universal postulate of legitimacy has a great sociological significance, which is not yet sufficiently acknowledged. It means that in all human societies moral tradition and law decree that the group consisting of the woman and her offspring is not a sociologically complete unit. The ruling of culture runs here again on entirely the same lines as natural endowment; it declares that the human family must consist of the male as well as the female.[40]

Recall that in the prehistory of marriage, according to those who have studied the evolution of our species, the primary reason for the emergence of human pair-bonding was to ensure that mothers do not raise children alone. The evolutionary record suggests that men and women developed an unusual way of living together, primarily because the human infant needs a father and the human mother needs a mate. The rule of legitimacy is the cultural expression of this evolutionary fact. It is society's way of *naming* that fact, of fully acknowledging it, and of creating the expectations and rules of conduct—the *social institution*—capable of responding to its requirements.

That social institution is marriage. Malinowski, seeing the whole issue in the person of the Trobriand father, put it simply: "The father is defined socially, and in order that there may be fatherhood there must be marriage."[41] That's the crucial linkage. In the Trobriands, where fatherhood lacks a biological basis, the dependence of fatherhood upon marriage is total and complete. The *only* way for a Trobriand man to be a father is to be married to the mother. But Malinowski—and many other scholars after him—have viewed Trobriand society as only one (albeit an extremely interesting) example of a universal or at least near-universal rule of human filiation and kinship.

Among scholars, belief in the universality of the legitimacy principle is not universal. As we'll see in the next chapter, there is some quarreling over close calls and hard cases. But the agreement (like the principle itself) is *close enough* to universal to be quite impressive, and the scholarly disputes surrounding it primarily concern qualifications and details, not the main point. The eminent sociologist Talcott Parsons writes that the nuclear family is "universal to all known human societies" and contains two core features. The first is a mother loving and caring for her child. The second is that the mother has "a special relationship to a man outside her descent group who is sociologically the 'father' of the child, and that this relationship is the focus of the 'legitimacy' of the child, of his referential status in the larger kinship system."[42] The prominent anthropologist A. R. Radcliffe-Brown, specializing in kinship structures, writes: "The almost universal rule is that an individual derives some elements of his status from or through his father, and others from or through his mother."[43]

Another highly respected anthropologist, Meyer Fortes, criticized some aspects of Malinowski's work but said in 1957 that "ethnographic evidence seems to support" the rule of legitimacy: "There is no doubt that the recognition of this principle has led to important discoveries about kinship."[44] More than a decade later, Fortes made it clear that he had become fully persuaded by the steady accumulation of scholarly evidence. Across time and cultures, the foundation of human filiation is "a package of credentials bestowed by parents acting as the agents of society." Accordingly, the "basic model" of human kinship is the "reproductive cohabitation" of the two parents who, as agents of society in the institution of marriage, bestow these emotional, moral, legal, and practical benefits on their offspring. For Fortes, the weight of evidence constantly

> brings us back to the proposition that no one can become a complete social person if he is not presentable as legitimately fathered

> as well as mothered. He must have a demonstrable *pater*, ideally one who is individually specified as his responsible upbringer, for he must be equipped to relate himself to other persons and to society at large bilaterally, by both matri-kinship and patri-kinship. Lacking either side, he will be handicapped, either in respect of the ritual statuses and moral capacities that every complete person must have ... or in the political-jural and economic capacities and attributes that are indispensable for conducting himself as a normal right-and-duty bearing person.[45]

For every child, a mother *and* a father. To meet this fundamental human need, marriage.

Particulars and Universals

Kind reader, we are on a trip together. Searching for the core meaning of human marriage, we have puzzled over some evidence from the prehistory of our species. We have visited the two river valleys where marriage as an institution first appeared in recorded history. And now we have traveled to the South Pacific and glimpsed the traditional way of life among some people on a few islands off the mainland of New Guinea, primarily in order to see what marriage looks like in a society that, as much as any society on earth, is unmarked by the patriarchal distortion regarding the origin of children. In the Trobriands we have learned that human beings across time and cultures have developed richly diverse ideas about where children come from, and that these ideas significantly influence how societies treat marriage, gender roles, and social structure.

We have also learned that, regarding many aspects of sexuality and courtship, the historic Trobriand Islands and the contemporary United States are more alike than different. Both societies have quite permissive sexual codes for the young. We have college dorms; they have the *bukumatula*. We have birth control; they are sure that sexual intercourse is not the cause of pregnancy. Neither society generally requires or even expects unmarried persons to refrain from sexual intercourse. In neither society does marriage effectively monopolize sexual conduct.

But the Trobrianders, unlike most of the voices in the current American debate, know that marriage is not just a series of private relationships. Trobriand marriage is a thick, rich *social institution*. It is much more than a name for an individual love relationship. It is far more substantial than those gauzy definitions of marriage offered up by many current commentators in the United States.

Trobriand marriage establishes clear rules and expectations, such that Trobrianders know what being married *means*. It is not only a personal decision, but also a shared way of living with a public dimension and authoritative guidelines. All Trobrianders know, for example, that having children outside of marriage is morally wrong, just as surely as they know that getting married means wearing longer skirts and receiving yams each year from the wife's brother. Marriage defines Trobrianders much more than Trobrianders define marriage.

Marriage *creates* Trobriand fatherhood. As an institution, it does not monopolize sex, but it does monopolize parenthood. Marriage in the Trobriands is not really a license to have sex; it is primarily a license to be a parent and start a family. Here is the rule: For every Trobriand child, both a mother and a father, via marriage. On this matter the Trobrianders are quite firm. This fact is all the more interesting—and all the more relevant to our search for marriage's essential, cross-cultural meaning—in light of their remarkable matriarchal bias and their generally strong emphasis on mother-right.

We have seen a fascinating variety of particulars. Matrilineal descent and spirit-babies. Men as the originators of children. A sexual double standard and restricted autonomy for women. Sexual equality and much higher status for women. Premarital chastity. Premarital sexual experience. Prostitution. No prostitution. Money. Yams. Cities. Villages. Millennia ago. Yesterday. But underneath these amazing and diverse particulars, there is a foundational human institution, called marriage. We are now ready to wrestle to the ground what that institution is.

5

What Marriage Is

IN ALL OR NEARLY ALL human societies, marriage is socially approved sexual intercourse between a woman and a man, conceived both as a personal relationship and as an institution, primarily such that any children resulting from the union are—and are understood by the society to be—emotionally, morally, practically, and legally affiliated with both of the parents.

That's what marriage is. It's a way of living rooted in the fundamental physiological and biochemical adaptations of our species, as developed over the course of our long prehistory. It first entered into recorded history in the two river valleys about five thousand years ago. It is constantly evolving, reflecting the complexity and diversity of human cultures. It also reflects one idea that does not change: For every child, a mother *and* a father.

The exact wording of this definition is my own, but the definition is anything but idiosyncratic. It rests on a large and growing mountain of scholarly evidence. It incorporates widely shared conclusions about the meaning of marriage reached by the leading anthropologists, historians, and sociologists of the modern era. As a result, I don't think that the essence of this definition should be controversial. Let me briefly explain each phrase.

Socially approved sexual intercourse between a woman and a man

In the history of the world, I have found only two examples of influential groups declaring that marriage is *not* fundamentally connected to sexual intercourse. The first is a group of Christian writers from the patristic and early medieval periods whose views on the definition of marriage stemmed largely from Christian doctrine concerning the relationship of Mary, Jesus' mother, to Joseph, her husband. For if Joseph and Mary were in fact husband and wife, and Mary was in fact a virgin, then it followed, for these early Christian thinkers, that sexual intercourse is not integral to marriage. Moreover, and relatedly, some of these same writers also viewed all human sexual intercourse as essentially impure and tending toward sinful. Even sexual intercourse between married spouses for the sole purpose of procreation constituted, in their view, a good use of an evil thing. For obvious reasons, this group of Christian writers also tended to view marriage itself with a certain amount of suspicion.[1]

The second example is the leading proponents of same-sex marriage in the United States today. As we saw in Chapter One, these advocates, including some state supreme court justices, studiously avoid any implication that marriage is connected to sex. Instead, they insist that marriage is an abstract and radically nonphysical "relationship" that is separate and apart from, you know, what people do in the bedroom.

These are the two exceptions. For nearly everyone else who has ever thought about it, marriage is deeply and inextricably connected to sex. For most people, not only in the United States but everywhere in the world, this linkage is obvious, a matter of everyday knowledge and common sense. Nearly everywhere, nearly all married couples are presumed to be in a *sexual* relationship. No one has to scratch his or her head and wonder what terms like "the marriage bed" and "consummating the marriage" mean.

Some scholars have tried to begin and end their definitions of marriage by describing its social functions. This approach is insufficient. What marriage *does*—what benefits it can bestow and what social needs it can meet—is an important question. We'll get to it shortly. But first we must state *what it is* that does these good things. And what it fundamentally is, according to almost all scholars, including those who can't agree on any other of its aspects, is socially approved sexual intercourse between a woman and a man.[2]

More than any other human relationship, marriage bridges the sexual divide in the human species. For this reason, sexual union is marriage's baseline activity. The anthropologist Robin Fox writes: "Copulation produces the relation between the mates which is the foundation of marriage and parenthood."[3] As we saw in the Trobriands, sex often occurs outside of marriage, but it nearly *always* occurs, and is always expected to occur, inside of marriage, which everywhere carries with it a clear set of sexual privileges and expectations. "Although one can have sex without marriage," notes the anthropologist Ladislav Holy, "one cannot, or at least one is not expected, to have marriage without sex."[4] Whatever else marriage is, concludes the anthropologist Jack R. Goody, it "involves the acquisition of relatively exclusive sexual rights."[5]

For anthropologists working from an evolutionary perspective, the linkage between marriage and sex could hardly be plainer—in part because for these scholars both sex and marriage are inextricably linked to procreation, which is the starting point for the study of human evolution and of human groups. Pierre L. van den Berghe writes:

> All known human societies recognize the existence of the sexual pair-bond and give it formal sanction in the form of marriage. With only a handful of exceptions presently to be examined, married pairs are expected not only to copulate with each other, but to cooperate in the raising of offspring and to extend each other material help.

He concludes: "Sex is culturally defined as a necessary but not sufficient condition for marriage, for marriage is explicitly, or at least implicitly, conceived as legally recognized kin selection and reciprocity."[6]

Reviewing similar bodies of evidence, the anthropologist Suzanne G. Frayser makes the same case with admirable brevity: "Marriage is a relationship within which a group socially approves and encourages sexual intercourse and the birth of children."[7]

In search of the core dimensions of marriage, the anthropologist Laura Betzig took a novel and revealing approach: She examined 186 societies to determine why people *divorce*. The number one reported reason was adultery. Coming in a close second was sterility. Betzig thinks, and I agree, that these findings suggest that marriage is fundamentally about sex and reproduction.

All the other marriage problems on the list—a total of 43—scored significantly lower than adultery and sterility as causes of divorce. They include: third, cruelty or maltreatment; fourth, displeasingness; fifth, mutual consent; sixth, elopement with a lover; and seventh (my favorite), laziness. Some of the other causes relate to sex and procreation: death of children ranked 15th; refusal to have sex, 17th; lack of virginity, 26th. Other reasons given include witchcraft (16th), bad temper (19th), and repressiveness (37th). Economic factors, Betzig remarks, "are less often reported as causes of conjugal dissolution than many might expect."[8]

This modern anthropological conclusion about the sexual basis of marriage echoes the conclusion reached by virtually all the early pioneers in the field. For example, George Murdock in 1949 called marriage a "relationship between a sexually associating pair of adults" that is "socially approved."[9] Edward Westermarck was only repeating the obvious in 1936 when he wrote that the "primary object of marriage has always been sexual union."[10]

The view that sex is foundational to marriage is as old as marriage itself, and the roots of this understanding go back even further. Recall the discussions in this book of marriage's prehistory, its development in the two river valleys, and its institutional shape in a matrilineal society in the South Pacific. If we removed from those chapters the material focusing directly or indirectly on sexual intercourse, there would hardly be anything left to read! On the other hand, calling marriage a close relationship takes only a moment. And because such a definition is so abstract and essentially lacking in content, it not only requires no elaboration—it does not even *permit* any.

In about the year 860 in France, a Christian archbishop, Hincmar of Reims, wrote an important and prescient public letter in which he sought to define marriage. On the evidence, the archbishop disagreed with some of his more sexually suspicious colleagues and predecessors who believed that it was possible to disconnect heterosexual intercourse from marriage. He wrote:

> A true coupling in legitimate marriage between free persons of equal status occurs when a free woman, properly dowered, is joined to a free man with paternal consent in a public wedding followed by sexual intercourse.[11]

The archbishop obviously was speaking more as a man of God than as a man of science. He was clearly the product of a specific time and place. But the main components of marriage enumerated in this spare, elegant definition are quite consistent, give or take a bit at the margins, with the broad understanding of marriage evidenced across world history and articulated over the course of many generations (including our own) by the leading women and men of science.

Regarding the specific issue of sexual intercourse in marriage, the archbishop clearly had a more valid argument than those who were trying, for ideological purposes largely removed from the actual lived experience of married life, to remove sex from our basic understanding of marriage. And of course, the archbishop's point about sex ultimately carried the day inside the church, just as it has always carried the day outside the church any time that serious people have tried to examine what marriage is.

Conceived both as a personal relationship and as an institution

In an influential article first published in 1955, the anthropologist E. R. Leach suggested that, instead of trying to formulate a universal definition of marriage, scholars should view marriage in each particular society as a "bundle of rights." For Leach, there are a number of important marriage rights. But nowhere do we find a marriage system that contains all of them, and the makeup of the bundle can vary considerably across societies. Leach enumerates what he views as the most important classes of these rights—sexual rights, the rights of legal maternity and paternity, the right to receive domestic labor from a spouse, the right to a spouse's property, the right of the couple to pass on property to their children, and family rights accruing to the wife's brothers—but he also speculates that more could probably be added.[12]

It is certainly true that marriage systems around the world, as Leach puts it, "do not all have the same legal and social concomitants."[13] Our comparison of ancient Mesopotamia and Egypt with the Trobriand Islands clearly demonstrates this point. And Leach's emphases on sexuality, legal parenthood, the creation and maintenance of a household, ties with other kin, and the ability to share and pass on property are both warranted and, as far as I can see, uncontroversial.

But I want to dispute the claim that marriage is best understood as a "bundle of rights." Speaking of marriage exclusively or primarily in terms of "rights" is misleading and I think also demeaning, because it obscures the human dimension. The term "bundle of rights" is often associated with the study of law and economics and commonly refers to rights connected with the ownership of property. In this regard, it can make perfect sense for me to claim my "property rights," since I am not in an interpersonal relationship with my property. But my spouse is not my property, and I am not hers. Marriage certainly involves rights, but marriage at its core is about *persons*, not rights.

Of course, as Leach and many others have pointed out, husband-wife relationships in Japan are typically going to look different from those in, say, Zimbabwe. Fair enough. But in both Japan and Zimbabwe, and pretty much everywhere else, marriage at its core is a woman and a man whose sexual union forms the basis of an important cooperative relationship. A foundational component of marriage is the interpersonal relationship between the wife and the husband.

At the same time, if the evidence presented in this book proves anything, it proves that marriage is also more than an interpersonal relationship. Defining marriage as a set of "rights" also obscures the fact that the married spouses are not simply rights-bearing individuals in an interpersonal relationship, but also agents of society in a vital *social institution*.

A social institution is not a "bundle of rights," but a pattern of rules and structures intended to meet social needs. Rights free me up. Institutions obligate me. Rights are about individual permission. Institutions are about social expectation. To break or get rid of rules, you probably need a right. To establish or maintain rules, you definitely need a social institution. Both rights and institutions are essential components of any good society. But they are separate things; neither can be reduced to the other. For this reason, it is highly misleading to suggest that a primary social institution such as marriage can be defined as a "bundle of rights."

This is more than an academic quibble about a definition. In today's discussion of marriage in the United States, by far the biggest problem is the widespread refusal to respect or even acknowledge the *institutionality* of marriage. It's as if we have forgotten what a social institution is.

Douglass C. North, who won the 1993 Nobel Prize in Economics, can help us with this problem. He succinctly describes social institutions as "the rules of the game" that "define the incentive structures of society." Institutions are

> the humanly devised constraints that structure human interaction. They are made up of formal constraints (e.g., rules, laws, constitutions), informal constraints (e.g., norms of behavior, conventions, self-imposed codes of conduct), and their enforcement characteristics.[14]

For North, social institutions are primarily about what one *may not* do.

Similarly, the anthropologist and marriage scholar A. R. Radcliffe-Brown reminds us that social institutions are "the ordering by society of the interactions of persons in social relationships." You know you are part of an institution when what you encounter is not "haphazard conjunctions of individuals," but instead situations in which "the conduct of persons in their interactions with others is controlled by norms, rules, or patterns." Accordingly, a sign and consequence of participating in a social institution is that "a person knows that he is expected to behave according to these norms and that other persons should do the same."[15]

Social institutions carry public meaning. Let's consider an example. Just for fun, we'll make it about sex. Let's say that I am a young adult who hopes and expects one day to marry. If I personally believe that sexual fidelity in marriage is important, that is a private opinion. But if the institution of marriage communicates to everyone that sexual fidelity is important, and if the institution rewards people who follow this rule and punishes those who flout it, that is a public meaning.

The difference between the two makes all the difference. The former is purely subjective and, as a practical matter, tends to be ineffective and isolating—in part because I am likely to meet many otherwise attractive prospective spouses who disagree with me on the issue of fidelity or who have never seriously thought about it, and in part because I can never assume that another person shares my view. Fidelity as a *public* meaning is much more objective and authoritative. It establishes an "ought" not just for me alone, but for everyone who is or wants to be a part of the institution, including (I have good reason to believe) the person I will marry.

To work at all, marriage *requires* this type of shared understanding. Without such public, institutional meaning, marriage (as distinct from intimate relationships) could not exist. That's why no marriage system anywhere in the world condones marital sexual promiscuity or regards it as normal, and why adultery is the world's leading cause of divorce.

Here is a thought experiment: If marriage were *not* a social institution, how would we know that it is not? Is it possible to imagine weddings taking place, and couples with marriage licenses living together, but without the social institution part—without clear rules and agreed-upon public purposes? Yes, it is possible. In fact, moving in that direction, which scholars call deinstitutionalization, is a primary goal of more than a few opinion leaders in the United States.

Let's imagine that these opinion leaders ultimately achieve their goal, so that we Americans, at some point in the foreseeable future, have successfully removed from marriage all or most of its institutionality. When that day comes, why would anyone bother to get married? What is the point of a public act that has no public meaning? If we can no longer credibly answer the "what" or the "why" of marriage, then the thing itself becomes pointless and even a bit ridiculous. If marriage is only a private relationship, there is no need for it. The clear logic of deinstitutionalization is not transformation or even redefinition, but extinction.

So here is the answer to our thought experiment: We'll know that marriage is no longer a social institution when most people stop marrying, and when those who keep doing so cannot say why and therefore are unable to treat their marriages seriously.

Children resulting from the union are—and are understood by the society to be—emotionally, morally, practically, and legally affiliated with both of the parents

A social institution—for what? *Why* do all human groups establish this institution and keep it around? Follow the basic steps: From sexual desire, the female and male of the species come together for sexual union, from which develops an interpersonal relationship and a shared way of life, which in turn every society surrounds with elaborate rules and invests with important meanings. *For what purposes?* Conversely, under what circumstances might a society stop caring whether or how people married?

Let's recall the basic development of marriage's long prehistory. A series of "biological innovations" made human beings very sexy creatures—not so that the mother and father will make a baby, but so that the mother and father will stay together to *raise* the baby. Let's also recall Lipit-Ishtar of Sumer and Akkad: "I made the father stand by his children. I made the child stand by his father."

The oldest marriage laws of India are the Dharmasutras, probably dating from the third or second century BCE, and the Law Code of Manu, probably from the first century BCE or the first century CE. A central preoccupation in these codes is the importance of procreation within marriage. For example, a husband is obligated to have sexual intercourse with his wife, particularly when she is fertile.[16] At the same time, "there is nothing in this world as sure to shorten a man's life as consorting with someone else's wife." Intercourse and pregnancy must take place only within a lawful marriage: "Women were created to bear children, and men to extend the line; therefore, scriptures have prescribed that the Law is to be carried out. . . ."[17] And: "The excellence of the marriage determines the excellence of the children that issue from it."[18]

Let's go to rural southern Europe in the 1980s. Here, the anthropologist Joan Frigole Reixach describes the centrality of procreation to her informants' understanding of marriage:

> Marriage, procreation, and family are conceptualized as intertwined phases which cannot readily be separated from one another. "Now we are a real family," says Giacomo to his wife immediately after the birth of his first son. My female informants declared: "A married couple without children is not a family, they are only a married couple." "Children make a marriage complete. A couple is family, but not really a family. They are lacking the children which make a marriage complete and which form a whole family."[19]

Across cultures, marriage is above all a *procreative* institution. It is nothing less than the culturally constructed linchpin of all human family and kinship systems. Marriage brings together biologically unrelated persons to produce the next generation, create fatherhood as a social role for men, and radically expand the reach and possibility of kinship ties. It brings together the two sexes in such a way that each child is born with two parents, a mother and a father, who are legally and jointly responsible for the child.

Human groups from around the world—despite their diversity in so many areas, including their views of where babies come from—*all* have fashioned kinship symbols and marriage rules aimed at guaranteeing that each child is emotionally, morally, practically, and legally affiliated with both parents. For instance, in the patrilineal tribes of southern Africa it is customary for the groom's family to present a gift of cattle to the bride's family at the time of the marriage. These gifts, called *lobola,* are not intended to buy the bride, but to secure two responsible parents for the child. As A. R. Radcliffe-Brown explains:

> One of the chief functions of *lobola* is to fix the social position of the children of a marriage. If the proper payment is made by a family, then the children of the woman who comes to them in exchange for the cattle belong to that family, and its gods are their gods. The natives consider that the strongest of all social bonds is that between a child and its mother, and therefore by the extension that inevitably takes place there is a very strong bond between the child and its mother's family. The function of the *lobola* payment is not to destroy but to modify this bond, and to place the child definitely in the father's family and group for all matters concerning not only the social but also the religious life of

> the tribe. If no *lobola* is paid the child inevitably belongs to the mother's family, though its position is then irregular. But the woman for whom the *lobola* is paid does not become a member of the husband's family; their gods are not her gods; and that is the final test.[20]

The specific customs, as well as the precise balance between mother-right and father-right, are almost infinitely variable, but marriages everywhere share a common goal: For every child, a mother *and* a father.

Probably the most widely cited and influential definition of marriage in the history of anthropology comes from the sixth and final edition of *Notes and Queries on Anthropology,* published in 1951. Prepared by a committee of distinguished British anthropologists, the book is intended as a practical guide for trained anthropologists doing field work. Their definition is brief: marriage is "defined as a union between a man and a woman such that children borne by the woman are recognized as the legitimate offspring of both partners."[21]

To me, this definition suffers from several shortcomings. The most important is that the definition says what marriage *does*, without specifying what marriage *is*. Second, the definition implies that the legitimation of offspring is the *only* cross-cultural purpose of marriage—an implication that, as we'll see in a moment, is probably misleading. Finally, the *Notes and Queries* definition offers only a faint suggestion that marriage is a complex social institution.

Yet these scholars clearly have gotten to the heart of the matter. Kathleen Gough, who had valuable questions of her own regarding the *Notes and Queries* definition, nevertheless agrees that "legitimizing children" is "to me the minimum necessary criterion applicable to all those unions which anthropologists customarily label 'marriage.'"[22] From an evolutionary perspective, Pierre L. van den Berghe, echoing Claude Lévi-Strauss and others, finds that marriage is "the cultural codification of a biological program," because marriage across cultures is "the socially sanctioned pair-bond for the avowed social purpose of procreation."[23] The 1994 *Companion Encyclopedia of Anthropology* states: "In an overwhelming majority of human societies, marriage is the mechanism which provides for the legitimation of children and defines their status in relationship to the conjugal family and the wider kin group."[24]

Social institutions exist to meet basic human needs. An institution that exists everywhere on the planet, in addition to whatever else it may be doing in this or that specific locale, is also obviously meeting at least one primary, cross-cultural human need. Regarding marriage, we have now identified that need. If human beings were not sexually embodied creatures who everywhere reproduce sexually and give birth to helpless, socially needy offspring who remain immature for long periods of time and who therefore depend on the love and support of *both* of the parents who brought them into existence, the world almost certainly would not include the institution of marriage.

Primarily

An important limitation of the *Notes and Queries* definition is its failure to include the word "primarily" between the phrases "a man and a woman" and "such that . . ." Marriage is fundamentally and everywhere a procreative institution, but that is by no means *all* that marriage is.

For example, marriage is typically an economic as well as a procreative alliance. Husband and wife, and often other relatives on each side as well—remember the Trobriand uncle and the *urigubu*—cooperate economically, dividing labor according to capacity and social roles and in effect establishing kin-based economic enterprises. For this reason, marriage in human societies is commonly a wealth-generating, asset-building institution. Even in the United States, where this dimension of marriage is seldom recognized and is less important than it is in village and tribal societies, research shows that, compared with similar people who are unmarried, married people earn more money and accumulate more wealth.[25] Moreover, in many societies (although not in the United States), children are viewed in economic terms more as assets than as liabilities—another example of the ways in which marriage cross-culturally tends economically to be a producing as well as a consuming institution. The economic dimensions of the marital bond typically both thicken and help stabilize marriage as a social institution.

Marriage in many, probably most, human societies establishes an alliance not only between the two spouses, but also between two organized groups of kin. We saw this phenomenon in ancient Mesopotamia. We saw it very clearly in the Trobriand Islands, where each individual is a member not only of a nuclear family, but also of a distinct matrilineage—each with its own history, customs, magic, and status—as well as a member of one of four totemic clans, which are also partly kin-based.[26] In traditional African societies, this dimension of marriage appears to be even more important. Each African marriage unites corporate kin groups—whether lineages, subclans, or clans—which function as basic components of political and social structure.[27]

Some scholars, including Claude Lévi-Strauss, have suggested that marriage itself can be understood fundamentally as alliances between kinship groups. This viewpoint is sometimes called the "alliance theory" of marriage, as contrasted to the more commonly advanced descent theory, which takes as its analytic starting point the two spouses and their offspring. My own reading of the evidence is that the alliance theorists often go too far. In their accounts, married couples themselves all but disappear. Also, in common with many Marxist scholars, alliance theorists frequently, and in my view wrongly, regard women essentially as passive objects whose "sexual services" are constantly being traded back and forth by groups of men.[28] Think about your own marriage, or about any other marriages that you have observed, or about the marriages that we glimpsed in the two river valleys or in the Trobriand Islands, and ask yourself if such harsh and impersonal theories of marriage accurately match what you know of the human reality, the lived experience, of marriage in diverse societies. To me, they do not.

The weight of evidence clearly supports the evolutionary scholars and the descent theorists. To understand marriage and the family, we begin with sex and birth—with the mother and her infant, and through her the possibility of social fatherhood, and with fatherhood the possibility of expanded family relationships. These must be our starting points, because these are the baseline dimensions of human generativity and family life. They are the core biological and social facts that have led all human societies to institute marriage. Corporate kin groups are certainly important, but analytically they must come later, because ultimately they are more additive than foundational.

At the same time, we owe the alliance theorists a lot. Even though they may accept the married couple and their offspring as a core form of human association, these and other scholars persuasively point out that the extended kin group—or perhaps more precisely, the extended kin group that is constituted largely of nuclear families nestled within it and at times in tension with it—is also a core form of human association. Especially from the perspective of the United States, where extended kin groups seldom mean much more than borrowing money from your father-in-law or visiting your relatives on holidays, it is important to remember that, for most couples in probably most societies, marrying a spouse also means becoming both a new member of an extended group of kin and a link between two such groups.[29]

Finally, marriage in many societies is also an institution that encourages, expects, and is partly defined by enduring emotional intimacy between the spouses. Today in the United States, of course, this idea will come as no surprise to anyone. Quite the contrary. While marriage as a primary social institution cannot be miniaturized and redefined as merely an affective relationship—as nearly everyone active in today's marriage debate seems to do—it does function in part, in some societies, as a vitally important affective relationship.

I have a standing quarrel with some of the great anthropologists cited in this book who pioneered the study of marriage in non-Western village and tribal societies, even though I revere their achievements. In what strikes me as over-eagerness to avoid sentimentality and concentrate only on structures and systems, these scholars rarely mention the affective dimension of marriage, and when they do, it is usually to remind us that this dimension is almost entirely absent from the institution of marriage in . . . (fill in the blank). Something tells me that they missed something. (Malinowski, who carefully describes the affection between Trobriand husbands and wives, is exempt from my complaint.)

For example, recall from Chapter Two the biochemistry of human pair-bonding. Don't the same hormones and neurotransmitters that cause people in Paris and Kansas City to fall in love and become addicted to one another's bodies also influence the emotions and feelings of tribal people in faraway villages? Surely the answer is yes. The pair-bond, emotions included, is a human universal. When a widow in the Trobriand Islands blackens herself with soot and grease, cuts her hair, wears mourning clothes, and lives by herself for up to two years, what do I as an outsider believe is happening psychologically? One answer is that she is in a "traditional" culture that requires her to participate in these rituals, irrespective of how she personally feels. Another answer—one that I favor—is that *she is also mourning the loss of her husband,* with emotions that may closely resemble those of widows and widowers in Paris and Kansas City. I suspect that the emotional dimension of marriage is deeper and more prevalent across cultures than many scholars have assumed.

Whatever emotional intimacy exists between the spouses is largely founded on, and never completely detached from, erotic attraction and sexual union. From this fact flows another: Marriage is the principle human institution through which women and men share a common life. Today in the United States, many people discussing marriage seem to believe that the principal sexual divide among humans is between gay and straight. But the principal sexual divide is between men and women. When it comes to sexual orientation, marriage as an institution is mute and insensible; it was never meant to address that issue. But when it comes to sexual embodiment, marriage is vocal and reactive; it was always meant to address that issue. Indeed, that is its *reason for being.* Marriage's affective dimensions are inextricably linked to its purpose of bridging the primary divide in our species.

All or nearly all human societies

The evidence that marriage as defined here is a universal human institution is overwhelming. In fact, especially in light of the vastness of the human historical record and the variety of human sexual experience, the power and prevalence of this one sexual institution across time and cultures is so noteworthy, and so empirically incontrovertible, that I am tempted simply to say "all human societies." Tempted, but not finally persuaded.

At issue are a very few hard cases and close calls. Let's review the most important of them, starting with the hardest.

The Nayars

Probably more than any other group, the Nayars of central Kerala, a region in southwest India, have been cited by scholars as evidence that defining marriage as I have done in this chapter is improper.[30] Are these scholars right?

To begin with, the Nayars do not constitute a society; they are persons in a category of castes within the larger Hindu caste system. The period under question is from about 1400, the time of the first useful scholarly account, until about 1800, the time of the British conquest of India and the consequent disbanding of the Nayar armies.

During this period, the Nayars constituted the ruling and military castes of three kingdoms of central Kerala. These centuries were ones of virtually continual war, interrupted only by the rainy seasons. The Nayar castes, constituting about 20 to 25 percent of the total population of the region, specialized in carrying out this warfare. As a result, most able-bodied Nayar men, most of the time, were largely preoccupied by the requirements of war and service to king. Fortunately for the Nayars, below them in social rank were castes of serfs and subtenants who did the bulk of the day-to-day work needed for the economic maintenance of the aristocratic Nayar households while the Nayar men were living in military barracks or away on wars. Above the Nayars in rank were only the Nambuduri Brahmins, from India's most elite caste. How elite? The Law Code of Manu announces that "the Brahmin is by Law the lord of this whole creation" such that the "whole world" is "the property of the Brahmin" and "it is by the kindness of Brahmins that other people eat."[31] Brahmin men often, and with social approval, impregnated Nayar women, whom they treated as concubines.

These highly unusual circumstances help to explain the Nayars' highly unusual marriage system. Each decade or so, under the supervision of elders, the young, prepubescent girls of a lineage were married to young men of socially linked and cooperating (*enanger*) Nayar lineages. Prior to her marriage ceremony, each girl was secluded for three days to observe ritual prohibitions connected to menstruation. The marriage ceremony itself consisted chiefly of the bridegroom tying a gold ornament (*tali*) around the neck of his bride. It's important to note that this "tying of the *tali*" was the central marriage rite among most of the castes in southern India. A married Nayar woman was expected to wear the *tali* throughout her life.

Following the ceremony, each newly married couple was secluded for three days in a room of an ancestral house, during which time fertility rites were performed and, if the girl was old enough, sexual intercourse could take place. On the fourth morning, the spouses took a purifying bath and ate a meal together. Afterwards in some (but not all) cases, the bridegroom tore into two pieces a portion of the lower gown worn by the bride during the couple's seclusion, keeping one piece for himself and giving the other piece to the girl.

These rituals essentially *concluded* the formal obligations owed by the married spouses to one another—with one exception. At the time of her husband's death, the wife and any of her children (whoever their biological father) were required to observe fifteen days of ritual mourning. And that, gentle reader, was how the Nayars married. The anthropologist Kathleen Gough understandably calls Nayar marriage "the slenderest of ties."[32]

After the marriage ceremony and seclusion, and after the bridegroom was on his way, free from further obligation and often never to be seen or heard from again, a married Nayar woman was permitted and expected to maintain informal and often temporary sexual liaisons (*sambandham,* or "joining-together" relationships) with one or more men from appropriate castes. These were typically sleeping-over relationships. The man would arrive at the woman's room after having eaten dinner in his natal home, and would leave her room the next morning before breakfast. Often, upon entering, he would leave his weapons outside the woman's door, in part to alert other male consorts that he was within. While these relationships lasted, the men were expected on occasion to give small gifts to the woman. These gifts were largely symbolic—bathing oil, bananas, wafer biscuits, betel leaves, and nuts—and were clearly *not* understood by anyone as economic maintenance of the woman or her children.

When a Nayar woman became pregnant, it was mandatory for one or more men of appropriate caste to acknowledge possible biological paternity. Any man who had had sexual intercourse with the woman in the right time period was expected to make this declaration, typically by giving small gifts to the woman and the midwife at the time of the child's birth. If no acknowledgment of possible paternity was forthcoming, the consequences for the mother and child were dire. Usually the mother was expelled by her caste and driven out of her home by her kinspeople. Funeral rites would typically be performed for her. She could also be sent into slavery or put to death. Why this harshness over the matter of declaring *possible* paternity? Because it was highly important for the elders of the lineage to make sure that the woman had *not* had sexual intercourse with a Muslim, a Christian, or a man from a lower caste.[33]

The legal guardian and the primary male authority figure for a Nayar child was the mother's brother. Like the Trobrianders, the Nayars determined descent on a matrilineal basis, and consequently the maternal uncle was a key figure in the life of a child. Among the Nayars, to an almost unparalleled degree, formal authority over land and families was exercised by brothers, not husbands. For example, a Nayar brother had the right to prevent a particular man from entering a *sambandham* relationship with his sister, or to dismiss him from the relationship at any time.

If a child of a Nayar woman knew its mother's ritual husband, as was often the case, the child would address that man as "father" (*appan*). If the child knew her biological genitor—one of the men of the *sambandham* relationship—the child would address that man with an honorific meaning "leader" or "lord" (*acchan*).

The *sambandham* father had no formal obligations to either the woman or her child; yet in practice, since we humans are a stubbornly pair-bonding species, affectionate and enduring *sambandham* relationships often *did* develop, both between the woman and the man and between the father and his offspring. But astonishingly, such emotionally intimate and long-lasting relationships, including any activities suggesting their institutionalization, were generally *discouraged* by the larger kin groups. The reason was that pair-bonding Nayar men were considered potentially weak and unreliable; they might falter in their loyalty to their natal kin group and in their devotion to their primary duties, which were warfare and service to king. As one author put it in the early sixteenth century, the distinctive Nayar way of mating is "a very ancient law among them," which "springs from the wish of a certain king to relieve the men of the burden of maintaining sons, and leave them ready for warlike service whensoever the king calls upon them."[34]

In fact, among the Nayars throughout this period, sorcery was sometimes practiced by kinspeople seeking to thwart a man's desire to bond more closely with a particular woman, even if that woman was the mother of his children. Conversely, the impregnation of a Nayar woman by a Brahmin man, even if that man refused any personal relationship with the mother and child, was highly prized by the elders of the lineage.

Some scholars, including Kathleen Gough, the leading authority on the Nayars, have suggested that the *sambandham* relationships, insofar as they require the admission of possible paternity, do establish a notion of fatherhood and do serve to legitimize children.[35] I wish I could accept this argument, but I find it largely unpersuasive. Alas, no matter how hard we look, the Nayars simply did not seem particularly interested in establishing the norm of one social father for every child. Quite the contrary. That's what makes their marriage system such a rarity. Admittedly, they did seem intensely interested in ensuring that their women were not impregnated by men of the wrong caste or religion. But this concern is not the same as seeking a responsible father for every child.

Gough also argues that the Nayars during this period effectively practiced a form of group marriage, in which the ritual husband symbolically represented *all* the eligible men of the appropriate caste. In this view, the marriage ceremony basically effectuated the union—the "marriage"—of the immature girl to the males of the caste group as a whole.[36] This interpretation has some merit, even as we must not overlook the fact that a legal marriage of one woman to one man, however flimsy, *did* take place and was viewed by the Nayars as mandatory. Other scholars, including Robin Fox, Claude Lévi-Strauss, and A. R. Radcliffe-Brown, have rejected the idea that the Nayars practiced a form of either group or plural (polyandrous) marriage.[37]

To me, the essential lesson of the Nayars is that it is possible for a human group—probably not an entire society, but a subgroup within a society—to shrink and alter marriage to such a degree that it becomes essentially a simulacrum of marriage. This radical devaluation occurs because the group is corporately preoccupied with other activities that conflict with full-bodied marriage and may be positively served by shadow-marriage.

Nayar men during this period were essentially warriors, not husbands. They had distant battles to fight and demanding kings to serve. They had socially inferior castes who would maintain their households economically. They had men from a socially superior caste who were more than willing to help them perpetuate their lineages biologically. They had a matrilineal descent system that emphasized the importance of the mother's brothers as male authority figures. In addition, these Nayar warriors needed only a marriage system that effectively relieved them of the obligations and pleasures of marriage and fatherhood, but permitted them informal sexual relationships with women, while still perpetuating the thin legal pretense that what was happening was "marriage." And that is exactly what the Nayars did.

The Nayars were thus an exception to the rule; but an exception does not prove that there is no rule! A possible deviation from the pattern does not prove that no pattern exists. For it is *only* the discernment of an underlying pattern that permits us to see those spots where the pattern may be broken. Scholars who trot out one or several ambiguous cases to suggest that marriage in human affairs has no coherent meaning—that it does not exist as a definable cross-cultural institution—are engaging in an unserious activity. They remind me of the old fundamentalist preacher who can "prove" anything by citing one isolated verse from the Bible.

Let's test the hypothesis that exceptions and rules make sense only when viewed together. What do you think happened among the Nayars of central Kerala after the British conquest around 1800 had resulted in the disbanding of the Nayar armies? The entire mating system that we have been struggling to comprehend "rapidly died out," according to Kathleen Gough. Within a few decades, monogamous marriage had become the norm and "fathers had assumed a definite role in the upbringing of their children."[38]

The Nuer

The rest of our hard cases are easier. The Nuer are a predominantly pastoral, cattle-herding people who live in what is now southeastern Sudan and western Ethiopia, mostly in savannah country around the juncture of the Nile, Bahr el Gazal, and Sobat rivers. The time period under consideration is about 1930–1950.

The Nuer are probably the most famous and carefully studied of those African societies that have historically permitted under certain circumstances what is often called "woman-woman" marriage.[39] In the context of today's debate on same-sex unions, the Nuer and this particular feature of their marriage system have become even more famous. But woman-woman marriage in Africa has nothing to do with homosexuality. Moreover, it arguably underscores, more than it violates, the principle that marriage is fundamentally a procreative institution aimed at securing a mother and a father for every child.

The Nuer are patrilineal, reckoning descent through the father. Patrilineages, or extended kin groups, are important Nuer family and social structures. Children in Nuer society are highly valued assets, and marriage is intimately linked to procreation. For example, a Nuer marriage is not considered to be final and complete—the spouses do not live together in their own hut as husband and wife—until the birth of the first child.[40] For the Nuer, like so many other cases we've seen, the legitimacy of the marriage, including the status of the children, is established partly through ritual and public ceremony and partly through a complex series of gift exchanges over time between the two family groups whose children are marrying. Among the Nuer, by far the most important marriage gifts are cattle, given by the groom's kin to the bride's kin.[41]

What appears to be essential for the Nuer regarding fatherhood is less physical paternity than social paternity—less who is the male inseminator, or genitor, than who is the legal and social father, or pater, and therefore whose lineage is the child's lineage. For example, if a wife is impregnated by a man who is not her husband, the husband has a grievance owing to the adultery, but the child born of the adulterous union is properly and by right *his* child, not the child of the inseminator.

So far, interesting but not unusual. However, a barren, affluent Nuer woman—a woman who cannot bear children but has acquired independent wealth through the ownership of cattle—can marry another woman. There is no sexual or pair-bonding relationship between the two women. The barren woman in this case is said to "count as a man."[42] She makes the requisite gifts of cattle to the bride's family. She participates with the bride in some of the marriage rituals. After the marriage she recruits a man—sometimes a relative, sometimes not—to cohabit with the bride, impregnate her, and assist her on a day-to-day basis in the maintenance of the home.

Yet the woman who counts as a man—the woman who gave the cattle to the bride's family and participated in the ceremony—is the legal "father" of the children born of the wife. She is the formal head of the family and the children show her great respect, sometimes addressing her as "father." Most importantly, the children born of the marriage are legally *her* children and they belong to *her* patrilineage. She participates directly in the renewal of her kinship group.

This Nuer way of thinking about procreation—in particular, the idea that one's parenthood ultimately derives from marriage more than from biology—is also evident in what E. E. Evans-Pritchard famously called Nuer "ghost marriage." In this arrangement, if a man dies without leaving a male heir, one of his male relatives may properly cohabit with his wife, impregnate her, and help her raise the child. But it is the dead husband, not the living genitor, who is the legal father of any child born of the union. The Nuer call this practice "kindling the fire" of the dead husband. The man who died without children becomes a legal father, much to his honor, after his death.[43]

Sometimes a woman-woman marriage and a ghost marriage can even blend together. On such (rare) occasions, a "woman who counts as a man" marries a woman in the name of her dead kinsman, usually her brother. The persons involved in this marriage are the dead or "ghost" husband, his surviving wife, the woman who counts as a man who marries the wife in her brother's name, and the man who is brought in to cohabit with the wife. Quite an arrangement! The resulting children are legally the heirs of the deceased husband and belong to his (and his counts-as-a-man sister's) patrilineage.[44]

As Evans-Pritchard sums it up, the Nuer "pay little regard to the manner of begetting so long as the legal fatherhood of the child is well established." Thus, from the mother's point of view, "The person in whose name she was married with cattle is the pater of her children whether he begat them or not, was dead or alive at the time of her marriage and the birth of her children, or is a man or a woman."[45]

Woman-woman marriages and ghost marriages are not common in Nuer society and are not present at all in the great majority of human societies. By any reasonable standard, woman-woman marriage is not a version or a precursor of gay marriage. But these forms of marriage do challenge the definition of marriage presented in this book.

In particular, despite the preoccupation with legitimizing children, neither of these arrangements embodies the idea that children need more than a formal and legal "father" and that father's kin group. Marriage typically means that children benefit enormously from a real, living, in-the-home man who is a companion to the mother and who helps bring the children into the world and raise them to adulthood. To the degree that ghost marriage and (especially) woman-woman marriage deviate from this norm, they are exceptions to the rule.

At the same time, both forms honor the principle that true parenthood comes from marriage, not a sexual act. Both forms insist upon the legitimation of children, the importance of legal fatherhood, and the principle that every child by birthright is a child of both her mother's people and her father's people. That's not everything, but it's a lot.

Ritualized Homosexuality

In the context of the debate over same-sex marriage now occurring in the United States, Canada, and elsewhere, some scholars have focused renewed attention on the prevalence of ritualized or institutionalized homosexual behavior in human societies. As a public argument, the main idea is that such socially recognized homosexual institutions can be viewed in some respects as precursors and prototypes of same-sex marriage. To me, this argument has some validity.

Institutionalized homosexuality in human societies appears to be almost an exclusively male phenomenon. In some societies—most of the studies I've seen focus on cultures in Africa and Melanesia—adult men under certain circumstances are permitted to have short-term sexual relationships with boys in ways that are ritualized and socially approved. These relationships do *not* mean that either the men or the boys are homosexual in their habitual sexual motivation or sex-object choice and identity. In fact, the men in these relationships are later expected to marry women and father children. So are the boys, but perhaps only after themselves spending some period of time as the men in men-boy unions.[46]

In 1930, E. E. Evans-Pritchard studied the (by then extinct) phenomenon of "boy marriage" among the Azande people of the Sudan in northern Africa. Evans-Pritchard pointedly uses the terms "wife," "husband," and "marriage" to describe this institution, since, as he put it, "the relationship was, for so long as it lasted, a legal union on the model of a normal marriage."[47] The man gave marriage gifts (usually spears) to the boy's family and was obligated to perform services for them, just as if he had married one of their daughters. Indeed, if things went well with the boy, sometimes the man *would* later marry one of their daughters! While the relationship lasted, the man and boy would sleep and have sex together, and the boy (who was called "woman" and "wife") would cook for and serve the man and in other ways act as a kind of wife-substitute, including, for example, speaking only softly or not at all when in the man's presence.[48]

Among the Azande, the institution of boy marriage was directly connected to groups of young adult male warriors living in sex-segregated, bachelor-only military companies. (Conventionally married, usually somewhat older warriors had their own, separate companies.) Evans-Pritchard argues that boy marriage as an institution thrived largely due to a lack of women. Opportunities to meet unmarried women were sharply restricted, in part due to the prevalence of polygynous marriage among the Azande elite. As regards adultery with married women, the punishments were severe and could include cutting off the offending man's ears, upper lips, genitals, or hands. In this context, for the men, temporary boy marriages were serviceable if imperfect substitutes for the heterosexual unions that were not (yet) attainable. For the boys, they seemed to serve as a kind of initiation or apprenticeship. Anyone who has read reminiscences—by George Orwell, C. S. Lewis, and others—of attending elite all-boys private schools in Britain in the early and middle decades of the twentieth century will immediately recognize at least some of the aspects of this phenomenon. Among the Azande, when the all-bachelor military companies historically came to an end, so did the practice of boy marriage.

On the other hand, in his study of ritualized homosexuality in Melanesia, Gilbert Herdt finds examples of similar institutions that do not appear to be linked to sexually atypical settings such as prisons, military camps, or plantations. Herdt argues that these arrangements in Melanesia are typically found in societies in which the status of women is quite low and in which gender roles are highly polarized and even antagonistic.[49]

Does the cross-cultural presence of formal homosexual unions require us to qualify, or at least add complexity to, the definition of marriage presented in this book? Perhaps. In describing the Azande institution, Evans-Pritchard uses the word "marriage" for a reason. In some ways these are clearly marriage-like, or at least marriage-imitating, social structures.

But in other ways—arguably the most important ways—they clearly are not. First, they are structurally defined as temporary, intended as one relatively short phase of life, not as an enduring way of living. Second, they are not procreative; children play no role at all in these institutions. Third, because they are prescriptively age-ranked, pairing adult men with adolescent boys, they are structurally inegalitarian in a way that marriage, at least formally, is not. Finally, and most importantly, in no society anywhere are these arrangements understood, either by the partners themselves or by the society, to be equivalent to, or even an acceptable long-term substitute for, marriage as defined in this book.

What are the take-away lessons? One is that homosexual behavior is an important and normal (expected) occurrence in human societies, and that homosexuality at times is expressed in and embodied by mainstream social institutions. These institutions have their own integrity and logic. They demand attention and, in many cases, respect. Another lesson is that marriage is a separate social institution.

The Navajo

In a recent essay arguing in favor of gay marriage and against the proposition that marriage can be defined, the anthropologist Linda Stone cites the Navajo as evidence that marriage across human societies is not *always* an institution through which children are legally affiliated with both of their parents. *Usually,* she says, but not always. Among the Navajo, she writes, "children born to a woman, married or not, become full legitimate members of her matriclan and suffer no disadvantages."[50]

Stone argues that marriage cross-culturally does not always and necessarily "establish the legitimacy or status rights of children."[51] In putting it this way, she seems to be focusing exclusively on the *jural* dimension of marriage as a procreative institution—that is, on the legal status and rights of the offspring. But as we've seen, this focus on legal rights, while important, is too narrow.

Marriage affiliates the child with both of her parents not only legally, but also emotionally, morally, and practically. *Emotionally:* The child has a complex and meaningful psychological connection to both of her parents. *Morally:* Her moral formation, or the development of her character and therefore of key dimensions of her personality, is significantly shaped by her connection to each parent and by the parents' connection to one another. *Practically:* In countless prosaic ways both large (economic provision) and small (helping her put on her moccasins), both of her parents contribute to her day-to-day survival and, one hopes, flourishing. Plus, as Stone rightly points out, there is the important legal part—but that is only *one part.* Guided by a more robust understanding of the concept of the child's "affiliation" to both of her parents by virtue of their marriage, let's look at the Navajo and at Stone's assertion about Navajo marriage.

The largest Native American group, the Navajo live primarily on the 15.5 million acres of the Navajo Reservation located in northeastern Arizona and parts of New Mexico and Utah. The time period under consideration is the recent past, roughly the 1940s through the 1960s. Like the Trobrianders and the Nayars, the Navajo reckon descent on a matrilineal basis. Although clans and subclans serve as key social units in Navajo society, their significance declined somewhat in the twentieth century. But the extended Navajo family, which typically operates as a kind of cooperative residential unit, remains very important.[52]

In general, modern Navajo marriage is a weak institution. Almost every Navajo during this period did marry, usually while quite young (a traditional Navajo saying is that "a girl's first bleeding is an order from the Holy People to marry").[53] But divorce and remarriage rates were high; only about 40 percent of Navajo children spent their entire childhood living with their own two married parents.[54] At the same time, the Navajo definitely distinguished legitimate marriages from informal or illegitimate unions. Most marriages, especially first marriages, were arranged by the parents and uncles, and were taken seriously. Typically, gifts were given and a formal ceremony took place.

Stone suggests that Navajo marriage, including the gifts from the groom's family to the bride's kin, was intended solely to guarantee the husband's "sexual rights" to his wife.[55] But surely this thesis is inadequate. Even leaving aside the fact that sex and procreation tend to go together, and cannot be conceptually split apart in the way that Stone suggests, it seems likely that the well-documented Navajo preference for marriage over informal unions would have something to do with the well-being of children. Dorothea Leighton and Clyde Kluckhohn point out that "from the Navaho point of view, it is precisely the exchange of property which regularizes the marriage, assuring respect for the wife *and security (economic and otherwise) for the children*" (emphasis added).[56]

Unwed childbearing was clearly viewed by the Navajo as harmful and undesirable. Some unmarried Navajo mothers practiced abortion or infanticide. A nonmarital pregnancy sometimes led to adoption, sometimes to the couple getting married, and sometimes to the boy's family paying a fine, historically a large one, to the girl's family.

The Navajo during this period used at least four terms to describe children born to unmarried mothers. One is *yotashkii*, which is derogatory, meaning "bastard." Another commonly used term is *johonaa ai ba'atchini,* meaning "children of the sun" or "nobody's children." The reference here is to the famous Navajo story of the birth of the children of Changing Woman, who was magically impregnated by the sun. In the story, when the children ask who their father is, they are told that they are *yotashkii.* A third term is *k'a bizhii,* meaning "braided arrow." It is also both derogatory and a mythological reference. A fourth term is *bizhe'e doo beehozinii,* meaning "his father is unknown."[57] The prevalence of these terms is difficult to reconcile with the notion that Navajo children born outside of marriage "suffer no disadvantages," as Stone asserts, or that getting married is all about the man's "sexual rights" and has nothing to do with children's status or well-being.[58]

Acceptance into the mother's clan is a birthright of every Navajo child, and it's fair enough to point out this fact. But this one fact tells us only a small part of the story. For example, what about the *father's* clan and *his* immediate kin? Obviously, if the father is not living with the child or is not known by the child or is not acknowledged by the relevant parties as the father—sometimes in such cases the father's clan is simply stated as "unknown"[59]—the child is unlikely to benefit as much as other children from close ties with either her father or his relatives. Such a glaring absence of fatherhood and of ties to paternal relatives might even qualify as a "disadvantage."

What if we assume that the father is nearby, accounted for, and a wonderful guy to boot, though unmarried to the mother? Are *his* children denied full access to his clan and his immediate relatives? It appears that scholars do not know. David F. Aberle, an authority on Navajo kinship, acknowledges that the answer to this question is not known, even as he hazards a guess: he does not believe that such a child would be "seriously handicapped" in relating to his father's kin, a belief he bases on the "exceedingly flexible" nature of modern Navajo kinship relations.[60]

But regardless of the answer, the matter of access to the father's clan doesn't tell us all or even most of what counts regarding the role of the Navajo father.

Let's start with a familiar topic: Where does a baby come from? The classic Navajo belief is that the baby is made from a mixture of the father's semen and the mother's menstrual blood. The Navajo teach that wrong behavior by either the wife *or* the husband while the woman is pregnant can harm the health and life prospects of the unborn child. They teach that each child is both "born of" her mother's clan and "born for" her father's clan. Here again is a beautiful cultural expression of what scholars call the principle of bilateral filiation. After *shima* ("my mother"), usually one of the first words a Navajo child learns to say is *shizhee* ("my father").

Navajo fathers by custom played important ceremonial roles connected to the birth of their children. A few weeks after the birth, the father was expected to make a cradle for the child from the finest pine wood—in this sense, the Navajo child was "born of" the womb and "born for" the cradle—and to recite a number of chants and prayers during the ceremony in which the baby was placed in his or her cradle. ("I have made a baby board for you, my daughter. May you grow to a great old age.") A Navajo baby, we are told, was frequently "held, touched, and talked to by the father."[61]

Fathers were expected to pay particular attention to moral education. When Navajo children during this period reflected on their moral training, they commonly described "what my father taught me." One little girl in the 1940s wrote:

> Father is the one who taught me to do the right thing, but my mother taught me how to boil coffee, tea, and how to fry bread, meat, teach me how to milk the goat. In winter she teaches me how to do things, and how to feed the baby sheep. I get punished when I do bad things and do not do what my father tells me to do.

Another girl, age ten, asked what makes her happy, said: "When my father brings me candy from the trading post." A seventeen-year-old boy answered: "When my father and I go to the Sing." A Navajo saying was that boys look like their fathers and their fathers' relatives, and young Navajo boys tended to "imitate their fathers in every detail of costume." Navajo fathers commonly oversaw hardiness training (such as racing and disregarding bad weather) for their children, especially sons.[62]

"In general, the relationship of a father to his children is one of affection, discipline, instruction, and economic assistance," writes

Gary Witherspoon in *Navajo Kinship and Marriage.*[63] Navajo men during this period did these things for their children first and foremost *by getting married.* Witherspoon points out that in Navajo society, with its matrilineal descent system and its high valuation of motherhood, the father-child relationship "is traced through another person, the mother." Therefore, "The father-child bond is really just another extension of the husband-wife bond."[64] The effectiveness, even the possibility, of Navajo fatherhood as a hands-on social role was intimately linked to the status of Navajo men as *husbands.*

Remember Malinowski: "The father is defined socially, and in order that there may be fatherhood there must be marriage."[65] In the matrilineal societies of the Navajo, as in the Trobriand Islands, the single most important precondition for effective fatherhood is marriage, and a primary purpose of marriage is to give children two responsible parents as a birthright.

What Good Is a Definition of Marriage?

Kind reader, I believe that we have found the core meaning of marriage. Can it serve us as a guide for the future?

Perhaps not. We Americans have never felt particularly constrained by history or tradition, even our own, much less the inherited ways of other peoples in far-off places. What counts for us is today and the future. Yesterday hardly seems to matter—Americans are probably less influenced by the past than any other people on earth. We also don't care much for authority. We don't like to bend the knee. If our institutions disappoint us, we change or scrap them, or at least try very hard to do so. As Harold Rosenberg put it, our tradition is the tradition of the new. Because I'm as American as the next fellow, I find much to admire in this way of thinking.

The rest of this book is about the future of marriage in the United States. What are the institution's strengths and weaknesses? Can it remain—can it more fully become—our society's most pro-child way of living? Or will it eventually become just an ersatz word, a Hallmark greeting-card word, used to name our private love relationships and perhaps qualify for some government benefits? Is it possible to reconcile our desire for equal treatment for same-sex couples with our desire to protect and renew marriage as our primary social institution?

Discerning the core meaning of marriage does not provide us with answers to these questions. Understanding our inheritance does not tell us what to do with it. At the same time, surely the understanding helps. It tells us what the stakes are. It contributes to moral and intellectual seriousness. As we debate the future of marriage in one society, surely recognizing the basic structure of marriage as a human institution offers us the right starting point, the best place to stand in order to gain the clearest view ahead and try to take our best steps forward.

At a minimum, we ought to consign to the cultural dustbin those comically inadequate definitions of marriage that currently dominate the debate in the United States. Chapter One contains many examples of what I mean. All of these definitions make the same basic point: Marriage is a private relationship based on mutual caring. Most of them even follow the same rhetorical style. They typically begin with the claim that marriage is constantly changing. Next they say that marriage in former days was really terrible; it was racist and sexist, and mostly it was all about property. From these insights, the conclusion is obvious: If the deepest meaning of marriage is that marriage is always changing, and if marriage historically has been pretty awful and crass, then why not say that marriage today is whatever we want it to be—especially if this formulation might help us achieve some useful social goal?

Here is an example of this idea, from Mike Anton, writing in the *Los Angeles Times* in 2004:

> Marriage as Americans know it today didn't exist 2,000 years ago, or even 200 years ago. Rather than an unbending pillar of society, marriage has been an extraordinarily elastic institution, constantly adapting to religious, political and economic shifts and pliable in the face of sexual revolutions, civil rights movements and changing cultural norms.

So that's what marriage is. Plus we learn:

> Throughout most of human history, a man married a woman out of desire—for her father's goats, perhaps. Marriage was a

> business arrangement. The bride was a commodity, her dowry a deal sweetener.[66]

Let's look at one more example, and see if our understanding of marriage's actual meaning can help us. In the introduction, I described my conversation over lunch in 2003 with Evan Wolfson, the executive director of Freedom to Marry and a prominent advocate of equal marriage rights for same-sex couples. After that discussion, I knew I wanted to write this book. A few months later, Evan published his own book, *Why Marriage Matters*. In the book, Evan defines marriage as "a specific relationship of love and dedication to another person." It also confers certain legal benefits. We also learn that "the history of marriage is a history of change." For example, throughout much of U.S. history, getting married turned women into "chattel." Also, Evan writes,

> you might be surprised to learn that, for example, the Catholic Church had nothing to do with marriage during the church's first one thousand years; marriage was not yet recognized officially as a Catholic sacrament, nor were weddings then performed in churches. Rather, marriage was understood as a dynastic or property arrangement for families. . . .[67]

Evan further advises us that marriage as a social institution is not about mothers and fathers for children, but instead about "parents." He assures us in the strongest terms that "leading experts and major studies do *not* say children fare better with a mother and a father." Instead, the scholars agree that "*two parents*" is the key. To illustrate this distinction, he cites the work of David Popenoe. According to Evan, some "right-wing figures" have "twisted" Popenoe's conclusions in the mother-father direction, but all that Popenoe "actually" says is that two parents on average are good.[68]

Almost everything that Evan says here is wrong. Let's start at the end and work back. David Popenoe is a friend of mine as well as a leading family scholar. In 1999 he wrote: "Based on accumulated social research, there can now be little doubt that successful and well-adjusted children in modern societies are most likely to come from families consisting of the biological father and mother."[69] More recently he has written: "Few propositions have more empirical support in the social sciences than this one: Compared to all other family forms, families headed by married, biological parents are best for children."[70] And again: "A central purpose of the institution of marriage is to ensure the responsible and long-term involvement of both biological parents in the difficult and time-consuming task of raising the next generation."[71] Based on this conclusion, he proposes a national strategy of "promoting marriage" in order to revive "the two-natural-parent" family.[72]

That's what David Popenoe thinks. Many "leading experts and major studies" agree with him. For example, in 2002 a group of researchers from Child Trends, a nonpartisan research center, concluded that "research clearly demonstrates that family structure matters for children, and the family structure that helps children the most is a family headed by two biological parents in a low-conflict marriage." And further: "Thus, it is not simply the presence of two parents, as some have assumed, but the presence of *two biological parents* that seems to support children's development."[73] Clearly "two biological parents" is scholar-speak for "mother and father." And as we've seen, while marriage across human societies has little to say about disembodied abstractions called "parents," marriage *is* centrally concerned with bringing together into a common life the mother and father who make the baby.

In no human society and in no period of history is it reasonable to view marriage primarily as a "property arrangement." Nor has marriage ever been viewed by any society primarily as a "dynastic arrangement." Marriage typically does involve property (as do religion, art, just about everything), but it can never be reduced to a matter of property.[74]

The claim that the Catholic Church had "nothing to do with marriage" during the Church's first millennium is preposterous. From the first century onward, starting with Jesus' teachings on divorce and remarriage, the clergy and theologians of the Church developed a robust theology and law of marriage. By the fifth century, after the Christianization of the Roman Empire, much of the Church's internal canon law of marriage had become Roman law as decreed by the emperors. This same body of law was then repeated and revised in the Germanic kingdoms.[75]

Christian marriage ceremonies built on Jewish prototypes may have been present in the Church as early as the second century. By the fourth century, marriage ceremonies in Christian churches were certainly occurring, and after the sixth century, a strong liturgical tradition of marriage is plainly visible.[76] St. Augustine had developed the concept of Christian marriage as a sacrament, particularly in the sense of an indissoluble bond between the spouses, by the early fifth century.

It is true that marriage for Christians was not formally established by the Church as a sacrament, understood (following the teaching of St. Thomas Aquinas) as containing a grace or a spiritual reality instituted or recognized by Jesus, until the decree "Tametsi" of the Council of Trent in 1563. But this fact did not prevent the Christian Church from involving itself in marriage from the beginning, with significant repercussions for the world. While marriage is a natural and social—and not primarily a religious—institution, across human societies it typically includes a sacred dimension and is commonly influenced by religious leaders or possessors of magic.

Apart from the deplorable history of slavery in the United States, there is no evidence that a married American woman could ever legitimately be treated by her husband, or by anyone, as "chattel" or personal property. We have seen that a society's marriage system can be an excellent barometer of prevailing gender roles and the treatment of women, as demonstrated by a comparison of patriliny and father-right in Mesopotamia and the Nile Valley with matriliny and mother-right in the Trobriand Islands. The anthropological record also clearly suggests that in no society anywhere has it ever been normative to treat a spouse as a thing.

Finally, to say that marriage is a "relationship of love and dedication" is sweet but virtually meaningless. I have precisely such a relationship with my parents and with several friends from childhood, but I am not married to any of them. So unless Evan can explain why and in what ways marriage is *not* merely a relationship of love and dedication, he has next to nothing to say about what marriage is.

I don't mean to single out as unusual, or as particularly flawed, this one description of marriage by Evan Wolfson. Countless others are equally flawed, and in pretty much the same ways. The result is a generalized conceptual disaster such that on one of the key issues of our day, we as a society often seem literally not to know what we are talking about. If this book captures with any accuracy what marriage is, the dominant definition of marriage in today's public debate is all but worthless. We must toss it out and start over. Then and only then can we dream marriage's future.

ʼeinstitutionalize Marriage?

Today in the United States, almost any public discussion of marriage becomes immediately embroiled in the controversy over same-sex marriage. The result is a kind of distortion. The tail is wagging the dog. What should be the main subject is reduced to either a vacuous afterthought ("marriage is the ultimate expression of love") or a means-to-an-end debating point. Both proponents and opponents of gay marriage typically approach the issue in this way. Almost always, the main focus is "gay," not "marriage."

It's time to turn that dynamic on its head. It's time for the gay marriage debate to illuminate marriage, not the other way around. In the remaining chapters, I want to treat the current controversy over gay marriage as a valuable opportunity to envisage, and make decisions about, marriage's future. I want to analyze the possibility of same-sex marriage in order to imagine what marriage can be in the United States in the twenty-first century.

The Rule

Dorian Solot and Marshall Miller, who are unmarried to each other, are poster persons for the idea that marriage is not a very good thing. With their book, *Unmarried to Each Other,* and the organization they founded, the Alternatives to Marriage Project, Solot and Miller have emerged in recent years as tireless campaigners for not-marriage. But if they are not for marriage, what *are* they for? Here are some clues: the "Hot Topics" at the Alternatives to Marriage website include "Cohabitation," "Marriagefree," "Polyamory," and "Unmarried Parenting."[1]

And how do these two who dislike marriage view the possibility of same-sex marriage? They view it *extremely* favorably. For example, in May of 2004, to "celebrate" the "joyful" arrival of same-sex marriage in Massachusetts, Solot and Miller announced that their project "firmly supports" same-sex marriage. (This was almost certainly a Solot-Miller first: the words "supports" and "marriage" in the same sentence without a "not" or a "but.") Gay marriage, they inform us, "is only one step in a broader movement toward recognizing family diversity in all its forms"—including cohabitation, marriagefree, polyamory, and unmarried parenting.[2]

Here is my dilemma: With every fiber of my being, I want to affirm the equal dignity of all persons and push for equal treatment under the law. Yet I'm also a marriage nut. I've spent most of my professional life arguing that marriage is important and that children need mothers and fathers.

Some people profess to see no conflict between these two ideals, and they argue that gay marriage would actually strengthen marriage as a social institution. If I could believe this, I would support gay marriage without reservation. Yet whenever I consider such a rosy scenario, I ponder the clearly stated intentions of Dorian Solot and Marshall Miller and many others like them, and my nightmare begins. These people dislike marriage intensely. They have spent years openly campaigning against it. They think marriage advocates like me constitute a genuine danger. And they *love* gay marriage! Moreover, they view gay marriage as one key step toward their larger goal, which is to knock the stuffing out of marriage as a social institution.

I believe that my nightmare can even be expressed as a sociological principle: *People who professionally dislike marriage almost always favor gay marriage.* Here is the corollary: *Ideas that have long been used to attack marriage are now commonly used to support same-sex marriage.* In this chapter we'll test this rule and its corollary against the evidence, to see what they mean both for the possibility of same-sex marriage and for the future of marriage as a pro-child social institution.

The Dream

Jonathan Rauch has a dream. His dream is also a prediction: that permitting same-sex couples to marry will *strengthen* marriage as a public norm. In his book, *Gay Marriage,* Rauch argues that "legalizing same-sex matrimony" would "shore up marriage's unique but eroding status as the preferred structure for two people who want to build a life together." First, he says, gay marriage would strengthen marriage by making it more universal, broadening its influence, and thus signaling society's clear preference for marriage over cohabitation. By reinforcing marriage's normative status, Rauch argues, gay marriage might slow or even to help reverse the current drift toward nonmarital cohabitation.

Second, gay marriage would undercut the main rationale for "marriage lite" alternatives such as civil unions and domestic partnerships. Such alternatives typically provide some (or most) of marriage's practical benefits, but without the full status of marriage and without the name "marriage." Much of the rationale for these rapidly proliferating legal arrangements is that they would help same-sex couples, who are not permitted to marry. In practice, however, many couples who seek out "marriage lite" alternatives are heterosexual. Rauch argues convincingly that establishing a clearer line of demarcation between marriage and nonmarriage would strengthen marriage's distinctive status. Permitting gays to marry, he concludes, would help to achieve that goal. He also argues that gay marriage would "immensely" diminish the legitimacy and public appeal of what he calls the alternatives-to-marriage movement—would make life harder for the Dorian Solots and Marshall Millers of the world—by causing a natural parting of the ways between gays and lesbians (who would now be free to marry) and those pressing for an increase in socially sanctioned alternatives to marriage.

Finally, gay marriage would strengthen marriage by making the institution more just. It would be an important victory for the basic American value, stated most famously in our Declaration of Independence, that all people are created equal. For Rauch, too many Americans, especially young Americans, view marriage as an outdated and illiberal institution, in part because marriage laws currently exclude same-sex couples. Changing those laws to permit gay marriage would improve marriage's public image. It might even make marriage as a way of life a bit more glamorous and sexy, since gays and lesbians these days are widely viewed as cool. (Think *Will and Grace* or *Queer Eye for the Straight Guy*.) For these reasons, Rauch concludes, gay marriage would not only be good for individuals—gay and straight—but also be good for marriage as a social institution.[3]

Jonathan Rauch's *Gay Marriage* is by far the most precise and serious argument to date in favor of the proposition that marriage supporters should accept gay marriage. Since his book came out, I've met Jonathan a few times, and I admire his integrity and good will. And how I wish he were right! If his basic thesis were convincing, or at least plausible, life for me and many other marriage advocates would be a lot simpler. We could be congratulating ourselves on our open-mindedness and saying "win-win."

But I've looked at the lay of the land as carefully as I can, and I believe that Jonathan Rauch is fundamentally mistaken. He can create and sustain his dream for the future only by writing as if he lived today in a dream world where the only thing that matters is his own logic, his own personal vision of the future. He gets around huge bodies of disconfirming evidence simply by ignoring them.

For example, recall the fundamental inquiry of the previous chapters: What is marriage? How did it come to exist? What are its fundamental features as a human institution? *Gay Marriage* basically ignores these questions, as if they didn't matter. "If I had to pare marriage down to its essential core," Jonathan writes, "I would say that marriage is two people's lifelong commitment, recognized by law and society, to care for each other."[4] This conclusion is little different from all those other wafer-thin formulations quoted in Chapter One. Regarding the entire anthropological and historical record on marriage, Jonathan has nothing to say—as if nothing that has happened before now were germane to assessing the future of the institution. Regarding the connection between marriage and children, he is virtually silent. His only real point about children, in a chapter called "Married, Without Children," is that current laws permit heterosexual couples to marry whether they intend to have children or not—as if that somehow settled the matter!

But most fundamentally, Jonathan casually glosses over the correlation of forces and the actual clash of ideas in today's marriage debate. He writes as if the nation's leading proponents of gay marriage agreed with him about the importance of strengthening marriage as a social institution. They don't. He imagines that the main ideas behind the push for gay marriage are consistent with recognizing and protecting marriage as a social institution. They aren't. He seems to believe that anti-marriage crusaders like Dorian Solot and Marshall Miller, in their strong support of gay marriage, are strategically naïve and don't realize what they are doing. They do.

Proponents

Judith Stacey is, to put it mildly, an unlikely marriage proponent. Search through all of her writings, and you'll find that she never met a divorce (or a divorce rate) that she didn't like. She views unwed childbearing with equanimity bordering on approval. She therefore believes that the real threat to society is not the weakening of marriage, but people who worry about the weakening of marriage. Currently a professor of sociology at New York University and formerly the Barbra Streisand Professor of Contemporary Gender Studies at the University of Southern California—I'm not making that up—Stacey is an activist as well as an intellectual. Her main project is to combine socialism with women's liberation. And in the sought-after Staceyan future of economic collectivism combined with radical sexual liberty, one thing that *definitely* does not fit is marriage as an authoritative social institution.

In the 1970s Stacey began, as she put it, "to explore the relationships among socialism, family transformation, and the liberation of women."[5] She casts a friendly eye toward Communist China in "When Patriarchy Kowtows: The Significance of the Chinese Family Revolution for Feminist Theory," published in a 1979 volume entitled *Capitalist Patriarchy and the Case for Socialist Feminism.*[6] In her 1990 book, *Brave New Families,* Stacey calls for much more "family diversity" in the United States, by which she basically means not-marriage.[7] In her 1996 book, *In the Name of the Family,*

Stacey renews her call for greater family diversity—one chapter is called "The Family Is Dead, Long Live Our Families"—and attacks what she calls "the neo-family-values campaign," by which she basically means the activities of people like me.[8] When my colleagues and I formed a Council on Families in the early 1990s, aimed at promoting marriage and criticizing the divorce revolution, Stacey and her colleagues responded by forming a Council on Contemporary Families—*contemporary*, get it?—aimed at promoting the divorce revolution and criticizing marriage.[9]

Today, however, after all those years in the anti-marriage trenches, publishing articles like "Should the Family Perish?" and "Good Riddance to 'The Family'" in journals like *Socialist Review*, Judy Stacey has suddenly found her pro-marriage voice. In her recent academic writings, in her newfound status as an "expert" frequently quoted in the *New York Times* and other publications, and in her civic activism, including providing expert testimony in marriage-related court cases, Stacey is today one of the nation's leading proponents of marriage. That is, of same-sex marriage.[10]

What led Stacey to this new position? Has she modified her long-held view that marriage is at best a dubious feature of American life, and that, if we keep the institution around at all, we should certainly overturn its rules, weaken its authority, and revolutionize its purposes?

Not in the slightest. Stacey is nothing if not clear regarding her reasons for advocating same-sex marriage. Early on, she came to view the fight for same-sex marriage as the "vanguard site" for "rebuilding family forms" in the United States. The struggles connected to gay marriage serve as vitally important "wedge issues in national politics and culture wars."[11]

Stacey recognizes that some of her friends disagree with her on this issue, and she respects their concerns. On the cultural left, there has been lively debate on this matter in recent years.[12] Stacey ably summarizes the three main positions. The first is that marriage is a fundamentally flawed and dangerous institution, and that nothing, including gay marriage, can redeem it.[13] The second position is that gay marriage is an important long-term goal, but should not become an immediate priority, due to public opposition and the possibility of a conservative backlash. A better strategy, in

this view, is to forgo for now the fight for gay marriage and instead wage "a multi-faceted struggle for family diversity." The third position—Stacey's own position—is that same-sex marriage is a goal worth fighting for today, both as a matter of equal rights and, just as importantly, as a powerful mechanism for transforming today's outmoded "conjugal institution" into tomorrow's "varied creative forms" of bonding and kinship.[14] How varied? Here are some possibilities:

> If we begin to value the meaning and quality of intimate bonds over their customary forms, there are few limits to the kinds of marriage and kinship patterns people might wish to devise.... Two friends might decide to marry without basing their bond on erotic or romantic attachment.... Or, more radical still, perhaps some might dare to question the dyadic limitations of Western marriage and seek some of the benefits of extended family life through small-group marriages arranged to share resources, nurturance, and labor.[15]

Stacey's main point here concerns what scholars call deinstitutionalization. Much of my argument in this book is devoted to establishing the fact that marriage is a social institution, and that its institutionality is inseparable from its fundamental purposes and meaning. But Judith Stacey does not believe that marriage should be an institution.[16] Yes, we can keep the "meaning and quality of intimate bonds," but those "customary forms" will have to go! Here Stacey lists three such forms. The first is the form of opposites: marriage is a man and a woman. The second is the form of two: marriage is for two people. The third is the form of sex: marriage is connected to sexuality and procreation. Stacey knows that these three forms depend upon one another. Knocking out any one of them weakens the overall institution—that's the whole point!—and makes it easier to knock out the other two.

For Judith Stacey, the strategic brilliance of campaigning for same-sex marriage—she also calls it a "paradox"—is that advocating the seemingly benign goal of extending marriage's benefits to an oppressed minority can, in the process, help to deconstruct marriage's "customary forms" for everyone in the society. That's a good day's work. She approvingly quotes Nan

D. Hunter, a professor of law, who argues that legalized same-sex marriage would have "enormous potential to destabilize the gendered definition of marriage for everyone." Stacey calls this strategy "using marriage" to both "change its context" and "reconstruct its meaning."[17]

Stacey reports that her position has carried the day, and she is right about that. Viewing same-sex marriage as a powerful tool for deconstructing (or deinstitutionalizing) marriage is now the dominant perspective of intellectuals and activists on the marriage-is-the-problem left, both straight and gay. (Stacey is straight.)

And what of Jonathan Rauch's argument that gay marriage will actually *strengthen* the institution of marriage? Stacey does not take it seriously. She points out that some people, including some of her anti-marriage friends and colleagues, view marriage as inherently oppressive. For them, gay marriage fundamentally means bringing more people into a bad institution. Others, among them Jonathan Rauch, view marriage as inherently civilizing. For them, gay marriage fundamentally means bringing more people into a good institution.

Stacey and her allies disagree with both of these perspectives. For them, gay marriage fundamentally means *transforming the institution.* In their view, marriage as a contemporary social construct is oppressive, but malleable. After all, marriage is ultimately a human creation, not an ever-fixed reality that is impervious to social and political pressure. Stacey argues that there is nothing "inherent" or unalterable about any of it. Marriage in the United States today may be unjustly defined and harmfully constrained by certain "customary forms," such as male-female, the rule of two, and the linkage to sexuality and children; but those forms are not unassailable. With effort, and over time, they were built up. With effort, and over time, they can be taken down.

Taking those forms down—deinstitutionalizing marriage—is the cause to which Stacey has devoted her entire professional life. For years she has been a determined cheerleader for divorce, unwed childbearing, and cohabitation. The results of these efforts have been mixed and limited. But today, her cause is winning new recruits and attaining new momentum. With the emergence of the campaign for same-sex marriage, Stacey has found what she (in my view, correctly) believes to be her main chance. She sees her opening and she is going for it.

Jonathan Rauch assures us that removing from our laws what is arguably the most fundamental of marriage's customary forms—the man-woman part—would not weaken the institution. It would not subvert marriage's basic public meaning or undermine its core purposes. It would not, as Nan Hunter hopefully put it, "destabilize" the definition of marriage for everyone. In fact, Jonathan assures us that gay marriage would have *exactly the opposite effect* on every score!

Stacey regards such talk with bemused disdain, mixed with a touch of cynical admiration. She judges the Rauchian thesis to be a particularly naïve version of "essentialism," which is the view that marriage will remain marriage no matter how we define it or what we do to it. It's the view that getting rid of the form does nothing to dilute the content. It's the view that changing a thing's public meaning does not change the thing. It's the view that if we redefine marriage as merely a private relationship (an "expression of love"), we have not at the same time fundamentally altered marriage itself—that we have not, in fact, deinstitutionalized it. Stacey presumably knows a thing or two about what it would mean to deinstitutionalize marriage, and she can hardly be bothered to take this argument seriously, except to point out its obvious value as a sell-it-to-Peoria rhetorical strategy.[18]

My friend Evan Wolfson, whose key role in the genesis of the campaign for same-sex marriage (and in the genesis of this book) I've mentioned previously, concurs with Stacey on this point. In 1994, in the early days of gay marriage as a national issue in the United States, Evan published an important article, "Crossing the Threshold: Equal Marriage Rights for Lesbians and Gay Men and the Intra-Community Critique," in a journal called the *Review of Law and Social Change*. The article is addressed less to the general public, or even to Evan's fellow lawyers, than to the organized gay and lesbian community and to political progressives such as Judith Stacey and her colleagues.

On the one hand, Evan offers yet another of those diaphanous, now-you-see-it, now-you-don't definitions of marriage: "a loving union between two people who enter into a relationship of emotional and financial commitment and interdependence." Marriage occurs when these two people "seek to make a public statement about their relationship."[19]

But, of course, the great majority of the world's loving and committed relationships are *not* marriages, and marriage is much more about society making a public statement to you than about you making a public statement to society. Evan's definition, like so many others we've seen, is insubstantial to the point of meaninglessness, primarily because it scrupulously avoids any hint of marriage's institutionality and public authority.

On the other hand, at some points in the article Evan reveals an understanding that he and his colleagues are seeking to engage and transform a substantial social institution. He believes it can be done. He argues that critics of marriage—people who believe that its customary forms render it hopelessly flawed—should not fall into the trap of "essentializing" the institution. Nothing is inherent. Basic change *is* possible. Marriage, he suggests, is "socially constructed, and thus transformable." Same-sex marriage is a pathway to that transformation.[20] "The brilliance of our movement's taking on marriage," Evan concludes, is that gay marriage as a social issue in the United States today is "both conservative and transformative, easily understood in basic human terms of equality and respect, and liberating in its individual and social potential." He sums up by calling the campaign for same-sex marriage "conservatively subversive."[21]

I think I understand. What Evan is calling the "conservative" part is "easily understood." It concerns equality and respect. Who could be against these ideas? The "transformative" and therefore "subversive" part, presumably less easily understood, involves the legal freeing of individuals and society from marriage's customary forms. That's the "potential" of the gay marriage campaign, and it really is "brilliant."

But if the "subversive" dimension of gay marriage is less "easily understood," one reason is that so many opinion leaders regularly serve up a description of marriage itself that is effectively meaningless! It's hard to evaluate the possible consequences of deconstructing a social institution when your basic conceptual framework doesn't even suggest to you that you are dealing with a social institution.

Jonathan Rauch sunnily predicts that after same-sex marriage is established, the influence of the "alternatives-to-marriage movement" will be "immensely diminished."[22] Maybe. But I seriously doubt it. More importantly, Jonathan misframes the question. I agree with him that after such a change, some of today's same-sex marriage advocates would be likely to pack up and call it a day—after all, they would have achieved their goal—and also that opponents of marriage as an institution would no longer be able to score points by calling marriage anti-gay. Fair enough.

At the same time, many intellectuals and activists seeking to deinstitutionalize marriage—supplant its customary forms, change its meaning and purposes, and weaken its public influence and authority—view same-sex marriage as an important step toward their larger goal. Winning same-sex marriage would be, in their view, a big victory for their cause. And in my experience, a big victory makes a social change movement stronger, not weaker.

Ellen Willis, a professor at New York University who writes and speaks frequently on these issues, does not like marriage one little bit. But she favors gay marriage as "an improvement over the status quo," because "conferring the legitimacy of marriage on homosexual relations will introduce an implicit revolt against the institution into its very heart, further promoting the democratization and secularization of personal and sexual life." She foresees other improvements: "For starters, if homosexual marriage is OK, why not group marriage—which after all makes a lot of sense when the economic and social fragility of the family is causing major problems?" Willis's ultimate goal is the full deinstitutionalization of marriage.[23]

Maria Bevacqua, a professor at Minnesota State University who studies women's issues, has a similar perspective. She insists that lesbian and gay marriage should be "inextricably bound to the ongoing critique of marriage as an institution." Since she and her colleagues "know that the institution of marriage needs to be radically transformed to rid it of inequality or abolished altogether," a primary task is to "call into question the very institution into which we seek admission."[24]

David L. Chambers, a law professor at the University of Michigan and a prominent advocate of same-sex marriage, argues that marriage law is best understood as the state seeking to respond justly to "persons who live together in enduring, emotionally based attachments." He favors gay marriage not only for its own sake, but also because it would likely "make society receptive to further evolution of the law." He tells us plainly what he has in mind: "If the deeply entrenched paradigm we are challenging is the romantically linked man-woman couple, we should respect the similar claims made against the hegemony of the two-person unit and against the romantic foundations of marriage."

Let's call this agenda "The Full Stacey." Goodbye to the form of opposites. Goodbye to the form of two. (Say hello to polyamorous or group marriage.)[25] And goodbye also to the form of sex. As Chambers puts it,

> By ceasing to conceive of marriage as a partnership composed of one person of each sex, the state may become more receptive to units of three or more (all of which, of course, include at least two persons of the same sex) and of units composed of two people of the same sex but who are bound by friendship alone. All desirable changes in family law need not be made at once.[26]

I doubt that Chambers—or Stacey, or Bevacqua, or Willis, or Solot and Miller, or many of their allies—would quit the fight or lose heart the day after gay marriage became legal. Quite the opposite. More importantly, would societal acceptance of same-sex marriage make their views about marriage in general appear more cranky and extreme, or more mainstream and plausible? I think that gay marriage would amount to an important (if incomplete) validation of their views. That's certainly what *they* think.

But what would happen to the anti-marriage movement *after* the advent of gay marriage is not really the issue. The main issue is what happens to *marriage* as a result of the *campaign* for gay marriage. The key time frame is not "after" and "later," but "during" and "now." As we've seen, many people now advocating same-sex marriage are consciously doing so, at least in part, in order to *change marriage.* And they don't have to wait until after the advent of same-sex marriage to think up some new plan to weaken the institution. They are implementing their plan right now.

Ideas

Institutions change primarily as our ideas about them change. External factors—wars, economic developments, new scientific discoveries—can obviously influence our ideas, but ultimately *what we think* is what drives social and institutional change. So if you are a marriage nut like me—or for that matter, if you are an anti-marriage nut like Judith Stacey—what ultimately matters are certain fundamental ideas about marriage. What is it? Why do we have it? What are its purposes? What are its essential features? What is its authority? The answers to these question account for marriage's public meaning, and for people interested in institutions and social change, public meaning is everything. All the rest flows from it.

In large measure, our current national debate about same-sex marriage is a conversation about marriage's public meaning. It's a much-needed conversation. We should be grateful for this opportunity to clarify the meaning of marriage in our society and determine its future. So let's now turn directly to the question of public meaning and focus on the ideas themselves. Forget for a moment who the proponents are, whether they do or do not like marriage, whether politically they are radicals or conservatives, and whether or not they view gay marriage as one step toward a larger goal. Assume for the moment that I am wrong about everything you just read regarding those anti-marriage activists who support same-sex marriage.

Let's just ask ourselves: Which ideas about marriage constitute the main argument for same-sex marriage? Which points about marriage seem to be conceptually the most important and the most frequently emphasized? If you knew nothing or almost nothing about marriage, and your only source of information were today's most influential arguments in favor of gay marriage, what conclusions would you reach about marriage's public meaning?

Here are fifteen summary conclusions about marriage that emerge from the public arguments in favor of same-sex marriage:

1. Marriage is an expression of love and commitment between two people.

2. Marriage confers social approval on the love between two people.
3. Marriage removes the stigma of nonmarriage.
4. Marriage civilizes relationships.
5. Marriage is how we distribute benefits to people who make a commitment to one another.
6. Marriage is not intrinsically connected to sex.
7. Marriage is not intrinsically connected to bridging the male-female divide.
8. Marriage is not intrinsically connected to bearing and raising children.
9. Marriage does not intrinsically seek to connect natural and legal parenthood.
10. Children do not necessarily need a mother and a father.
11. The idea of marriage as a bond between a man and a woman is a religious idea.
12. Marriage needs to be more separated from religion.
13. Historically, marriage has been a bad institution.
14. Marriage has become much weaker—and that's a good thing.
15. Marriage has become much weaker—and that's a reason for gay marriage.

These fifteen ideas can be divided into three broad categories. The first five *define*—they say what marriage is. The next five *disconnect*—they say that some things that formerly were intrinsic parts of marriage no longer are. And the final five *evaluate*—they make moral judgments about marriage's past, its relationship to religious faith, and its current status. Let's explore these ideas more fully.

Ideas That Define

1. Marriage is an expression of love and commitment between two people. Defining marriage in this way has become both our dominant national idea about marriage and our single biggest failure in understanding what marriage is and can be.

The gay marriage debate did not produce this idea. It's been around for decades, used primarily by people seeking to explain or justify the spread of divorce, unwed childbearing, nonmarital cohabitation, and other manifestations of marriage's declining institutional authority. But if today's national discussion of same-sex marriage did not originate the notion of marriage as essentially a private love relationship, that discussion certainly has reinforced and enshrined the idea to an extent that would have seemed inconceivable only a few years ago. Proponents of gay marriage repeat it endlessly. Courts adopt it routinely. Most people who use it regularly seem to understand—correctly, in my view—that it is a debate-shaping idea. They typically say it first because they regard it as the most important thing they can say, since everything else follows from it.

The idea's fundamental implication is deinstitutionalization. If you take away the institution part from marriage, what's left is an expression of love and commitment between two people. If this idea wins, so many other ideas necessarily go down, including the idea that marriage has a shared and authoritative public meaning.

What also logically goes down is Jonathan Rauch's rose-colored prediction that marriage, once reconceptualized in this way and therefore accepting of same-sex couples, will serve as our society's newly refurbished "gold standard" of committed relationships.[27] The opposite would be much more likely to occur. Such a radically minimalist idea of marriage obviously champions the values of privacy and diversity, not uniformity or standards. We can't have it both ways. To the degree that marriage becomes merely a matter of private ordering, constructed by couples themselves for their own purposes, unguided by public meaning and without any socially defined content other than the presence of "love and commitment," *marriage in social terms is not any kind of standard at all.* From society's perspective, marriage defined in this way would serve much more as the voiding or negation of a standard.

2. Marriage confers social approval on the love between two people. In an essay called "Love and the Lexicon of Marriage," Kevin Bourassa, a leading Canadian gay marriage advocate, calls marriage "the gold standard in relationship recognition."[28] The Ontario Court of Appeal clearly agreed with this idea in its famous *Halpern* decision of 2003, which effectively inaugurated same-sex marriage in Canada, and in which Kevin Bourassa and his partner Joe Varnell were plaintiffs, because the justices used almost identical language to convey what they viewed as the essential meaning of marriage. Marriage, which is "one of the most significant forms of personal relationships," the justices say, occurs when "society publicly recognizes expressions of love and commitment between individuals, granting them respect and legitimacy as a couple."[29] (By the way, Judith Stacey came up from the United States to serve as an expert witness in this case.)

What is so striking here is the notion that one of marriage's core institutional features—perhaps even its *primary* institutional feature—is conferring social approval on the couple. Jennifer Vanasco, a Chicago-based writer who visited Toronto with her girlfriend after the *Halpern* decision to consider getting married there, argues that marriage is more than being eligible for certain benefits. It is even more than "a public witnessing of love and commitment." Marriage is above all an occurrence that "validates membership in society." Vanasco writes: "We validate the institution at the same time it validates us."[30] John Corvino, who teaches philosophy at Wayne State University in Detroit, outlines a strategy to fight for "civil unions now and marriage later." He repeatedly describes the ultimate goal, the main prize, as securing "social endorsement."[31]

Again, gay marriage advocates certainly did not invent this idea. It's been around, quietly gnawing away at marriage's cultural normativity, for quite some time. Moreover, as we saw in Chapter Five, marriage *does* involve social approval of a sexual relationship. But the idea that marriage's essential social function is to bestow approval on undefined private relationships—that a marriage is less about society guiding the couple than about the couple gaining society's endorsement of their relationship—is peculiarly prominent in today's arguments for same-sex marriage. I think I know why. The queer theorist Michael Warner writes that many same-sex couples conceive of marriage in social terms largely as "an intensified and deindividuated form of coming out."[32]

This view is understandable: marriage as validation, as a badge of equality, as a symbol of acceptance, as an occurrence through which society recognizes the dignity of homosexuals and the legitimacy of homosexual relationships, as a socially blessed coming-out ritual for lesbian and gay couples.

Irene Javors is a lesbian therapist and community organizer who does not like marriage very much. She believes strongly that "the individual and not the state has the right to define significant relationships" and that, in addition, "all such constructions should be equal to one another" as regards public policy. (The Full Stacey!) Accordingly, on "philosophical grounds" she herself would never choose to marry, even if she were legally permitted to do so. Yet Javors is also a vigorous and public proponent of same-sex marriage. In fact, for several years she served as president of United for the Freedom to Marry, a grassroots lobbying group advocating for same-sex marriage. Why? In part, she tells us, because gay marriage would change marriage: "In my view, if we gained access to marriage the whole institution would be turned upside down. For that perverse reason alone, I wholeheartedly support our right to marry."[33]

Javors' main reason for becoming a leader in the campaign for same-sex marriage also stems from her understanding of what marriage is. "As a therapist," she writes, "I have counseled many people who desperately want marriage because of the social validation it offers for their lives and their relationships." Because so many gays and lesbians "deeply crave public recognition of their relationships," same-sex marriage would meet a vital need in the gay and lesbian community. Thus, a primary rationale for gay marriage is "conferring society's blessing on the fortunate couple." Javors specifically relates gay marriage to "the coming out process."[34]

If I were gay, I might well view the prospect of marriage in exactly these terms. Paul Varnell explains his thinking about marriage as a route to social equality:

> I suspect that our new ability to marry, even in just a few states, will inevitably encourage most heterosexual people to take us, our lives, and our partnerships more seriously. If the law stipulates that our partnerships are the legal equivalent of theirs, that will be considerable encouragement for them to begin thinking of us and our lives as equal to them and their lives. Far more than non-

> discrimination laws, that is pretty much exactly what our long-sought goal of social equality consists of.[35]

As an idea about homosexuality, this one is poignant and understandable. But as an idea about marriage, it is fundamentally misguided. Whatever one thinks about the idea that society should systematically confer approval on committed relationships as such, that has never been, and never should be, marriage's purpose. Marriage's aims are sterner and much more specific. As a result, for those seeking to revitalize marriage as a social institution, this idea is not part of the solution. It is part of the problem.

3. Marriage removes the stigma of nonmarriage.

Proponents of same-sex marriage frequently point out that in some respects American society still looks down on unmarried people. Fair enough. We have all probably heard such comments and insinuations. Single adults are not yet fully grown up. They haven't settled down properly. They must not be attractive or winning enough to find a spouse. They must be lonely. Surely they are living incomplete lives. Surely they wish they were married. What's wrong with them?

For gays and lesbians, who are legally prevented from marrying anyone to whom they are attracted, this lingering social stigma resulting from nonmarriage is particularly arbitrary and even cruel. Permitting gay marriage would therefore remove a stigma that makes life harder and less pleasant for many gays and lesbians, just as it would more generally represent greater social acceptance of gay and lesbian relationships.

4. Marriage civilizes relationships.

By far the most frequently voiced public arguments for gay marriage are those stressing the importance of equal rights, equality under the law, justice, and nondiscrimination. Both morally and legally, the basic framing of the issue is that of civil rights.[36] At the same time, a number of same-sex marriage advocates, most prominently Jonathan Rauch, Andrew Sullivan, Bruce Bawer, and William Eskridge, have argued that just as marriage appears to improve the lives and relationships of heterosexuals, it will do the same for homosexuals.

Under this general theme, perhaps the most frequently voiced specific prediction is that gay marriage will improve and stabilize the relationships of gay men. For example, William Eskridge of Yale Law School says that marriage is "good for gays" in large part because it "civilizes gays" by coming closer to ending their "outlaw status" and by encouraging "a greater degree of domestication." He adds: "To the extent that males in our culture have been more sexually venturesome (more in need of civilizing), same-sex marriage could be a particularly good commitment device for gay and bisexual men."[37]

On the surface, at least, this thesis has considerable merit. Scholarly research does show that participating in the institution of marriage—being subject to its rules and incentives and being guided by its public meaning—adds stability and longevity to a relationship. After all, that's one of the main purposes of the institution.[38] More generally, a large and growing body of social science research finds that, compared with similarly situated unmarried persons, married people are happier and healthier, live longer, are more fulfilled sexually, earn more and accumulate more wealth. Of course, some of the differences between the two groups are attributable to what scholars call "selection effects"—the fact that people who marry also, at the time of marriage, already tend to be better off in areas such as educational achievement, wage rates, health status, and others. At the same time, the key finding in study and after study is that *marriage itself*—the lived reality of being married—contributes significantly both to the relationship's stability and to the spouses' health, happiness, and prospects for economic success.[39]

Marriage advocates have been making these arguments for years. Now these same arguments are being used to support gay marriage.[40] Fair enough. The thesis that marriage would strengthen gay and lesbian relationships and improve the well-being of gay and lesbian married persons seems plausible.

Plausible, but not self-evident. For example, some of the documented advantages of marriage stem from its role in bridging male-female differences. Would these same advantages accrue to same-sex married couples? Researchers do not know. For example, marriage's well-documented role in reducing male sexual venturesomeness does not stem only, or probably even primarily, from an abstract, gender-neutral public norm of marital "domestication." Instead, much of marriage's vaunted public power in this area stems from the fact that it constantly exposes males to strong influences from *females*. Whether and to what degree a similar dynamic of domestication would occur in cases of male-male marriages is not known.

More importantly, this thesis conveniently presumes that changing marriage to include same-sex couples does not really change marriage. It presumes that adopting same-sex marriage would not contribute to a weakening of marriage's institutional authority or public meaning—the very features that confer all these advantages on individuals in the first place.

The evidence presented in this chapter suggests that we should be quite skeptical about this presumption. If it turns out to be invalid, all bets about those wonderful advantages of marriage are off—not just for gays and lesbians, but for everyone. For if "marriage" in the future became merely a pretty label for a private relationship, then everyone who married under such a regime would essentially get only the advantages of a private relationship.

5. Marriage is how we distribute benefits to people who make a commitment to one another.

After the argument that marrying the person of your choice is a basic civil right that should not be denied to anyone, probably the most widely repeated argument in support of equal marriage rights for gays and lesbians is that being married entitles spouses to a range of practical benefits in areas such as taxation, immigration, private employee benefits, Social Security, housing, hospital visitation rights, and others. Many of these benefits are conferred by the state. The core argument here is one of simple justice: Withholding these benefits from some couples on the grounds that they are not married, while at the same time legally preventing them from getting married, is unfair and cries out for remedy.[41] As an argument about justice, much of this reasoning is compelling and persuasive.

At the same time, what does this overall idea, framed in this way, tell us *about marriage*? Two basic themes stand out. One is clearly pro-marriage: that society recognizes and values marriage in part by giving specific, concrete benefits to married couples. The second, and more troubling, component of this thesis is that society confers all these advantages on marriage because society has decided that it wishes to support close personal relationships! If we need yet another example of this way of thinking, here is Andrew Sullivan, one if the nation's leading proponents of same-sex marriage. Arguing that the state should be "neutral" as regards all the inner dynamics of marriage, Sullivan recently insisted that the only legitimate purpose of marriage law is to encourage "social support for relationships as such."[42]

Relationships as such? Sullivan is proposing an entirely new and untested rationale for this institution. No society anywhere or at any time has ever established marriage in order to encourage "relationships as such." The whole notion boggles the mind. Accepting this idea necessarily means rejecting any concept of marriage as a coherent social institution, established by society for important public purposes that can be specified. It means that "marriage" and "close relationships" are the same thing, so we might as well just say, "Society supports and provides benefits to close relationships." What we used to call marriage is now completely deinstitutionalized.

Ideas That Disconnect

6. Marriage is not intrinsically connected to sex.

In the previously mentioned *Halpern v. Canada* court case, which led to the recent legalization of same-sex marriage in Canada, the lesbian and gay couples who sued the government submitted a brief to the Ontario Superior Court of Justice in which they spelled out their understanding of marriage. The "very heart" of marriage, they said, is "love and commitment." Getting married is also a "fundamental personal choice," a means of achieving family "security," an occasion for others to support the loving relationship, and "a celebration of a life of commitment to the relationship."[43]

What about children? The plaintiffs' answers are that "procreation is not the purpose of marriage" and that "procreation is not essential to marriage, in reality or law." What about sex? The plaintiffs tell us unequivocally: "Intercourse is not an essential marker of a marriage."[44] Marriage, they say, is a committed personal relationship that is supported by the society. And *sex has nothing necessarily to do with it!*

As we saw in Chapter Five, with the exception of a small number of early Christian theologians, who viewed sex as basically sinful and marriage as deeply problematic, no influential persons in the history of the world have *ever* argued that sex is not an intrinsic part of marriage—until now. The idea is a radical act of disconnection. It boldly asserts: Everyone has always presumed that A is a natural part of B, but it is not! From now on, the two are conceptually separate and distinct. Any overlap is purely a matter of coincidence and private choice, not public meaning or shared social norms.

When scholars use the word "deinstitutionalization," this is exactly the process they have in mind—amputating from the institution one after another of its core ideas, until the institution itself is like a room with all the furniture removed and everything stripped from the walls. No one knows anymore what this room was for, or why we might gather here as opposed to some other room. That's deinstitutionalization. The Full Stacey. Insisting that sex and marriage don't necessarily fit together is a giant step toward that end.

Regarding a number of other ideas on this list, I've made clear that they predate the gay marriage controversy. The campaign for gay marriage is employing and spreading these ideas, but it did not create them. But the one about sex is new, and it derives specifically from arguments supporting same-sex marriage. It is true, of course, that marriage in our society no longer has (if it ever did have) a working monopoly on sexual intercourse. But no one anywhere in nearly two millennia has seriously proposed that having sex is not an intrinsic or natural part of being married. Until now.

Let's reflect on what this idea might mean. If sexual intercourse is hereby disconnected from marriage's public meaning, what about the old idea of sexual faithfulness within marriage? Does that go, too? Is monogamy another one of those "customary forms" that marriage would be better off without?

William Eskridge and others argue that gay marriage would provide "a greater degree of domestication" to gay and lesbian relationships. He may be right. But social change on this issue is just as likely to flow in the other direction.

Jonathan Katz directs a lesbian and gay studies program at Yale University. In 2004, he told a National Public Radio interviewer, "I would never five years ago have defined myself as an advocate of marriage. In fact, the very institution smacked of precisely that which I lived my life in opposition to." But now he strongly favors same-sex marriage. He gives four reasons for his change of heart. First, gay marriage has become "the litmus test of civil rights now." Second, marriage "carries real social benefits." Third, gay marriage "furthers the uncoupling of the state and the church in this country," which Katz strongly favors. And fourth, gay marriage could "revolutionize the institution of marriage itself." Katz foresees that gay marriage could "redefine an institution that is increasingly viewed by many in our culture as having outlived its usefulness." More specifically, he believes that same-sex marriage would likely

> move the state perspective on marriage by virtue of our inclusion towards a much broader, more capacious view. I'm thinking even of the fact of monogamy, which is one of the pillars of heterosexual marriage and perhaps its key source of trauma. Could it be that the inclusion of lesbian and gay same-sex marriage may, in fact, sort of de-center the notion of monogamy and allow the prospect that marriage need not be an exclusive sexual relationship among people? I think it's possible.[45]

When I had lunch with Evan Wolfson of Freedom to Marry in 2003, I casually used the word "monogamous" in describing what I viewed as an important norm of marriage. Evan asked, "Do you mean monogamous, or exclusive?" I had no idea what he was asking me, and I must have looked puzzled, so he explained: Monogamous means that you are committed to one person. Exclusive means that you have sex only with that one person. The two are not intrinsically connected. A couple could be monogamous but not exclusive; it all depends on how they privately define their relationship.

Separating "monogamous" from "exclusive" is another act of radical disconnection. Until a moment ago, we had one idea: monogamous. Then we decided to split this idea into a sex part and a commitment part, separate and distinct. Now we have two ideas—and apparently a lot more for couples to discuss at night!

I don't want to hit this point too hard. Certainly heterosexuals have done more than enough all by themselves to devalue the norm of sexual faithfulness in intimate relationships. Moreover, while I believe that there are strong reasons to question the wisdom of legalizing same-sex marriage, I do not, when all is said and done, believe that the real or alleged promiscuity of homosexuals is one of them. My concern instead is how we as a society think about marriage. And to me it is distressing that, in using the new language that Evan introduced to me, we are once again, at least potentially, entering into the institution of marriage to break apart things that used to fit together. Over here is being committed. Over there is being exclusive. What'll it be for us, honey? And amidst this conceptual disconnection, where is marriage as an institution that has public meaning and generates shared norms? The answer: It is no longer an institution.

7. Marriage is not intrinsically connected to bridging the male-female divide.

Almost by definition, advocating for same-sex marriage means advocating that we remove the "male-female" part from our legal and public understanding of marriage. Making the case for gay marriage *requires* one to argue that bringing together the male and the female into a common life should no longer be an intrinsic component of marriage's public meaning.

Here is another act of radical disconnection. All of a sudden, what was heretofore a foundational component of marriage no longer is. The process of deinstitutionalization here is like turning off lights, one after another—we get rid of one defining idea after another—until it's dark enough to suit us. To remove the male-female part from our public understanding of marriage would be to turn off marriage's single brightest and most unmistakable light.

Many advocates of gay marriage appear to be quite confident about declaring that sexual embodiment and gender should be irrelevant to our understanding of marriage. Much of their argument comes in the form of angry attacks on "gender roles" and on the "gendered" meaning of marriage—by which they mean any roles and expectations within marriage linked to sexual embodiment. Thus Gretchen Stiers says proudly, in *From This Day Forward:* "By claiming the legal right to have a commitment or wedding ceremony, lesbians and gay men challenge the gender component of marriage as well as its underlying procreative function."[46] Similarly, here are Jeffrey Weeks, Brian Heaphy, and Catherine Donovan in their introduction to *Same Sex Intimacies:*

> Overwhelmingly, our interviewees feel that being lesbian, gay, bisexual or queer opens opportunities for more equal and fulfilling relationships than are available to most heterosexuals. This is because non-heterosexual relationships can be based on choice, and because they can escape the rigid assumptions about gender which continue to confine heterosexual relationships.[47]

In this view, the problem in family life today is institutional structures, kinship understood as biological ties, and gender roles. The solution is the elimination of gender roles and the expansion of choice. These authors agree with the British sociologist Anthony Giddens that "same sex couples are in the vanguard of these changes, pointing the way forward to their less advanced heterosexual brothers and sisters."[48]

Mary Bernstein, who teaches at Arizona State University, has a similar perspective, arguing that same-sex marriage "challenges the gendered basis of the heterosexual nuclear family." And she thinks that's good. (No gender roles, please!) One important aspect of getting rid of gender roles is getting rid of the notion that there is anything special about merely *biological* parents. This would mean, for example, that society must accept the legitimacy of artificial insemination for lesbian couples who want children. More fundamentally, society must rid itself of the idea—we might call it a "gendered" idea—that there is anything optimal about a child growing up with her own two biological parents. Bernstein concludes: "Such changes in law and policy pose the ultimate threat to conservatively defined 'family values' that view two parents of the opposite sex as necessary for a child's proper gender and sexual development."[49]

Follow the logic here. The premise is no gender roles. Therefore sexual embodiment is irrelevant. This requires an end to society's privileging of biological parents, which shows that a mother and father together are not necessary for a child's gender and sexual development, which in turn suggests that a mother and father together are not necessary. Knock out the male-female part, and look where we end up.

8. Marriage is not intrinsically connected to bearing and raising children.

- Andrew Sullivan: "The heterosexuality of marriage is intrinsic only if it is understood to be intrinsically procreative; but that definition has long been abandoned in Western society."[50]
- William N. Eskridge Jr.: "In today's society the importance of marriage is relational and not procreational."[51]
- Dale Carpenter: "Marriage is not *essentially* about procreation because procreation is not essential to any marriage."[52]
- Twenty-six big-name professors, in a brief to the Massachusetts Supreme Judicial Court when those justices were considering the *Goodridge* case, which led to the inauguration of same-sex marriage in Massachusetts: "Procreation, on the other hand, is not fundamental to marriage."[53]
- The Massachusetts Supreme Judicial Court, in its *Goodridge* decision, responding to the state's idea that procreation is fundamental to marriage: "This is incorrect."[54]

These authorities all seem to be quite sure on this question. To support their conclusion, they cite three facts. First, society does not, as a condition of marriage, legally require couples to bear and raise children. Second, if a married couple does not produce offspring due to either infertility or choice, society does not for that reason seek to invalidate or revoke their marriage. Finally, marriage is about other things, such as financial cooperation and emotional intimacy, that are not necessarily connected to bearing and raising children. Case closed, it would seem.

By the way, did you know that cars are not intrinsically connected to driving? When you acquire ownership of a car, society does not impose upon you a binding obligation to drive it. If you buy a car but fail to drive it, the state does not for that reason revoke your driver's license or refuse to grant you one, or take your car away. If you do not drive, but do collect antique cars, there is nothing wrong or illegal about it. Cars can be about many things, including pleasure, aesthetics, economic gain, and social status. Driving is therefore not fundamental to cars.

Did you know that art museums are not intrinsically connected to viewing art? When you pay your fee to join a museum, the museum does not require you, as a condition of membership, to promise to view the art. When you enter the museum, no one ensures that you visit the galleries, as opposed to the restaurant and the gift shop. No law stipulates that art museums are never, under any circumstances, about anything other than viewing art. And it's possible to view art without going to an art museum! Some argue that viewing art is fundamental to museums. This is incorrect.

A few years ago, I visited a small town in the Shenandoah Valley of Virginia to give a speech about fatherhood. I asked the guy driving me around to tell me about the place. "It's a nice little town," he said. "Even the atheists here go to church." Don't you agree that churches are not intrinsically connected to worshipping God?

This way of arguing is clearly preposterous. That it is widely employed by prominent journalists, eminent judges, and tenured professors does not make it any less preposterous. We can either think like analysts looking at a social institution, or think like lawyers looking for a loophole. The evidence presented in this book shows overwhelmingly—I believe beyond any reasonable doubt—that marriage as a human institution is intrinsically connected to bearing and raising children. To argue otherwise is to argue like a lawyer looking for a loophole; it is not intellectually or morally serious, at least insofar as we actually care about the institution we are discussing.

Marriage's main purpose is to make sure that any child born has two responsible parents, a mother and a father who are committed to the child and committed to each other. To achieve this goal, it has never been necessary, and it would never be possible, for society to require that each and every married couple bear a child!

Here's a thought experiment. What if society *did* seek to prove beyond any legal doubt that marriage is connected to procreation by legally requiring *all* married couples to have children? As a practical matter, we could never do such a thing. Many couples' views about when and under what circumstances to have children have not been finalized prior to marriage, and may well change over time as a result of many factors, including the experience of marriage itself. Their procreative intentions could never be stipulated in a legally binding way as a condition of marriage. Similarly, requiring legal proof of fertility prior to marriage, or prohibiting infertile couples from marrying, or invalidating the marriages of couples who fail to conceive, would all be practical impossibilities in the vast majority of cases, since infertility is rarely a clearly fixed or unalterable status.

But even to engage in such a thought experiment is to grant far too much to the argument. There is an obvious reason why no society ever has or ever would require certificates of fertility as a condition of marriage, or invalidate the marriages of childless couples. *There is no need!* The human desire to procreate is typically quite strong. When women and men bond with one another and have sex together, babies are an unexceptional and even quite predictable result. Society does not need them to submit fertility certificates to the state, or to swear in legal documents that they will do their best to produce children. They just do it.

In the long span of marriage's history, the institution's legal, intellectual, moral, and religious custodians have never felt obliged to act as if these simple facts did not exist, or could not be generally presumed. Nor have they ever in the past perceived a need to erect a legal firewall protecting the institution from conceptual assaults by lawyers insisting that even the smallest exception to the procreative norm invalidates the norm, or from brazen assertions that marriage is fundamentally disconnected from procreation—a claim that was never even raised, much less taken seriously, until about five minutes ago.[55]

In today's argument for same-sex marriage, the single most radical assertion regarding marriage has nothing to do with homosexuality. The most radical assertion—the one most likely to inflict further damage on marriage's capacity to serve as our society's most important pro-child institution—is that marriage and children are now basically disconnected, with marriage as a close personal relationship over here, and children's well-being as a social priority over there. Does any child advocate out there really want to sign on to this proposition?

9. Marriage does not intrinsically seek to connect natural and legal parenthood.

In March of 2005, Canada's federal government proposed legislation to establish same-sex marriage throughout Canada. The bill, called the Civil Marriage Act, contains three sections. The first, in which each paragraph begins with "Whereas," lays out the arguments for same-sex marriage. The second section, which begins with "Therefore," briefly declares the basic transformation that should occur. Marriage is to switch from "a man and a woman" to "two persons." The final section is called "Consequential Amendments." This section concerns the details. It lays out the specific changes that must occur in order to implement the new law faithfully.

Let's look at one of those details. The proposed legislation would remove the term "natural parent" from Canadian law and replace it with the term "legal parent." That sound you just heard is the earth shifting.[56]

A fundamental purpose of marriage as a human institution is to unite the biological and social dimensions of being a parent. Marriage boldly declares: The two of you whose physical union made the baby are simultaneously a social partnership responsible for raising the baby. In this bringing together of male and female, of nature and nurture, of the biological and the social, the great beneficiary is the human infant.

As we've seen, the great advantage for the child is not, as Evan Wolfson would have it, merely "two parents." Nor is it even "a mother and a father" in some abstract sense of "a male parent figure" and "a female parent figure," or what Mary Bernstein derisively calls "two parents of the opposite sex." In fact, the issue runs much deeper than either opposite-sex or same-sex. The great advantage for the child is to love and be loved by the two specific individuals whose physical union made the child.

Marriage does many fine things for human beings, but this one is probably the finest: It gives me as a child the mother and the father who made me. I have been studying what's good for children since the late 1980s, and if any gift to the human infant is more basic than this one, and more integral to the possibility of full human flourishing, I have not yet discovered what it is.

Accepting same-sex marriage would require us, in our laws and in our public norms, to disavow the importance of that gift. Instead of seeking to unite the natural and social dimensions of being a parent, gay marriage explicitly requires us to break the two apart—another act of radical disconnection—and then to choose one over the other. From now on in Canada, as a legal matter, apparently there is no such thing as a natural or biological parent. There are only "legal" parents, which is another way of saying that, from now on, a parent is whoever the state says is a parent.

The new norm of the "legal" parent represents such a radical change that it would probably take decades to come to terms with its myriad consequences. For example, when a lesbian mother marries a woman, does that woman automatically become the legal parent of the child? David L. Chambers, the law professor cited earlier, specifically argues that in a regime of equal marriage rights for same-sex couples, lesbian couples would need access to "automatic registering of parenthood for the nonbiological female partner."[57] And what about the men in these cases who—as anonymous sperm donors, as friends, or as ex-husbands or ex-boyfriends—biologically help to make these children? Can a child have more than two "legal" parents?[58] How many would be too many? No one really knows.[59]

What about the consequences for heterosexuals? For example, in cases of remarriage today, a man who marries a mother does not, by virtue of marrying her, become a legal parent of her child. He can seek to adopt the child (if the existing father gives up legal rights or has them severed), but adoption is an arduous process, not an "automatic registering." It *should* be arduous. Why? Because we see the threat to children in casually throwing around the word "parent." We recognize the meaning and importance of the natural parent. And we understand that the biological and social dimensions of being a parent stand best when they stand together. Marriage as a social institution supports these ideas. The logic of same-sex marriage requires us to reject them.

This logic is blatantly contrary to the interest of our children. The fading out of the biological parent and the rise of the "legal" parent clearly point to a new understanding of "parent" essentially as whoever happens to be around the child at the moment. I fear that we are about to revoke one of the greatest gifts that we as a society give to our children.

10. Children do not necessarily need a mother and a father.

In February of 2005, Governor Mitt Romney of Massachusetts summed up his opposition to same-sex marriage by saying, "Every child has a right to a mother and a father."[60] The *Boston Globe*, the governor's hometown newspaper, reacted with outrage. "Not Fair, Governor," was the title of the *Globe*'s editorial. According to the editors, Romney was "peddling ignorance" and "practicing divisive, mean-spirited politics."[61]

A few years earlier, state officials in Hawaii, as part of their (unsuccessful) attempt to defend the premise that viewing marriage as an opposite-sex institution is constitutionally permissible, had argued that "a child is best parented by its biological parents living in a single household." Evan Wolfson, who served as co-counsel for the plaintiffs in that court case (*Baehr v. Lewin*), angrily dismissed this line of argument, saying, "This proposition is both offensive and unproven."[62]

Ignorant and mean-spirited? Offensive and unproven? *Unfair*?

As we've seen, the idea that the human child needs to love and be loved by her own mother and father—and that in a good society this amounts to a birthright—is a very old idea. (Remember Lipit-Ishtar: "I made the father support the child.") It is also nothing less than marriage's central idea and its most important reason for existing. To repudiate this aspect of marriage's public meaning is to rob the institution of its core rationale.

Unproven? We saw in the previous chapter, when he was misreporting the scholarly views of my friend David Popenoe on exactly this subject, that Evan is not well informed on this matter. In fact, as David and many other scholars have shown, when it comes to the family structure that is generally best for children, there is proof aplenty for those who care to look.[63] The *New York*

Times summed up the weight of scholarly evidence in a front-page story in 2001: "From a child's point of view, according to a growing body of social research, the most supportive household is one with the two biological parents in a low-conflict marriage."[64]

Offensive? Since when is it offensive to discuss what is best for our society's children? I think I know the answer: It is offensive when doing so runs contrary to the wishes of a vocal group of adults.

Mean-spirited politics? Perhaps this means that marriage nuts are making up this stuff about children for political reasons, and dwelling on it only to prevent gays and lesbians from getting married. Now it's my turn: Unfair![65] The idea that children need mothers and fathers is anything but a new anti-gay tactic. People who care about marriage have been saying it for centuries, long before anyone imagined same-sex marriage.

I began saying it publicly in the late 1980s, when the scholarly debate about the social consequences of unwed childbearing and the divorce revolution was in full swing. I wrote a book on the subject in 1995, just when scholarly opinion was clearly shifting toward a new consensus regarding the importance for children of growing up with their own, married mother and father. During those years, despite many baptisms by fire, I never quite overcame my surprise at the fact that one can not only earn a living, but also earn a reputation as a controversialist, by saying in public that every child deserves a mother and a father. At that time, most people who criticized this idea—think Judith Stacey—did so in order to defend, or at least put a happier face on, the nation's high and growing rates of family fragmentation via divorce and unwed childbearing. More than a few times, we marriage advocates were told that our point about children needing mothers and fathers was "unfair."

Today, however, arguments in support of gay marriage are dramatically increasing both the visibility and the social impact of the idea that children do not necessarily need mothers and fathers. Every day, we hear that children do just fine, thank you, in all kinds of diverse arrangements. We hear that it's "unfair" to say something about children's basic needs that was viewed as nothing less than common sense until a generation ago, and that was recently reclaimed as a legitimate and important insight by leading social scientists. As a result, the recent and encouraging pro-child consensus in our national intellectual life may already be fading out—not because the evidence has changed, but because the push for gay marriage has changed its social context. I personally know more than a few scholars and leaders who strongly believe that every child deserves a mother and a father, but who simply will not say it out loud anymore. For to say it publicly today is, in all probability, to invite denunciation for bigotry and hate speech.

A business in New Jersey called Family Evolutions sells T-shirts, bibs, and other items for children being raised by lesbian couples. One T-shirt says: "Let My Parents Marry!" Another says: "My Daddy's Name Is Donor."[66] Proponents of equal marriage rights seem to realize that same-sex marriage is essentially incompatible with the idea that every child has a right to a mother and a father. They are probably correct about that. So we must choose.

Ideas That Evaluate

11. The idea of marriage being between a man and a woman is a religious idea.

As the Harvard law professor Alan Dershowitz puts it, "Those who oppose gay marriage believe deeply that marriage is a *sacreda divine,* a blessed sacrament between man and woman as ordained in the Bible." Such a particular conception, Dershowitz concludes, is fine as a private religious conviction, but should never become the basis of public policy in a society "which recognizes the separation between the sacred and the secular, between church and state."[67]

Alisa Solomon, a professor at the City University of New York, agrees: "Marriage itself violates the establishment clause by defining matrimony according to particular religious beliefs." She continues: "Take the sacral out of the state, and what reason can it give for preferring hetero to homo coupling? Not a one."[68] Jo Ann Citron of the Women's Studies Department at Wellesley College similarly argues that marriage as it is currently defined is "a religious institution."[69]

This thesis is about as intellectually weak as an idea can be. Marriage as a man-woman bond is fundamentally a natural and social institution—what Claude Lévi-Strauss calls "a social institution with a biological foundation"—that exists in all or nearly all human societies. It was not created by religion, and it certainly does not owe its definition or existence to any particular religion or to religion in general. Obviously, religion influences marriage, just as it influences every important sphere of human life. But calling man-woman marriage a "religious institution"—created by and intelligible to only those people who embrace a certain religious doctrine—is wildly off the mark. It's distressing that so many people with access to a microphone repeat it so often and with such gusto.

12. Marriage needs to be more separated from religion.

There are two reasons for the strenuous insistence that marriage—specifically, *man-woman* marriage—does not derive from society as a whole, but instead is a purely religious idea. First, if marriage is merely a religious doctrine, then it does not merit the protection of law; or as Alan Dershowitz puts it, marriage understood in a religious (man-woman) way "has no place in our civil society."[70] In one fell swoop, marriage is thus transformed from a universal human institution into a private religious prejudice. (Emergency! Call in the separation-of-church-and-state lawyers!) The second reason is that if man-woman marriage is merely a religious doctrine, then people who oppose same-sex marriage are almost by definition religious zealots who want to impose their doctrines on others.

And what is the solution? If the problem is that marriage as it actually exists is a narrow religious doctrine, one tactical solution is relentlessly to attack the "religious right" as the enemy of civic tolerance. A more fundamental solution is to insist that the big problem with marriage today is *too much religion.*

According to David Moats, the author of *Civil Wars: A Battle for Gay Marriage,* "one of the challenges facing the gay rights movement has been how to break the grip of religion on our secular democracy."[71] Steve Swayne, a professor at Dartmouth who writes frequently in favor of legally recognizing gay unions, similarly argues that "we would all benefit from a separation between church and state when it comes to marriage."[72] Just as getting a birth certificate is now completely separate from the religious ceremony of baptism, Swayne argues that legal marriage, or what he calls "the certificate," should become completely separate from any religious observance, or what he calls "the ceremony."[73] Dershowitz, Solomon, and Citron, cited above, also advocate widening the gap between marriage as a societal and legal matter that concerns all of us, and marriage as a private religious rite, left up to the wishes of each individual.

Andrew Sullivan, arguably the nation's most visible proponent of gay marriage, has gone so far as to propose an entirely new vocabulary. In his writing and public speaking, Sullivan almost never uses the simple term "marriage" anymore; it's usually "civil marriage," and occasionally "legal marriage." The purpose of the adjective is to demonstrate in everyday speech that "civil marriage," which is the good thing that we all want, is different from the old thing, "marriage," which is all tangled up with, you know, *religion*.

Kind reader, do you believe that what's ailing marriage today, and ailing our civil society more generally, is that too many Americans are too religious? That religious believers thought up this man-woman definition of marriage and are imposing it on everyone else for theological reasons? That the religious threat to marriage's integrity has become so dangerous that we must *completely* evict religious meanings and symbols from our shared understanding of marriage? That we now require a new, this-is-not-religious warning label to be stuck in front of that venerable old word, marriage? ("I love you. Let's get civilly married.") That conceptually breaking up marriage into different fragments—one civil, one religious—is likely to strengthen marriage as a pro-child social institution?

I don't believe so. I certainly understand why many gays and lesbians feel alienated from organized religion, which is often inhospitable to them, and why they strongly dislike the anti-gay statements and activities of some religious leaders. I don't like those statements and activities either. But I don't believe that we will solve those problems by pretending, against all evidence, that religion invented the man-woman basis of marriage, or that marriage will be improved by getting rid of any traces of religious influence. Do you?[74]

13. Historically, marriage has been a bad institution.

Call me overly sensitive, but I am bothered by the fact that public arguments in favor of gay marriage almost always include a dismissive denunciation of the entire history of marriage as a human institution. When the subject is the alleged noninstitutional "essence" of marriage as an expression of love, the words flow all soft and syrupy. But when the subject is the actual lived experience of marriage in human societies, the words become both vague and accusatory. Vague: marriage as an institution is always changing. Accusatory: up to now it has been a pretty terrible business.

The Canadian gay marriage advocate Kevin Bourassa, while stressing that marriage "has always been an evolving institution," repeats the charge that "marriage was at one time about property and chattel."[75] Andrew Sullivan similarly informs us that marriage as a social institution "was instituted many centuries ago to solve political problems—to annex one family to another, to settle dynastic disputes, to distribute property."[76] And that is why humans started marrying. One doesn't know whether to laugh or cry.

Advocates of gay marriage repeatedly insist that marriage as an institution is essentially racist and sexist, perpetrating economic inequality and dealing mainly in "property" and "chattel." The late Thomas B. Stoddard, who was director of the Lambda Legal Defense and Education Fund and an early public advocate of same-sex marriage, emphasized both "the oppressive nature of marriage historically" and "the general absence of edifying examples of modern heterosexual marriage." For these reasons, he said, "I am no fan of the 'institution' of marriage as currently constructed and practiced."[77] (Notice the scare-quotes around the word "institution.") So when Stoddard predicted that the campaign for gay marriage would transform this "institution" that he so disliked into "something new,"[78] he meant, I believe, exactly what scholars call deinstitutionalization.

The essential proposition here is that marriage *as it has actually existed* in human societies is a harmful institution. The hope for "something new," stemming in part from the adoption of same-sex marriage, lies in removing the institution part of marriage and replacing it with the understanding that marriage is how society affirms private relationships of commitment.

Criticism of marriage is easy, and some of the criticism is justified; like any human arrangement, it is far from perfect. But is there a *better* arrangement for bringing together women and men in a shared life and for protecting the human infant? These root-and-branch denunciations are aimed at deinstitutionalization—the melting away of marriage as an authoritative, pro-child social institution.

14. Marriage has become much weaker—and that's a good thing.
Today's intellectual and grassroots movement to strengthen marriage, of which I am a part, is united around the goal of reducing unwed childbearing and unnecessary divorce so that each year, as we put it in a joint statement in 2004, "more children are raised in nurturing homes by their married mother and father."[79] Our larger vision is what a group of us, the Council on Families, in 1995 called "recreating a marriage culture," by "reversing the trend of family fragmentation and reinstitutionalizing marriage."[80]

But as we are seeing, ideas in support of gay marriage aim in precisely the opposite direction. Instead of striving to reinstitutionalize marriage—to bolster its public meaning and authority—or even to maintain what is left of its institutionality, the arguments for same-sex marriage overwhelmingly favor the almost complete deinstitutionalization of marriage.

Margaret Gullette, a scholar at the Women's Studies Research Center at Brandeis University, was for many years "a rebellious critic" of the institution of marriage. But today she is "a vocal and explicit advocate." What changed her mind was, in part, the campaign for same-sex marriage. Seeing lesbian friends and relatives insist upon the right to marry, she says, caused her to reconsider her dim view of marriage. But Gullette also argues that marriage has *already* changed, and for the better. Divorce has become much easier. Sexuality outside of marriage has become far more acceptable. Raising children outside of marriage, and without fathers, is no longer a scandal.[81]

Gullette heartily approves of these changes. She realizes that marriage as an institution has weakened substantially in recent decades, so that people increasingly can approach it with "unshackled feet." The institution is gradually giving way to the possibility of the "pure relationship." Therefore, "Staying in a marriage has come closer to being an existential decision." This is all very good, in her view. These changes make gay marriage plausible, and gay marriage in turn would take us as a society further in this direction.[82]

Richard D. Mohr, a professor of philosophy at the University of Illinois who writes frequently in support of gay marriage, asks, "Should marriage as a legal institution simply be chucked, given the emptiness of its standard justifications?" His answer is: "Not quite."[83] But almost! Pardon the pun, but Mohr wants less. For starters, marriage must shed its "definitional entanglements with gender and procreation." Insisting that: "monogamy is not an essential component of love and marriage," Mohr says that "the law should acknowledge this possibility more generally." Committed relationships today increasingly require "a certain amount of open texture and play at the joints," he argues. "This strongly suggests that legal marriage ought not to enforce any tight matrix of obligations on couples if their long-term happiness is part of the law's stake." Policies aimed at discouraging unwed childbearing are definitely out. So are policies aimed at discouraging divorce.[84]

As Mohr sees it, marriage is "an evolving institution," and when it comes to deinstitutionalization, "family law reform has generally been moving in this direction."[85] He concludes that legalizing same-sex marriage would take our society *much* further down this path. He is almost certainly correct.

15. Marriage has become much weaker—and that's a reason for gay marriage.

In 2003, as I was struggling to think through the issue of gay marriage, I wrote to Andrew Sullivan asking him to clarify a point he had made in one of his articles. He sent a courteous reply and asked if I supported equal marriage rights for gays and lesbians. I replied that I was undecided—that I was a Morally Anguished Fence Sitter. I was worried, I told him, that such a transformation would weaken marriage as a pro-child social institution. He wrote back: "But isn't widespread no-fault divorce worse?" The question stunned me. It still does.

Sullivan and others make this point regularly in public arguments in support of gay marriage. Right after Vermont instituted civil unions for same-sex couples in 2000, Andrew wrote: "If any legal change truly represented the 'end of marriage,' it was forged in Nevada, not Vermont."[86] A year later, responding to the proposition that gay marriage would be likely to weaken marriage, he wrote:

> But isn't this backwards? Surely the world of no-strings heterosexual hookups and 50 percent divorce rates preceded gay marriage. . . . All homosexuals are saying, three decades later, is that, under the current definition, there's no reason to exclude us. If you want to return straight marriage to the 1950s, go ahead. But until you do, the exclusion of gays is simply an anomaly—and a denial of basic civil equality.

Here Andrew clearly implies that the case for gay marriage makes the *most* sense in a world where marriage as a pro-child institution has been weakened, and the *least* sense in a world of stable marriages, low divorce rates, and little unwed childbearing. Quite an admission.[87]

In this light, it is understandable that Andrew heartily approved of an essay by a Methodist pastor, Donald Sensing, that appeared in the *Wall Street Journal* in March 2004, called "Save Marriage? It's Too Late." According to Sensing, the rapid spread of unwed childbearing, along with "rampant, easy divorce without social stigma," meant that "talk in 2004 of 'saving marriage' is pretty specious. There's little left to save."[88] His tone was one of sadness bordering on despair. Andrew wrote that he himself is constantly making "the same point," and concluded:

> It's for these reasons that I find drawing the line at gay couples to be so morally troubling. Enforcing one rule for the majority and another rule for a tiny minority is so gratuitously unfair that it runs the risk of being understood as pure prejudice.[89]

There are deep problems with this argument. Let's begin with the question of consistency. On Mondays, Wednesdays, and Fridays, Andrew declares in purple prose that he loves marriage, reveres it as an institution—as "the highest recognition of personal integrity"[90]—and wants its wonderful benefits to be extended to everyone. But on Tuesdays, Thursdays, and Saturdays, he declares that marriage is dead already, beyond saving as a coherent pro-child institution, and therefore gay marriage couldn't hurt (much) and is inevitable anyway as a matter of basic equality. I cannot figure out how anyone can honestly believe both of these propositions at the same time.

Also, did you get the memo announcing that marriage is beyond saving? I didn't. Andrew and Pastor Sensing both seem quite sure about this point, but the last time I looked, most children in the United States were still living with their own two married parents. Divorce rates are actually declining modestly. Teen pregnancy rates are dropping dramatically. Rates of marital happiness have stabilized and may be increasing. The proportion of African American children living in two-parent, married-couple homes has stabilized and may actually have increased in the late 1990s.[91] Numerous states are experimenting with legal reforms aimed at strengthening marriage and reducing unnecessary divorce.[92] These trends are partly due to the dedicated work of thousands of marriage leaders and educators in communities across the country, who also never got the memo saying that marriage is beyond saving.

Andrew reports that he finds "morally troubling" the idea of "drawing the line" between, on the one hand, heterosexuals who want the freedom to trash the institution at will, and on the other, homosexuals who are told that permitting them to marry would weaken the institution. So do I! I certainly do not believe in "drawing the line" there either, and I do not know a single marriage advocate who does. That's why we marriage promoters spend most of our time arguing against *heterosexuals* who favor or acquiesce in trends that weaken marriage. We insist on "drawing the line" between, on the one hand, *anyone* pushing for the weakening of marriage, and on the other, *anyone* promoting the strengthening of marriage. As a debating point, Andrew's argument makes sense only if he is confronting someone who doesn't care about marriage and who could never imagine lifting a finger to try to strengthen the institution. Are you such a person, kind reader?

And while we're on the subject of what is "morally troubling," consider the implication of Andrew's question, "But isn't widespread no-fault divorce worse?" Think about that. If A has hurt marriage, and B is also likely to hurt marriage, but probably less than A, then people who support marriage should support B! Because divorce on demand and related trends have already harmed society's most pro-child institution, it is acceptable to *harm it fur-*

ther in order to advance the goal of gay equality. Morally, that is the essence of Andrew's claim. It is clearly a demand that we worry less about children and more about adults in general and "me" in particular. For this reason, it is a claim reeking of narcissism—the conviction that one's own needs and desires are the axis of the universe, around which all other values and considerations must revolve.

Andrew Sullivan and others have put down this extraordinary marker and, in doing so, have called on us to make a choice. So we must choose.

Should Marriage Fade Away?

These fifteen ideas in support of same-sex marriage overwhelmingly endorse or presuppose the deinstitutionalization of marriage. These ideas aim to change marriage's public meaning by effectively removing any notion of institutionality from our cultural and legal understanding of what marriage is.

Accepting these ideas would mean accepting something like a post-institutional understanding of marriage. It would mean the Full Stacey. Instead of society's most pro-child social institution, marriage would become a word that we use to name private relationships of commitment that are not really about sex, not about procreation, not about recognizing the double (male-female) origin of each child; that should have nothing to do with religion, should be almost completely open and unstructured, and should have no public goal or purpose that we can collectively specify, other than supporting "relationships as such."

I don't think there can be much doubt that this post-institutional view of marriage constitutes a radical redefinition. Prominent family scholars on both sides of the divide—those who favor gay marriage and those who do not—acknowledge this reality. Andrew Cherlin of Johns Hopkins University, a supporter of same-sex marriage, describes "the movement to legalize same-sex marriage" as "the most recent development in the deinstitutionalization of marriage" in the United States.[93] Norval Glenn of the University of Texas, who has voiced reservations about gay marriage, similarly observes the current shift in our society from an institutional to a couple-centered conception of marriage, and points out that

> acceptance of the arguments made by some advocates of same-sex marriage would bring this trend to its logical conclusion, namely, the definition of marriage as being for the benefit of those who enter into it rather than as an institution for the benefit of society, the community, or any social entity larger than the couple.[94]

So we are left with the biggest question of all: Do we believe that deinstitutionalizing marriage is a good goal, or a bad one?

Recall our definition from Chapter Three: A social institution is a pattern of rules and structures intended to meet basic social needs. Institutions are fundamental enablers of human sociality. They give humans the gift of knowing what to expect of others and what others expect of us. By reducing the burden of choice and permitting us to take some things for granted, institutions are essential pathways to higher and more complex forms of human creativity, deliberation, and cooperation. Finally, institutions guide behavior in specified pro-social directions. They wield authority in two ways. The first is when institutions provide meaning and aspiration that we experience as both natural and desirable. The second is when institutions pressure and coerce us.

This second form of institutional authority is obviously harder for us freedom-loving Americans to accept. As Peter L. Berger and Thomas Luckmann remind us, institutions at times can be "experienced as existing over and beyond the individuals who 'happen to' embody them at the moment," and as "possessing a reality of their own, a reality that confronts the individual as an external and coercive fact."[95] In the case of marriage, this external and coercive authority is wielded primarily in the interests of children.

The opposite of marriage as an institution is marriage as what the British sociologist Anthony Giddens calls "pure relationship." It's an idea we've encountered many times in this chapter. A pure relationship is just us, for us, made by us, and without the encumbrances of socially defined meanings, forms, and purposes. A pure relationship, says Giddens, "is one in which external criteria have become dissolved."[96] It is "entered into for its own sake, for what can be derived by each person from a sustained association with the other." Its central motif is the search for emotional intimacy.[97] Two of its primary traits are instability and impermanence: "It is a feature of the pure relationship that it can be terminated, more or less at will, by either party at any particular point." Giddens reports, not surprisingly, that enshrining the pure relationship as our primary model of intimacy not only seriously undermines marriage as an institution, but also is likely to prove "a subversive influence on modern institutions as a whole."[98]

Marriage can remain, and become even more, our society's most pro-child social institution. Or it can be redefined as merely a private committed relationship. Gay marriage would take us decisively in the latter direction, toward deinstitutionalization. Nothing is preordained or inevitable. We must choose.

7

Goods in Conflict

THE CENTRAL ARGUMENT for gay marriage is not an argument about marriage. In the previous chapter, we saw what many leading proponents of same-sex marriage are saying about marriage itself. We saw that the people who have devoted much of their professional lives to attacking marriage as an institution almost always favor gay marriage. Indeed, the most energetic crusaders *against* marriage in its customary forms appear to be among the most energetic crusaders *for* same-sex marriage. And the arguments that for years have been deployed to attack marriage, and in particular to plead for its further deinstitutionalization, are now routinely deployed to support same-sex marriage. These facts should worry anyone concerned about child well-being and the future health of our most pro-child social institution.

At the same time, for many—I believe most—people who support same-sex marriage, the single biggest and most deeply felt reason is less about marriage itself than it is about something else. That something else is human dignity. The central argument for gay marriage is not an argument about marriage, but an argument about basic rights.

In late 2005, I participated in a public conversation with Andrew Sullivan about same-sex marriage. It was a spirited debate. I wanted to discuss marriage, and Andrew fully obliged, repeating many familiar themes: Marriage is constantly changing. Marriage is a close relationship between two people. Marriage originally was all about property. Marriage is not really about children.

Marriage historically was pretty awful. On each of these points and more, Andrew expressed himself succinctly and forcefully.

But his heart was clearly elsewhere. Near the end of the debate, I told him as much, and read to him from one of his essays, in which he speaks directly to

> a young [gay] kid out there who may even be reading this now.... I want to let him know that he doesn't have to choose between himself and his family anymore. I want to let him know that his love has dignity, that he does indeed have a future as a full and equal part of the human race. Only marriage will do that.[1]

Not too many years ago, Andrew *was* that "young kid out there," struggling to know that his love has dignity and that he is a full and equal part of the human race. *That* is the heart of the matter for Andrew—not so much a cluster of intellectual concerns about what marriage as an institution is or should be, but instead, a bone-deep, fighting-for-my-life desire to be accepted by others as a child of God who can love with dignity and who is worthy of love. *That* is his motivation, his true and deepest need. Or so I suggested at the close of our debate. When Andrew responded, his eyes were filled with tears as he stressed again the idea that "only marriage" can meet such a basic human need. We didn't agree on that point, just as we hadn't agreed on much else. To my disappointment, we seemed to spend much of the conversation talking past one another. But at least we had agreed on what, for him, was the fundamental issue.

And not just for Andrew. For many—probably most—proponents of gay marriage, the essential fact is equal human dignity. Therefore the essential demand is for justice, and the essential argument is about human and civil rights.

The Analogy

We often hear that the struggle for equal marriage rights for gays and lesbians today is morally and legally analogous to the struggle for civil rights for African Americans in the 1950s and 1960s.

More specifically, we hear that today's effort to permit same-sex couples to marry is morally and legally analogous to yesterday's effort to permit interracial couples to marry.

For example, the title of a column in the *Boston Globe* announces: "Echoes of Racism in Gay Marriage Ban."[2] In the *Washington Post,* the columnist Colbert I. King elaborates:

> A host of state anti-miscegenation laws—strongly backed by white public sentiment—were upheld in state courts well into the 20th century. The reasoning was simple and absolute: Marriage between the races defied the natural order; intermarriage bans had legitimate historical roots and were based on a "divinely ordained" scheme. Conclusion: Government had the right to define marriage as a union of two persons of the same race.
>
> It remained that way for generations, until 1967, when the U.S. Supreme Court, in *Loving v. Virginia,* ruled that state laws setting forth who can marry whom violate "one of the vital personal rights essential to orderly pursuit of happiness by free men"—marriage—and "the principle of equality at the heart of the Fourteenth Amendment.... How will future generations view our present-day fight against allowing monogamous couples with life commitments to each other to marry?[3]

Gail Mathabane's column in *USA Today* declares that "Gays Face Same Battle Interracial Couples Fought." She writes, "Before the U.S. Supreme Court delivered the landmark Loving decision, interracial couples were in the same boat that same-sex couples are in today." Her conclusion: "Like interracial marriages, same-sex marriages are bound to become legal sooner or later...."[4]

Here is the columnist C. W. Nevius in the *San Francisco Chronicle:*

> There's no economic or public safety reason to keep two people who love each other from getting married. It just comes down to "I don't like the idea so you can't do it." Which, when you think about it, was pretty much the argument against interracial marriage.[5]

A judge on the Supreme Court of the State of New York invoked the analogy in a 2005 ruling:

> Marriage is no more limited by the historical exclusion of same-sex marriage than it was limited by the exclusion of interracial marriage. . . . The challenge to laws banning whites and non-whites from marriage demonstrates that the fundamental right to marry the person of one's choice may not be denied based on longstanding and deeply held traditional beliefs about appropriate marital partner.[6]

Here is the writer Steve Swayne: "Eventually gay couples will achieve full legal equality throughout America, just as interracial couples achieved equality."[7] Here is Kim Gandy, the president of the National Organization for Women: "In the 1960s, the civil rights movement fought for interracial couples to have marriage rights—and won. We're fighting for marriage rights again, this time for same-sex couples. We'll win this struggle too."[8]

This analogy has become a powerful shaper of our national conversation. It is repeated constantly. As far as I can tell, from the earliest proponents to the most recent, hardly *anyone* seriously proposing same-sex marriage in the United States has failed to assert, typically with great gusto, as if playing a surefire trump card, that prohibiting gay marriage is basically the same as prohibiting interracial marriage.

The analogy is moral dynamite. It forcefully links gay marriage to the African American civil rights movement—possibly the most morally compelling movement for social change of the past century in the United States. It also directly links opponents of gay marriage with a particularly despicable idea, racism, and with a particularly ugly period of our national history. All in all, this is a powerful tactic.

But the analogy is false—not simply intellectually weak, not merely confusing or misleading, but entirely and totally false. The fact that so many highly credentialed people in our society regularly shout it from the rooftops does not make it any less false. It is false at two levels. First, two men (or two women) seeking to marry one another is not remotely similar to a black person of one sex seeking to marry a white person of the other sex. At a deeper level, yesterday's proponents of anti-miscegenation laws have more in common with today's *proponents* of gay marriage than with those who oppose gay marriage.

Recall the basics. Across history and cultures, marriage is socially approved sexual intercourse between a woman and a man. Marriage is in part a private relationship, but it is also, and fundamentally, a social institution, with rules and forms that create public meaning intended to solve important problems and meet basic needs. The core problem that marriage aims to solve is sexual embodiment—the species' division into male and female—and its primary consequence, sexual reproduction. The core need that marriage aims to meet is the child's need to be emotionally, morally, practically, and legally affiliated with the woman and the man whose sexual union brought the child into the world. That is not *all* that marriage is or does, but nearly everywhere on the planet, that is *fundamentally* what marriage is and does.

Accordingly, it is *not* true that the only constant in the history of marriage is that it is always changing. It is *not* true that marriage is only incidentally connected to sex, or to children, or to bridging the male-female divide. Most of all, it is *not* true that marriage in essence is an expression of love, a private relationship of commitment between consenting adults.

Put somewhat differently, in the United States today, there are two competing and quite different conceptions of what marriage is. One view says that marriage at its core is a pro-child social institution. The other says that marriage at its core is a post-institutional private relationship. The latter view certainly has many advocates, but the former view is, well, correct. At a minimum, let's assume that it's correct for the purposes of examining the analogy.

Let's get specific. If a white person of one sex aims to marry a black person of the other sex, we have not the slightest reason to believe that marriage's fundamental forms are being weakened or violated, or that the institution's fundamental purposes are being challenged or denied. On the contrary, we have every reason to assume that such a marriage would be fully consistent with the core forms, meanings, and purposes of marriage as a human and social institution. But whenever someone seeks to *prevent* an interracial couple from marrying—say, by passing anti-miscegenation laws—that person is weakening the institution of marriage, because *promoting racism by enforcing racial separatism is not one of marriage's public purposes.* Accordingly, people who use marriage laws to promote racism are corrupting marriage by grafting onto it a public value that is alien and even hostile to the institution's core forms, meanings, and reasons for being. They are manipulating marriage for their own purposes, turning an institution designed to bring women and men together into one that often keeps them apart.

That's why Mildred Jeter and Richard Loving, a black woman and a white man, did a good deed for the social institution of marriage when they told the sheriff who arrested them in 1958 for violating Virginia's anti-miscegenation statutes that *they were married.* And that's why Sheriff R. Garnett Brooks, and the legislators who made the law he was enforcing, and the people of Virginia who supported that law, by their actions during that time all did significant harm to marriage as a social institution. This case led to the famous *Loving v. Virginia* decision of the Supreme Court in 1967, which overturned all bans on interracial marriage in the United States.[9]

This example of twentieth-century U.S. anti-miscegenation laws is far from unique. There are many episodes in the history of marriage in which interested persons—for racial, economic, religious, or other reasons—have sought to use marriage for essentially alien objectives, or twist marriage into something other than what it fundamentally is. Often these efforts have been successful, at least for a time, but usually they do not last. To see how this phenomenon can work, let's glance again at two examples from Chapter Five.

Early Christian fathers. As we saw, some important Christian writers during the Church's patristic and early medieval periods viewed all sexual intercourse as impure and tending toward sinful. In several creative ways, these Church fathers sought to graft this view of sex onto the institution of marriage. The most astonishing result of this effort was the notion, propagated by a number of these writers, that marriage is not intrinsically connected to sexual intercourse. Another result, which first appeared in the third century, was the idea of "spiritual marriage," in which Christian clergy and ascetic men could live intimately, but without engaging in sexual intercourse, with nuns or other consecrated female virgins. A third result was decrees, including one from the Council of Elvira in the early fourth century, stating that legally married

Christian clergy must abstain from sexual intercourse with their wives.[10] This novel view of the relationship of sexual intercourse to marriage, as well as the marriage rules and practices that stemmed from it, did not last.

The Nayars. Recall that marriage among the Nayars of India from at least 1400 to about 1800 was highly unusual in practice and institutionally wafer-thin. As a result, fatherhood among the Nayars, in the sense of one social father for every child, hardly existed at all. Nayar males during this period were highly specialized fighting men, far too preoccupied with war and rulership to become ordinary marrying men. Consequently, the Nayars invented a radically watered-down, structurally altered, and astonishingly flimsy version of marriage that both reflected and served these *military* goals—all of which came to an abrupt halt and quickly reverted back to normal marriage in the early nineteenth century, as the British conquest caused the disbanding of the Nayar armies.

In most respects, early Christian clerics do not have much in common with Hindu castes of Nayar warriors. But for our purposes, they are quite similar! Both groups of men were elite and highly specialized. Both were fundamentally preoccupied with callings that appeared to them to be inconsistent and even incompatible with marriage as a natural social institution. As a result, both groups sought effectively to change marriage's public meaning, by eviscerating one or more of its core purposes or by eliminating one or more of its basic forms. The Church fathers wanted to get rid of the form of sex. The Nayars abandoned not only the form of sex, but also the idea of marriage as a personal relationship and the idea of a mother and a father for every child.

Both groups reshaped marriage in order to use it for other purposes. For the Church fathers, that purpose was celibacy in the service of religious devotion. For the Nayars, the purpose was war. Both groups wanted to redefine marriage—lop off some features and restructure the rest in ways that would help them achieve extramarital social objectives—while still continuing to call it "marriage." Both of these projects succeeded for a while, then collapsed.

Does any of this sound familiar? In the same tradition, today's proponents of same-sex marriage in the United States are seeking to restructure marriage and use it for a special purpose. That purpose is to gain social recognition of the dignity of homosexual love. Or as Andrew Sullivan puts it, the purpose is to win acceptance of gays and lesbians as full and equal members of the human race. I endorse that purpose, but I do not endorse using marriage to achieve it. There are four main reasons why.

First, using marriage to achieve that good purpose would require eradicating in law, and weakening in culture, the form of opposites (marriage as man-woman), which arguably is marriage's single most foundational form.

Second, using marriage to achieve that good purpose would also mean largely eradicating in law and public discourse the form of sex (marriage involves sexual intercourse). For as we've seen, although their reasons are different, today's civic and judicial proponents of gay marriage easily rival the most sex-averse early Christian fathers in their adamant insistence that marriage is not intrinsically connected to sexual intercourse. So two of marriage's three basic forms have already been taken down. Whether the form of two (marriage is for two people) could remain standing once the other two basic forms have been tossed aside is at best an open question—especially since many proponents of gay marriage are earnest opponents of this form as well.

Third, using marriage to achieve the good purpose of full acceptance for lesbians and gays would require publicly and legally renouncing the idea of a mother and a father for every child. Across history and cultures, as earlier chapters demonstrated, marriage's *single most fundamental idea* is that every child needs a mother and a father. Changing marriage to accommodate same-sex couples would nullify this principle in culture and in law. For me, and for many other child advocates, this issue is more crucial than any other.

Finally, and more generally, using marriage to achieve that good purpose would mean marriage's complete or nearly complete deinstitutionalization. It would be like going from room to room turning off the lights, since many of the rooms would no longer be necessary. In the end, we would be wandering around a building that has been largely abandoned. The public meaning of marriage would become much thinner and weaker. The idea of marriage as a pro-child social institution would be replaced by a much smaller idea: marriage as another name for a private committed relationship.

We as a society can and should accept the dignity of homosexual love and the equal worth of gay and lesbian persons. But must we shrink and restructure *marriage* in these institution-maiming, child-threatening ways in order to achieve this social process? I do not suggest that the answer is easy. But to me, the answer is no.

Marriage exists for public purposes that can be specified. *Diminishing homophobia is not one of marriage's public purposes.* Marriage is institutionally alive to the fact of sexual embodiment and, flowing from it, sexual reproduction. Regarding the subjective and often complex issue of sexual orientation, marriage is institutionally deaf, blind, and dumb. It doesn't ask, tell, require, record, stipulate, accept, judge, or reject on the basis of individual sexual desire. Asking marriage to do so now—asking marriage to reconstitute itself according to the criterion of sexual orientation, and in doing so to help change public attitudes about orientation—is asking marriage to do something entirely unprecedented, and something for which the institution is radically ill equipped.

When people seek to reshape and use marriage for a bad purpose, such as fostering racism through anti-miscegenation laws, the moral judgment is easy. When a major social institution is threatened for a *good* cause, the moral judgment becomes difficult and painful, because doing more of one good thing requires doing less of another. That is our predicament today regarding same-sex marriage. There is no true analogy between yesterday's racists and today's defenders of marriage's customary forms. The only accurate analogy is between the advocates of anti-miscegenation laws and the advocates of same-sex marriage, since each group wants to recreate marriage in the name of a social goal that is fundamentally unconnected to marriage.

The Right to Marry

When Andrew Sullivan insists that "only marriage" can make it possible for a young gay man to know that "his love has dignity," he is grounding the plea for same-sex marriage in one of humanity's most powerful ideas. That idea is that all persons possess equal dignity, and therefore that all are entitled to equal moral regard. Philosophers increasingly view this idea as the essential universal moral law—the starting point of almost all liberal moral thought and the necessary foundation of any philosophical stance consistent with basic human values.[11]

In the modern era, the idea of equal human dignity has been expressed most concretely, and has achieved its greatest impact, through the development and practice of human rights. The most seminal human rights document in the world today, the United Nations 1948 Universal Declaration of Human Rights, begins its preamble with these properly famous words: "Recognition of the inherent dignity and of the equal and inalienable rights of all members of the human family is the foundation of freedom, justice and peace in the world." The first sentence of the Declaration's first article reads: "All human beings are born free and equal in dignity and rights."

This concept of human rights based on inherent human dignity is changing the world. Increasingly, talking about rights is the way that we talk about many of our most important needs and aspirations. Both in the United States and internationally, the language of rights has become a primary language for expressing our ideas of the good, especially regarding standards of justice. As the Canadian human rights scholar Michael Ignatieff puts it,

> Rights are not just instruments of the law, they are expressions of our moral identity as a people. When we see justice done—for example, when an unjustly imprisoned person walks free, when a person long crushed by oppression stands up and demands her right to be heard—we feel a deep emotion rise within us. That emotion is the longing to live in a fair world. Rights may be precise, legalistic, and dry, but they are the chief means by which humans express this longing.[12]

The modern human rights revolution carries powerful implications for the institution of marriage. The most important is that marriage is a fundamental human right, stemming from the equal dignity of all persons. The Universal Declaration of Human Rights establishes this point clearly in Article 16: "Men and women of full age, without any limitation due to race, nationality or religion, have the right to marry and to found a family." Today, and partly as a result of the Declaration, the right to marry is recognized in most of the world, by national and transnational political and judicial authorities as well as by religious groups and other institutions of civil society, as a basic human right.[13]

Does this right to marry imply—logically and by simple justice—the right to marry a person of the same sex? For proponents of gay marriage, the answer is easy. Indeed, of *all* public arguments favoring same-sex marriage, the most frequently repeated and the most rhetorically powerful one is the argument that the right to marry, if it means anything, means the right to marry the person you choose.

To me, this argument is mistaken and begs for reflection on what "the right to marry" means. Is it something like a generic permission slip to do what you choose?

To explore this issue, there is no better place to start than the Universal Declaration of Human Rights, the foundational document of the modern human rights revolution and the primary source for human rights instruments now in effect in countries around the world. What does the Declaration tell us about the right to marry?

First, *the right to marry is a compound right.*

When the Declaration affirms that men and women "have the right to marry and to found a family," it indicates that this is a compound right. The right to marry implies and carries with it the right to bear and raise children. The institution of marriage as understood by the Universal Declaration is intrinsically connected to parenthood and to the values, norms, and social expectations associated with bearing and raising offspring.

Today's proponents of same-sex marriage frequently and adamantly insist that marriage is *not* intrinsically connected to bearing and raising children. The weight of evidence overwhelmingly does not support this thesis. Now we know that the Universal Declaration of Human Rights also clearly disavows it.[14]

Second, and more broadly, *marriage as a right is closely linked to marriage as an institution.*

Overall, the drafters of the Universal Declaration of Human Rights did a masterful job of producing an integrated, holistic statement of human rights. As the legal scholar Mary Ann Glendon puts it, when we read it as a whole, we find that "the Declaration's vision of liberty is inseparable from its call to social responsibility." She states:

> When read as it was meant to be, namely as a whole, it is an integrated document that rests on a concept of the dignity of the human person within the family. In substance, as well as in form, it is a declaration of interdependence—interdependence of people, nations, and rights.[15]

So let us examine more fully what the Declaration tells us about the right to marry and to found a family. Here is Article 16, the one concerning marriage, in its entirety:

> Men and women of full age, without any limitation due to race, nationality or religion, have the right to marry and to found a family. They are entitled to equal rights as to marriage, during marriage, and at its dissolution.
>
> Marriage shall be entered into only with the free and full consent of the intending spouses.
>
> The family is the natural and fundamental group unit of society and is entitled to protection by society and the State.

Here we see six important ideas. Marriage is intrinsically linked to children. Men and women have equal rights in marriage. Marriage requires the spouses' free consent. The natural family is society's basic group unit. The institution of the family deserves protection. And, marriage is a fundamental human right.

The key point is that each of these ideas is connected to all the others. Freedom is linked to solidarity. Marriage is linked to family. Rights imply responsibility. Institutions are not wished away; they exist, and they matter. Together, these six ideas are not perfect and do not tell us everything about marriage, but they ably suggest marriage's fundamental shape and public purpose. Above all, the Declaration clearly does not intend for these ideas to be pulled apart and isolated from one another. It is certainly not saying, or even remotely implying, that the master idea, the one right, is that anyone has the right to marry anyone.[16]

Note especially the linkage in the Declaration between the right to marry and the idea that "the family is the natural and fundamental group unit of society." When Article 16 says "natural," it is making two interconnected claims. In one respect, "natural" refers to the dimension of the family that we today would more likely call biological. A "natural" parent, in this sense, is a biological parent. The second meaning of "natural" refers to marriage. The Declaration is suggesting that marriage is a "natural"—universal, existing everywhere—human institution. Thus the Declaration affirms that the basic social unit among humans is the biological mother married to the biological father, together raising their children. Marriage is a human right precisely, or at least primarily, because it is integral to this fundamental social unit.

In the Declaration, the right to marry is a thick idea, not a thin one. It is sociologically concrete, not abstract and free-floating. It concerns society as well as individuals, children as well as adults, responsibility as well as freedom. As a result, the right exists in a coherent institutional context—the right to the thing is bound up with the thing itself, which has public purposes that can be specified. In particular, the Declaration forthrightly refuses to sever marriage from parenthood, which is another way of saying that it refuses to sever marriage from its single most important public purpose.

In the world's most important articulation of human rights to date, the right to marry recognizes fully, but also recognizes only, *the right to participate in the institution of marriage*. It does not recognize the right to turn marriage into another word for any private adult relationship of choice.

Rights Claims in Conflict

Let us stipulate that many people today, including many policy makers, simply do not agree with the understanding of marriage found in the Universal Declaration of Human Rights. For the future, they want something quite different. They want society to adopt a much more flexible definition of the right to marry and to found a family. What exactly would this new, streamlined definition say?

For many people, the right to marry at its core should simply mean *the right to marry the person you choose.* As long as the person is an adult, consents to the marriage, and is not a biological sibling or parent, you have the legal right to marry that person.

In addition, any revised formulation of the right to marry must have something to do with parenthood, or what the Universal Declaration calls founding a family. After all, under nearly any foreseeable future arrangement, marriages would still have something to do with families, and families would still have something to do with children. In any legal regime in which marriage exists, marital status and rights would continue to overlap with and affect parental status and rights. In this regard, no one denies that extending marriage rights to same-sex couples would mean greater social acceptance and more legal protections both for same-sex couples already raising children and for those wishing to become parents. Indeed, proponents of gay marriage frequently point out that gaining more support for gay and lesbian parenting is a major reason to support same-sex marriage. *Whenever we change marriage, we are also changing parenthood.*[17]

Because same-sex pair-bonding cannot produce children from the union of one spouse's eggs with the other spouse's sperm, parenting by same-sex couples in every instance relies decisively on at least one of three additional factors. The first is any of a growing number of assisted reproductive technologies. The second is the involvement of third-party participants such as sperm donors, egg donors, or surrogates. And the third is the granting of parental status to at least one member of the couple who is biologically unrelated to the child.

Embracing these trends as normative clearly necessitates a redefinition of parenthood itself and therefore a thorough reformulation of the right to found a family. Here is the simplest way to say it: *Individuals have the right to form the families they choose.* The idea of gay marriage carries with it the idea that individuals have the right to form families of their own choosing and bear children in the way that they wish, with the support of available medical and scientific technologies and without restriction or interference by society.

Now let's put the two rights claims together and get the new proposal: *Adults have the right to marry the person they choose and form the families they choose.* Robert Goss sums up this new rights claim admirably in *Our Families, Our Values,* where he proposes that everyone "has the right to create family forms that fit his or her needs to realize the human potential for love in non oppressive relationships." And: "Everyone has the right to define significant relationships and decide who matters and counts as family."[18]

Kath Weston succinctly conveyed this idea in the title of her influential 1991 book, *Families We Choose.*[19] In 2001, praising the gay and lesbian community's "growing tendency to affirm positively both the right to parent, and the responsibilities that this entails," Jeffrey Weeks, Brian Heaphy, and Catherine Donovan, in a chapter called "Families of Choice," strongly endorsed the validity of "claiming as 'family' whatever our own arrangements are."[20]

Similarly, Mary Bernstein reminds us that same-sex couples as parents "imply the separation of sexuality from procreation," just as partners' parental rights and the use of surrogates, sperm donors, and the new reproductive technologies for gay and lesbian couples "separate children from procreation." For Bernstein, all this separation is not only necessary but also good, insofar as it challenges "hegemonic notions of family."[21] In the same vein, Cheshire C. Calhoun argues that same-sex couples wishing to bear and raise children are properly insisting that "in spite of their multiple deviations from norms governing the family, their families are nevertheless *real* ones and they are themselves naturally suited for marriage, family, and parenting, *however* these may be defined and redefined."[22]

Proponents of this new rights claim are actively pursuing it today in the courts. In the spring of 2005, attorneys for Basic Rights Oregon, a group of lawyers representing same-sex couples, sued the State of Oregon, as the *Portland Mercury* put it, "over what constitutes legal parenthood." In the first of what the group says will be a series of such legal challenges, a lesbian mother, who had conceived the child through artificial insemination, wants her partner (whom she also wants to marry) to be automatically recognized in law as the child's second parent, in just the same way that a married man is legally presumed to be the father of his wife's child. The mother's partner, Jeana Frazzini, could have tried to adopt the child through a process called second-parent adoption, and probably would have succeeded, but she decided against that course of action on the grounds that, as she put it, "we had already decided that this was our family." Her lawyer added: "We shouldn't have to adopt our own children."[23]

So here is the new claim: A woman in a close relationship with a mother is automatically the parent of that mother's child. Why? Because she and the mother say that she is. She is not just a caregiver, not just the mother's lover and partner. *She is the child's parent.* She should not have to suffer the indignity of seeking to adopt the child, because she and her partner have "already decided" the issue of parentage, and parents do not need to adopt their own children! As we saw in Chapter Six, the law professor David L. Chambers, a prominent supporter of this claim, describes such a reform as the "automatic registering of parenthood for the nonbiological female partner."[24] The philosophy professor Julien S. Murphy similarly sees the need to "alter perceptions of lesbian reproductive capacities" and "obtain parental rights for nonbirthing partners."[25]

Now we can see more clearly the essential dimensions of the new rights claim coming from proponents of same-sex marriage and from others seeking to reformulate the right to marry and found a family as stated in the Universal Declaration of Human Rights. Compared with the current right, the proposed revision is much simpler. It retains none of what the current right implies about marriage's structure, institutionality, or public purposes. Instead, the new claim fundamentally privileges the values of privacy, autonomy, and personal choice. Probably the most consequential implication of the new claim concerns parenthood, which must be radically redefined. Above all, the new idea embraces the norm of adult individual freedom.

Michael Ignatieff, a human rights scholar (and a former teacher of mine), strongly endorses the new rights claim as a key part of "the rights revolution in private life." Referring to this revolution-in-progress, he concludes that "it is hard to imagine that it will not run its full course." He explains, "The reason is simply that the human rights revolution appeals to the idea of equality and against this idea there is no remaining court of appeal."[26]

He may be right. A newly formulated right to marry the person you choose and form the family you choose does appeal unmistakably to important human goods. It appeals to freedom, which

Michael rightly calls modernity's core value. It declares that the individual has agency. I can shape my life the way I want to shape it. And it appeals to equality, saying that, insofar as policy can make it so, gay and lesbian couples by right can do whatever heterosexual couples can do, including marrying and bearing and raising children.

Whatever else it is, this idea is deeply American. Our nation's central idea is freedom. Our Declaration of Independence, itself a divorce document, affirms that all persons are created equal. Writing in *Harper's Magazine,* Fenton Johnson captures an important truth when he describes gay marriage as a "logical culmination of the American democratic experiment, which provides its citizens with an open playing field on which each of us has a responsibility to define and then respect his or her boundaries and rules."[27]

Appealing to the basic American values of freedom and equality is a powerful argument for a reformulated right to marry and to found a family. But is its eventual success, as Michael Ignatieff suggests, all but inevitable? Is there any legitimate court of appeal?

There should be. For no single good thing, no matter how good it is, should override all other good things. Here is a key principle of human rights: *A right exists only in community with, and at times in tension with, other rights.*

Freedom of speech is a very good thing, but so is public safety, which is why I cannot walk into the proverbial crowded theater shouting "Fire!" Parental rights are a good thing, but I cannot torture my child. We cannot understand any human right by imagining that it stands by itself, in splendid isolation. Rights exist only in relationship to other rights. Moreover, no single human right, no matter how important, is the lodestar for all other related priorities, which can also be expressed as rights. The inevitable result of these facts, in free societies, is the phenomenon of rights in conflict. Often enough, an important right comes into genuine conflict with another important right.[28]

So we must ask ourselves whether today's proposed reformulation of the right to marry and found a family—*I have the right to marry the person I choose and form the family I choose*—comes into conflict with any other important human goods or bumps up against any other basic human rights.

It does. It bumps up against the rights of children. Adults certainly have rights. But so do children. As societies change and philosophies evolve, adults can and do make for themselves new rights claims to fit new situations. But they also, in response to changing circumstances, can and do make new rights claims *on behalf of children*. For when it comes to human rights, everyone, including the children, gets a seat at the table.

At times, these new rights claims will inevitably come into conflict with one another. When this happens, all that we can do in a free society is consider the claims *together*, weighing the human good at stake on all sides, and seeking to arrive at an ethically responsible resolution.

When it comes to the adult right to marry and found a family, we therefore need to think carefully about the complementary rights of children. Let's start with the U.N. Convention on the Rights of the Child. Adopted by the United Nations in 1989, this Convention is intended to elaborate, develop, and enforce legally the principles of the Universal Declaration of Human Rights and its direct cognates insofar as those principles apply to the world's children. Here is the first section of Article 7:

> The child shall be registered immediately after birth and shall have the right from birth to a name, the right to acquire a nationality, and, as far as possible, the right to know and be cared for by his or her parents.

Every child in the world has three birthrights. She deserves a name. She deserves to be a citizen of a nation. And she deserves her two parents.

Let's consider what is meant by "his or her parents" and "as far as possible." As we've seen, the Universal Declaration of Human Rights plainly suggests that society's basic ("natural") social unit is the biological mother married to the biological father, together raising their children. So when the Convention says "his or her parents," it is clearly talking about the two natural parents, the biological mother and the biological father.

"As far as possible" is an important qualification and exception. It is intended to recognize the reality of human failure and loss, while providing protection for the child. Sometimes natural parents die. Sometimes they do not or cannot competently parent their child. Sometimes they become threats to their own children. In such cases, society can and must intervene directly on behalf of the child, primarily through institutions such as adoption and state-run residences for children. "As far as possible" is *not* an escape clause for indifferent policy makers or for parents who would rather do whatever, but is instead a sober recognition by the state that sometimes, tragically, children are denied their birthright to their two parents.

The United Nations Convention declares that *I have a right as a child to the mother and father who made me.* I am owed this right "as far as possible"; the only exception is when, due to tragedy, it is either not possible or not in my best interests to be raised by my natural parents. This right is as essential to me as having a name.

Yet across the world today, and especially in the rich countries of the West, children are increasingly denied this basic birthright. The divorce and unwed childbearing revolutions of recent decades mean that, with each passing year, more and more of our children are *not* living with and being cared for by their own two natural parents. In the United States, for example, the astonishing truth is that the proportion of all children who do *not* grow up living with their own mothers and fathers is now roughly as large as the proportion who do.[29] We are witnessing, with a considerable degree of indifference, a widespread and growing breach of a basic human right. This fact alone ought to concern anyone who cares about children—and anyone who cares about human rights.

But today, a new and potentially lethal threat to this right is emerging and gaining momentum. We can see the threat in any number of recent policy recommendations, commercial ventures, court decisions, interest group claims, and expert arguments, in the United States and in several other countries as well. The threat is the proposed elimination in law of the idea that there is something normative or desirable about a child being raised by her natural mother and her natural father. According to the researcher Frank Furstenberg and colleagues,

> Numerous studies have shown that individuals generally fare best both in childhood and in later life when they grow up with

> both of their biological parents.... Put simply, children benefit from the economic and emotional investment of parents who reside together continuously, and these investments are generally higher among biological than among surrogate parents.[30]

Until now, all cases of a child being denied its two natural parents have been viewed by international law and civil society, *without exception*, as something profoundly unfortunate and therefore as something that "as far as possible" should be avoided. But this idea is now under direct assault. The proposed replacement idea is that it doesn't really matter.

In "The Other Mother," a 2004 article in the *New York Times Magazine*, Peggy Orenstein writes about the growing use of sperm donors, egg donors, embryo donors, surrogates, and other third-party participants by same-sex couples wishing to become parents. These children by definition will not be raised by two natural parents. Does it really matter? To give us the answer, Orenstein quotes Leonard Glantz, a professor of health law at Boston University: "Once you have legalized adoption, that's the end of the picture in terms of genetics. It's a very broad statement of social policy by legislature that genetics and parenthood are different issues."[31]

In my public discussion with Andrew Sullivan on gay marriage in 2005, I said that I was alarmed by the fact that Canada, as a part of its implementation of same-sex marriage, was eliminating the term "natural parent" from Canadian law and replacing it with the term "legal parent." That is a hugely important change. It stems directly from—in Canada it is literally a part of—the adoption of same-sex marriage. This change demonstrates incontrovertibly that, at least in Canada, *changing marriage changes parenthood,* not just for a few children, but for all Canadian children. For same-sex marriage advocates who so frequently and confidently ask, "Where's the threat?" one answer is: *Right there!* Before same-sex marriage, Canadian law gave specific recognition to natural parents. Now, with same-sex marriage, it no longer does. The change could not be any plainer or any bolder. For anyone who believes that children have a birthright to their own two natural parents, it is most definitely a threat.

But Andrew saw it differently. Just like Professor Glantz, he responded to this entire issue by bringing up the subject of adoption. By definition, adoptive parents are not biological parents, and yet we as a society don't feel threatened or alarmed by adoption. So where's the problem? Being a parent is one thing, and "genetics," as Glantz calls it, is a "different issue." Adoption proves that the two are not really connected.

Here is how the argument works: First, identify two dimensions of parenthood—the natural dimension and the social/legal dimension—that typically go together and that all or nearly all human societies have strongly insisted *should* go together. Then, as casually as saying the word "adoption," break them apart and pit them against one another! Insist on this disconnection and polarization, justified by a small piece of evidence taken completely out of context, in order to destroy a big idea: that children have a right to their own mother and father.

In more general terms, declare that any exception to the rule means that no rule exists. Then declare that any complicating feature of a social institution—in this case, the role of adoption within the institution of parenthood—proves that the institution itself has no fixed or intrinsic meaning. Such an argument is easy enough to make. But it is intellectually vacuous.

Adoption is a wonderfully pro-child act. Adults respond to a child's loss with altruistic, healing love. Spouses who are not biologically related to the child promise to act as if—and are viewed by society essentially as if—they were the child's natural parents. Adoption does not deny but in fact presupposes the importance of natural parents.

For this reason, despite all the good it does, adoption is ultimately a derivative and compensatory institution. It is not a standalone good, primarily because its existence depends upon prior human loss. Almost everyone believes that in a good society, the great majority of children should be cared for by their own two natural parents. But it would never occur to anyone to believe that, in a good society, all or most children should be adopted.[32]

Leonard Glantz's and Andrew Sullivan's proposition about adoption is therefore utterly specious. The idea that the world's children have a birthright to know and be cared for by their two natural parents is not invalidated merely by pointing to the existence of adoption. Legalized adoption does not mean that parenthood is one thing and "genetics" is something entirely different. It does not imply that there is nothing distinctive or normative about natural parents. Nor does it mean we must pretend that adoption is unconnected to loss. Most of all, the existence of adoption does not mean that society is obliged to smile benignly and pretend that all is well when individuals or couples decide to take unprecedented steps—not as an altruistic response to a child's loss, but as a personal prerogative for which they seek society's support and collaboration—to bring into this world children who by definition can never be cared for by their two natural parents. So much for the argument based on adoption.

Some proponents also try to justify the new rights claim—both explain its inevitability and insist that there is nothing really novel about it—by invoking the reality of divorce and unwed childbearing. Both of these practices undermine the child's right to her two natural parents, yet we as a society tolerate them. Few if any of us are prepared to outlaw them. So proponents of the new rights claim pose this challenge: Isn't the new assertion about family formation just a bit more of the same—a further expression of essentially the same cultural values?

It is true, of course, that all three of these behaviors result in higher numbers of children in nontraditional family structures. But the right to marry the person you choose and form the family you choose departs sharply, and in the most alarming possible way, from the already disturbing cultural precedents set by the spread of divorce and unwed childbearing.

Divorce is failure, an unhappy ending. No one gets married planning or hoping to divorce. Almost no one denies that divorce is a major cause of childhood suffering today.[33] Although divorce is sometimes necessary, and even at times can open a pathway to future adult flourishing, a choice to divorce can never be anything better than the least bad choice. As the novelist Pat Conroy put it, "Every divorce is the death of a small civilization."[34]

Conversely, the new rights claim concerns a novel approach to *founding a family*—a birth, not a kind of death. It is not about what we sadly must do, but instead about what we joyfully want to do, and therefore what we want and expect society to recognize and assist. Creating a family is not anchored in loss and suffering; it models for individuals and society what we aspire to, for ourselves and for our children.

When a divorce results in a child no longer living with both of her natural parents, today's basic understanding is that something bad has happened. We as a society have failed to sustain an important relationship. We are witnessing loss. But if tomorrow a couple intentionally brings into the world a child with no chance of being raised by two natural parents, the new right to form the family you choose would suggest that something *good* has happened. We as a society are sustaining an important relationship, one that is worthy of recognition and support. We are witnessing human flourishing. This astonishing claim requires an enormous change in our evaluation of natural parenthood. What was, in the case of divorce, a partial failure to meet the norm is now *an entirely new norm.*

The world's main human rights statements say that children have a right to their two natural parents. The divorce revolution has weakened that right by separating too many children during too much of their childhood from at least one of their parents. But the moment we collectively declare, as a matter of principle, that adults forming their families can get babies any way they choose and define parentage any way they choose, with society's full recognition and acceptance, we have done more than weaken that right. Legally and culturally, we have fully overturned it.

In the case of unwed childbearing, family formation itself occurs in a way that undermines the institution of marriage and is likely to make children vulnerable. The children of unmarried parents are far more likely than children of married couples to spend at least some of their childhood living apart from one or both of their natural parents.[35] And since unmarried parents never made a legal promise in the first place, unwed childbearing probably outdoes divorce in weakening the child's right to her two natural parents.

Yet as a social phenomenon, unwed childbearing is much closer to divorce than to surrogate or contract pregnancy, the use of third-party sperm or eggs, or other forms of what the legal scholar John

A. Roberts (who supports the trend) terms "collaborative reproduction."[36] From the perspective of a child hoping to be raised by her two natural parents, unwed childbearing is a risky business, but it is not a final verdict. Many unmarried parents do live together and raise their children together, and some eventually marry. Societies typically expect, and in some instances compel, both of the unmarried parents to help care for their offspring. Whenever an unmarried parent walks away from his or her offspring, both law and custom typically view that conduct as reprehensible and possibly criminal. Tolerating unwed childbearing does not require us to renounce the principle that children have a right to be cared for by their two natural parents.

Accepting "collaborative reproduction" as a human right, flowing from the right to marry the person I choose and form the family I choose, clearly *would* require us to renounce the principle that children have a right to be cared for by their two natural parents. It would create a new standard in which individual adults have the approval of society and the support of scientific technology to do *anything they want to do* regarding the production and rearing of children. If you were a child coming into the world today and were able to understand your interests, how would you feel about such a standard?

In fact, what if you were born *today* in Britain? British law used to require doctors who facilitated conception through procedures such as anonymous sperm donation at least to consider, as an ethical matter, the welfare of the child who may be born, including specifically "the need for a father." But those words are now being scrapped. Apparently the whole idea has become too inconvenient for the adults involved. The old regulation was "judgmental and insulting," according to one activist who fought to get rid of it. The father reference had become "nonsense," according to another activist. The headline in *The Times* of London tells the story well enough: "No Father Needed."[37]

Recently the Law Commission of New Zealand recommended several key legal changes to help New Zealand move beyond what the "strict two-parent model" of what is desirable and normative for childrearing. In the area of parenthood, if you want to permit adults to move beyond the strict rule of two, you can either go down to one, or up to three or more. The recommended changes in New Zealand are intended to facilitate and normalize both options.

For example, depending on the wishes of the adults involved, egg or sperm donors may elect to "opt out" of legal parenthood. In recognition of this option, the Law Commission helpfully recommends several changes in New Zealand's birth certificates. For example, instead of reporting that the father of the newborn is "unknown"—the commission reports that some mothers find such terminology unpleasant—a mother could instead request that the birth certificate simply stipulate that the child was born of the mother and "by donor." The commission also recommends in such cases that the birth certificate inform the child—"the person whose certificate it is"—that "other information" about the child's origins may be available from the federal Register of Births, Deaths and Marriages. Such "other information" could include the fact that the father—excuse me, the donor—"opted out" of legal parenthood. ("Tough luck, kid, sometimes they opt out!")

On the other hand, if a sperm or egg donor reaches such an agreement with the intended parental couple—either heterosexual or homosexual, married or unmarried—the Law Commission also recommends permitting the egg or sperm donor to "opt in" to parenthood. In these cases, the child in question would have *three* legal parents. Four or more parents might be possible in some cases. Exactly how many would depend on the agreements reached by the collaborating adults.[38]

So, if some children in New Zealand are going to have three legal parents, why can't those parents all marry one another? Allowing three persons legally to co-parent a child but not to marry would surely constitute arbitrary discrimination against those parents, wouldn't it? Please whisper hello to group marriage.

Of course, in the public debate on same-sex marriage and the alleged right to found families of choice, anyone who brings up polyamory or polygamy is usually chastised harshly for offering "slippery slope" arguments. But as we've seen, legal scholars are already publishing articles in law journals making the case for legally recognized polyamory. I'll bet that these advocates, who are just as passionate and serious about their goal as gay marriage proponents are about theirs, are delighted to see that New Zealand has apparently decided it's fine for one child to have three parents. Will someone please explain why this child's parents cannot marry?

Same-sex marriage, by tossing out both the rule of opposites (marriage is man-woman) and the rule of sex (marriage involves sexual intercourse), renders the one big rule left standing, the rule of two, largely incoherent and increasingly vulnerable to assault. Now we can see the full threat to the form of two. The threat comes not only from "I can marry whomever I choose," but also, and *especially,* from "I can form the family I choose."

Regarding childbearing, the critics of the rule of two are anything but shy or subtle. The philosopher Cheshire C. Calhoun has clearly run out of patience with what she calls "the rule of one-mother, one-father per child." Here is how she puts it:

> As a result of remarriage, semen donation, and contract pregnancy, the rule of one-mother, one-father per child (both of whom are expected to be biological parents) that has dominated legal reasoning about custody and visitation rights has ceased to be adequate to the realities of many families. Multiple women and/or multiple men become involved in children's lives through their biological, gestation, or parenting contributions.[39]

An article by the influential Canadian legal scholar Alison Harvison Young is revealingly titled: "This Child Does Have 2 (or More) Fathers."[40] Any questions?

Marriage is a compound right. Erasing the rule of two parents therefore aids the process of erasing the rule of two spouses. The reverse is also true. Either way, the final result is likely to be the same. If the proponents of the new rights claim have their way, the form of two in marriage and parenthood is going down.

If this happens, some children will indeed have "2 (or More) Fathers," but a far greater number will have no father at all. For if we smash the form of two, almost certainly the single most important consequence will be the further weakening of fatherhood as a social role for men and a great increase in the proportion of children growing up without fathers. In Chapter Six, I mentioned a New Jersey company, Family Evolutions, that sells T-shirts for children. One says "Let My Parents Marry!" and another says "My

Daddy's Name Is Donor." The founder of the company, in fact, has a child by donor insemination. Whenever her son asks about a father, she tells him that he came in part from "some chemicals from a guy."[41] Is that really what we think a father is?

In a powerful phrase, the feminist philosopher Sylviane Agacinski insists that each child has a right to its "double origin." Humanity is divided into male and female. Each new child is born of one man (its father) and one woman (its mother). In a good society, the double origin of every child is recognized and respected. Unalterably denying or effacing a child's double origin in the name of adult freedom is morally wrong.[42] For those who ask "Where's the harm?" regarding same-sex marriage, here is the inescapable fact: Changing marriage changes parenthood, and changing parenthood in ways that permit and even encourage adults to wipe out the double origin of some children is a threat to all children.

In light of today's trends, ethicists such as Margaret Somerville of McGill University in Canada are urging the world community not only to maintain but also to strengthen and further specify the right of children to their natural parents. The Universal Declaration of Human Rights and the other main rights instruments of the modern era affirm that every child has the right, insofar as society can make it possible, to know and be raised by its two natural parents, except when it is contrary to the child's best interests. The clear implication is that society should recognize and seek to strengthen marriage, our only social institution that seeks fully to unite, in the persons of the spouses, the biological, social, and legal dimensions of parenthood.

In view of the emerging threat to children's interests posed by both collaborative reproduction and the subjective redefinition of parenthood, here for the twenty-first century is a proposed new elaboration of the child's right:

- Every child has the right to a natural biological heritage, defined as the union of the father's sperm and the mother's egg. Society as a rule should not intentionally deny or efface a child's double origin.
- Every child has the right to know his or her biological origins. Society should typically refrain from creating what Somerville

calls genetic orphans, or children who do not and cannot know their natural origins.[43]

- Children have the right to be heard. Today, the rights claims of adults come through loud and clear, but children's voices are much harder to hear. That could and should change.

In a good society, when it comes to making new rights claims, everybody gets to play.

So here are two basic but conflicting rights claims:

1. *I have the right as an adult to marry the person I choose and form the family I choose.*

2. *I have the right as a child to be cared for by my natural mother and father.*

The conflict is not between good and bad—each claim affirms valuable human goods. But the conflict can't be wished away. And so we must choose. For me, sustaining the right of the child to her two natural parents is ultimately more important than granting adults more freedom of choice. There are three reasons why.

First, virtually all of our religious and secular moral traditions emphasize that when we are forced to make hard choices between competing interests, we should seek first and foremost to protect the interests of those who are less able to protect themselves. In this case, that means children.

The second reason relates to the principle of the greatest good for the greatest number. The proportion of homosexuals in society is small. The proportion of homosexuals who would choose to marry is smaller. The proportion of homosexuals who would choose to marry and raise children together is almost certainly still smaller. On the one hand, the impact of the right to marry and to form families of choice would almost certainly be large and positive for that minority. So let's stipulate that a few in society would benefit greatly.

On the other hand, changing marriage, regardless of why we do it, changes marriage for *everyone*. In particular, it changes parenthood for everyone.[44] When Canada, by way of implementing same-sex marriage, erased the concept of natural parent from basic Canadian law, there was no asterisk saying "for gay and lesbian couples only." The idea of the natural parent got wiped out in law for every child and every couple in Canada.

Changing a public meaning is a collective event; the meaning changes for *everyone.* If the child's current right to her two natural parents goes down completely, as the proponents of the new rights claim insist that it must, then that right as a societal promise will no longer pertain to any child.

When a change of this sort takes place, we as a society seldom feel an immediate impact. It's not like an earthquake, but more like the imperceptible shifting of the earth's tectonic plates. Our foundations change, as deviancy is defined down.[45] The movement is slow, but powerful and ultimately determinative. On the principle of the greatest impact on the greatest number, and with what I hope is full knowledge of and respect for the competing goods at stake, I conclude that we ought to elevate the rights of the children over the freedom of the adults.

The third and final reason concerns the core purposes of marriage in human societies. The single most important purpose is to give to the child the mother and father who made the child. Marriage does not exist in order to address the problem of sexual orientation or to reduce homophobia. Marriage does not exist in order to embody the principle of family diversity or to maximize adult choice in the area of procreation and childrearing. A case can be made for each of these latter objectives, but marriage as a human institution was never intended to pursue any of them. It makes better sense to ask an institution to do what it is built to do, rather than something it was never meant to do. I conclude again that sustaining children's rights in this regard should outweigh new adult freedoms.

"Where's the Threat?"

A gay man writes in to *USA Today:* "Please clarify for me: How exactly would my marrying my partner of more than four years threaten the institution of marriage?"[46] In a similar tone of exasperation and bewilderment, a guest columnist for the *Los Angeles Daily News* writes: "I truly do not understand the argument that same-sex marriage somehow dilutes the institution of marriage.... How loving and committed gays or lesbians living together and creating homes and families threatens anyone is beyond me."[47]

In July of 2004, about four months after officials in Multnomah County, Oregon, issued some three thousand marriage licenses to gay couples—the Oregon Supreme Court later voided those licenses—the editors of the *Statesman Journal* in Salem, Oregon, wondered where the harm was: "We have yet to hear of a happily married straight couple who called it quits because marriage licenses have been issued to gay couples in Oregon.... Those licenses did not entice straight people to suddenly 'turn gay.'"[48]

Similarly, Norah Vincent asserts: "There is no objective reason to believe that legalizing gay marriage would adversely affect traditional marriage."[49] And Jonathan Rauch: "Would millions of straight couples flock to divorce court if they knew that gay couples, too, could wed?"[50]

In court opinions on same-sex marriage cases, judges regularly pose this same basic question. For example, a justice of the Supreme Court of Canada writes, "it eludes me how according same-sex couples the benefits flowing to opposite-sex couples in any way inhibits, dissuades or impedes the formation of heterosexual unions. Where is the threat?"[51] A superior court judge in Seattle opines:

> It is good for children to be raised in stable families with a father and a mother. There is not the slightest question about this. But, can it be said that fewer children will have this stability because couples consisting of two men or two women are allowed to have a relationship that is state-sanctioned? There is no reasonable explanation for why this would be so. There is no reasonable expectation that, should such a legal result come to pass, married mothers and fathers will abdicate their parental responsibilities or young would-be parents will defect from the ranks of heterosexuals.[52]

No mad rush to divorce courts. No sudden upsurge of parental neglect. No mass defections from heterosexuality. So what possible objection could there be? Where is the threat?

Would now be a good time to take this subject seriously? As we see from these examples, this "Where's the threat?" question is almost always intended as purely rhetorical. The answer is apparently presumed to be so self-evident, so obvious to any rationally thinking person, that merely asking the question is sufficient to clinch the argument.

But we know already that the answer is *not* self-evident. It's not enough merely to ask the question. So let's try in good faith to answer it.

There's the Threat

I have suggested that permitting same-sex couples to marry would threaten the institution of marriage in two fundamental ways.

First, the deep logic of same-sex marriage is deinstitutionalization. This fact, it seems to me, is essentially beyond dispute. Deinstitutionalization may not require same-sex marriage, but same-sex marriage plainly presupposes and requires deinstitutionalization. Do we want, in pursuit of a good cause, to transform marriage once and for all from a pro-child social institution into a post-institutional private relationship?

Second, same-sex marriage would require us in both law and culture to deny the double origin of the child. I can hardly imagine a more serious violation. It would require us to change or ignore our basic human rights documents, which announce clearly, and for vitally important reasons, that every child has a birthright to her own two natural parents. It would require us, legally and formally, to withdraw marriage's greatest promise to the child—the promise that, insofar as society can make it possible, I will be loved and raised by the mother and father who made me. When I say, "Every child deserves a mother and a father," I am saying something that almost everyone in the world has always assumed to be true, and that many people today, I think most people, still believe to be true. But a society that embraces same-sex marriage can no longer collectively embrace this norm and must take specific steps to retract it. One can believe in same-sex marriage. One can believe that every child deserves a mother and a father. One cannot believe both.

Surely we can at least recognize that same-sex marriage is not a simple issue of good versus bad, enlightened versus reactionary. The real conflict is between one good and another: the equal dignity of all persons and the worth of homosexual love, versus the flourishing of children. On each side, the threat to something important is real. It wastes everyone's time to pretend that this question is an easy one, and that only bad people can fail to see the right answer.

Is there some way to reach a balanced assessment, systematically adding up the pros and cons on each side and, on that basis, striving to see the issue whole? That is exactly what was attempted in 2004 when I co-convened and chaired three one-day seminars for researchers and family scholars on the topic of gay marriage—one in New York City, one in Washington, D.C., and one in Atlanta, Georgia. Altogether, about forty people participated, including a number of the nation's leading family scholars. Of that total, a few had already spoken out publicly in favor of gay marriage, and a few against, but most of the participants at the time of our meeting had taken no public position on the issue, and most of them, I believe, were genuinely undecided.

Each meeting followed the same format. After some introductory discussion, in which each participant expressed her or his primary questions and concerns, we conducted a group thought experiment. The game had three rules. First, we stipulated that gay marriage, like almost any major social change, would be likely to generate a diverse range of consequences, some of which would be positive and some negative. Second, we agreed to work together as a group to specify as many of those likely consequences as possible, both good and bad. Third, we agreed that everybody's ideas count.

On chalkboards and poster paper, we worked together for hours to come up with three lists. The first list was called "Positive Consequences": In what ways would legalizing same-sex unions be likely to *improve* our society? The second list was called "Negative Consequences": How would adopting equal marriage rights for same-sex couples be likely to *harm* our society? The third list was called "Other Consequences," including social changes that would likely occur as a result of adopting gay marriage, but that we as a group could not agree whether to label as positive or negative.

Positive Consequences

1. Same-sex marriage would meet the stated needs and desires of lesbian and gay couples who want to marry. In doing so, it would improve the happiness and well-being of many gay and lesbian individuals, couples, and family members.
2. Gay marriage would extend a wide range of the natural and practical benefits of marriage to many lesbian and gay couples and their children.
3. Extending the right to marry to same-sex couples would probably mean that a higher proportion of gays and lesbians would choose to enter into committed relationships.
4. Same-sex marriage would likely contribute to more stability and to longer-lasting relationships for committed same-sex couples.
5. Same-sex marriage might lead to less sexual promiscuity among lesbians and (perhaps especially) gay men.
6. Same-sex marriage would signify greater social acceptance of homosexual love and the worth and validity of same-sex intimate relationships.
7. Gay marriage would be a victory for the worthy ideas of tolerance and inclusion. It would likely decrease the number of those in society who tend to be viewed warily as "other," and increase the number who are accepted as part of "us." In that respect, gay marriage would be a victory for, and another key expansion of, the American idea.
8. Gay marriage would reaffirm society's commitment to social justice and equal treatment under the law.
9. Gay marriage, by establishing marriage for same-sex couples as a human right, would expand the concept of human rights for gays and lesbians and, at least indirectly, for all persons.
10. Gay marriage might contribute over time to a decline in anti-gay prejudice as well as, more specifically, a reduction in anti-gay hate crimes.
11. Because marriage is a wealth-creating institution, extending marriage rights to same-sex couples would probably increase wealth accumulation and lead to higher living standards for these couples as well as help reduce welfare costs (by

promoting family economic self-sufficiency) and decrease economic inequality.

12. Because gay marriage would allow into marriage a group of people who, until now, have largely and effectively been kept out, it would make marriage as a way of living less exclusive and more universally accessible.
13. Adopting same-sex marriage would demonstrate that marriage can be an adaptive social form that is responsive to new societal needs and requirements.
14. Adopting gay marriage might slow down or stop altogether the legal proliferation of "marriage lite" schemes such as civil unions and domestic partnerships, which can harmfully blur the distinctions between marriage and nonmarriage and can contribute (among straights as well as gays and lesbians) to nonmarital cohabitation. In this respect, gay marriage would make marriage, and marriage alone, society's standard for socially approved committed relationships. An important likely result of such a development would be less nonmarital cohabitation than would otherwise have occurred.
15. Extending marriage rights to same-sex couples would probably reduce the proportion of homosexuals who marry persons of the opposite sex, and thus would likely reduce instances of marital unhappiness and divorce.
16. Adopting same-sex marriage would almost certainly reduce the proportion of Americans, particularly younger Americans, who believe that marriage is an outdated and discriminatory institution. This change might encourage more couples to choose marriage over cohabitation.
17. Especially by increasing the proportion of couples eligible to marry, gay marriage, to the degree that it produced more marriage in society, might increase the (currently quite low) birth rate, especially among the highly educated and more affluent.
18. By increasing the number of married couples who might be interested in adoption and foster care, same-sex marriage might well lead to fewer children growing up in state institutions and more growing up in loving adoptive and foster families.

19. Adopting same-sex marriage would likely be accompanied by a wide-ranging and potentially valuable national discussion of marriage's benefits, status, and future.
20. Adopting gay marriage would largely, over time, put an end to today's socially divisive and distracting debate over gay marriage.
21. Gay marriage would challenge and possibly reduce gender stereotypes.
22. Gay marriage would probably expand the possibility and likelihood of new scholarly research on a variety of topics related to marriage and parenting.
23. Same-sex marriage, to the extent that it would be adopted on a state-by-state basis (as against being established by Congress or the federal courts), would create a process of potentially valuable local experimentation in matters of marriage and marriage law.

Negative Consequences

1. Adopting gay marriage would contribute significantly to changing the public meaning of marriage from a structured social form to a private relationship, from an institution with defined social purposes to a right of personal expression.
2. To the degree that adopting same-sex marriage requires the further deinstitutionalization of marriage, adopting same-sex marriage would be likely to contribute over time to a further social devaluation of marriage, as expressed primarily in lower marriage rates, higher rates of divorce and nonmarital cohabitation, and more children raised outside of marriage and separated from at least one of their natural parents.
3. Accepting same-sex marriage would require explicit public endorsement of the idea that a child does not really need a mother and a father. The main likely consequence would be fewer children growing up with fathers.
4. Gay marriage would eradicate in law and weaken further in culture the idea that what society favors—that what is typically best for the child and the community—is the natural

mother married to the natural father, together raising the child. This change would likely result over time in smaller proportions of children being raised by their own, married mothers and fathers.

5. Same-sex marriage would likely mean, to some measurable degree, publicly replacing the idea that parenting is largely gendered (the sex of the parent matters a lot) with the idea that parenting is largely unisex (the sex of the parent is not very important). The main likely consequence would be that fewer men will believe that it is important for them to become active, hands-on parents.
6. Adopting same-sex marriage probably means supporting and subsidizing a range of reproductive technologies—including donor insemination, the sale of eggs, contract pregnancy, and other forms of third-party-participant procreation, as well as newer technologies up to and likely soon including reproductive cloning and creating a child from the genetic material of two persons of the same sex—all of which share one feature: almost by definition, the resulting child will not be raised by her own mother and father.
7. Adopting gay marriage will likely contribute to replacing the norm of the natural parent with the norm of the legal parent. The two main probable consequences of this change would be: a growing disjuncture between the biological and the legal-social dimensions of parenthood; and correspondingly, a significant expansion of the power of the state to determine who is a parent.
8. A likely consequence of shifting from a man-woman to a two-person conception of marriage is that U.S. law would effectively be viewing the homosexual experience, rather than the heterosexual experience, as its baseline model for evaluating the meaning and public purposes of marriage.
9. Social acceptance of same-sex marriage would likely increase the social acceptability of other alternative marriage forms, in particular polyamory and polygamy.
10. Gay marriage might encourage some U.S. Muslims and Mormons with historical and current ties to the institution of polygamy to press for its legal acceptance.

11. Adopting gay marriage would legally enshrine the principle that sexual orientation (as opposed to sexual embodiment) is a valid determinant of marriage's structure and meaning—even though orientation is more complex and subjective than embodiment, arguably much more fluid, and a subject about which our social understanding remains fragmentary and provisional.
12. If same-sex orientation becomes a legitimate grounding for same-sex marriage, it is likely that bisexual orientation could become a legitimate grounding for group marriage.
13. Insofar as society's endorsement of same-sex marriage would also signify society's endorsement of leading gay and lesbian understandings of the couple, sexual expression, and kinship, same-sex marriage would likely contribute to a further decline of the norm of sexual fidelity within marriage and a further weakening of the norm of marital permanence.
14. Adopting gay marriage would likely require all relevant branches and agencies of government formally to replace the idea that marriage centers on opposite-sex bonding and male-female procreation with the idea that marriage is a private relationship between two consenting adults.
15. Gay marriage would likely mean that the public socialization of heterosexual young people into a marriage culture—in children's books and entertainments, in church teaching, in school curricula, in youth organizations, and in the popular culture—would either end altogether or be significantly diluted in order to avoid what would have become the possibly illegal suggestion that marriage fundamentally concerns heterosexual bonding and procreation.
16. Adopting gay marriage might cause many Americans who dissent on gay marriage to abandon some or all of those public institutions that champion the new definition of marriage and declare the old one to be morally and legally repugnant, which probably would result in the weakening of those institutions and a further rending of our common culture.
17. The redefinition of marriage from man-woman to two persons implies that the understanding of marriage embraced by millions of orthodox Christian, Jewish, and Muslim

Americans would no longer be legally or morally acceptable, thereby probably forcing many of these Americans to choose between being a believer and being a good citizen.

18. Adopting gay marriage might lead to new state-imposed restrictions of religious freedom and freedom of expression.
19. Adopting same-sex marriage might mean that some religious organizations now receiving public support to provide services to the poor and to others would no longer provide them, due to state disqualification over refusing programmatically to endorse same-sex marriage.
20. Adopting gay marriage might catalyze an anti-gay backlash.
21. Adopting gay marriage could contribute to the public belief that marriage in our society is now politicized.
22. Especially if same-sex marriage is established primarily through court decisions, it would be likely, at least in the short term, to create a significant gap between legal and public understandings of marriage.
23. If same-sex marriage is established primarily through court decisions, the issue could contribute to public loss of confidence in, and resentment of, the judicial branch of government.
24. To the degree that adopting same-sex marriage means that marriage under the law becomes primarily a right of intimate expression, largely disconnected from defined public purposes, unmarried people might increasingly, and logically, complain that the legal and practical benefits currently attached to marriage properly belong to everyone, not just married people. Many single people also have interdependent personal relationships.

Other Consequences

1. Adopting same-sex marriage would likely increase the public visibility and social significance of same-sex couples and of gay and lesbian culture generally.
2. Adopting gay marriage might contribute over time to an increase in homosexual conduct.

3. For gays and lesbians, the right to marry a person of the same sex might serve over time to reduce some of the distinctiveness of gay and lesbian culture, thus possibly creating in both the gay and lesbian community and the society as whole less diversity and less respect for diversity.
4. Insofar as marriage has been a significant shaper of heterosexual identity, adopting gay marriage might challenge and complicate that identity.
5. Adopting same-sex marriage would likely mean that a higher proportion of all children would be raised by gays and lesbians.
6. Adopting same-sex marriage would likely lead to greater diversity in childhood experiences.
7. Adopting same-sex marriage might lead to a higher proportion of "intentional" children—that is, a higher proportion of children whose births are the result of specific planning.
8. Adopting same-sex marriage might contribute to the adoption of new policies aimed at imposing parental obligations, especially financial obligations such as child support, on more categories of biologically unrelated adults, including stepparents, partners, and ex-partners.
9. Adopting same-sex marriage would likely bring the United States closer to the European marriage model.
10. Adopting gay marriage would likely undermine some core tenets of the Jewish-Christian-Muslim conception of marriage and thereby contribute to the secularization of U.S. marriage.
11. Adopting gay marriage would probably reduce the influence of evangelical Christians in U.S. public life.
12. Adopting gay marriage would likely encourage some evangelical Christians to be more accepting of diverse and changing sexual and family norms.

These long lists of incommensurable goods are not exhaustive or scientifically exact. But as far as I am aware, they represent the best—in fact the *only*—effort by serious scholars and leaders to wrestle systematically with this issue whole, trying to see it as clearly as possible from both sides, and consciously avoiding the temptation simply to make the best lawyer's case for one foregone conclusion or the other. What do these results tell us?

First, many people who favor the reform insist that permitting same-sex marriage would affect only a small minority and would not constitute a major social change. It would be closer to a modest adjustment, they say, letting just a few more people into the main room. Our lists indicate that this argument is wrong. Whether we ultimately favor gay marriage or not, let us recognize that the idea being proposed is a big one. These three lists add up to quite a bit of significant social change, affecting many aspects of our society. Not all of these predicted consequences are inevitable, but most of them do seem likely. A few might be considered relatively trivial, but most clearly cannot. Many of them are quite far-reaching. A few on each side are genuine culture-changers. Plainly, the stakes on this issue are extremely high.

Second, many people on both sides seem genuinely to believe that this issue is morally easy. For some, homosexual orientation is intrinsically wrong, homosexual conduct is shameful, and gays and lesbians should either change or live deep in the closet. For them, the issue of gay marriage hardly requires serious analysis; it's simply a *bad* idea. On the other hand, for many others who take general acceptance of homosexuality in our society as their starting point, establishing the right of gays and lesbians to marry the person they choose is nothing more or less than a matter of simple justice. If you are a bigot, you are against gay marriage. If you are not, you are for it. What other morally sensitive position could there possibly be?

I believe that both of these positions are wrong. One side makes the issue easy to decide by judging an entire demographic group as blameworthy on the basis of a dimension of personality that, as best I can tell, is closer to being a given than a choice. I am a Christian. I take the Bible seriously, and I know what the Bible says about homosexuality. I disagree with the Bible on this point. Or, if you'll permit me, I believe that Jesus' teachings are inconsistent with the idea that today in the United States we should judge people as blameworthy just for being gay or lesbian.

The other side makes the issue easy to decide by imagining that marriage is not a social institution but an expression of love, a committed personal relationship. If marriage is the public recognition of a private bond, what could possibly be wrong with recognizing same-sex bonds? Much of this book has been a quarrel with this basic thesis. If I have persuaded you that marriage in human societies is both a private relationship *and* a pro-child social institution, we can agree that wishing away its institutionality might make everything appear simple, but it is not intellectually or morally serious. If marriage is fundamentally a pro-child social institution with clear and vital public purposes, then it simply cannot be true that the master idea, the one goal that trumps all other goals, is public recognition of the freedom of adults to do what they want.

This consideration leads to the third general conclusion from our seminars: Whenever important goods conflict, it's inevitable that any resolution, no matter how carefully arrived at, will carry with it elements of loss and even tragedy. Some people argue that our main moral priority in this case should be the gays and lesbians who want to marry the person they choose and form the families they choose. They are the victims of injustice, the ones whose needs demand our response.

I have argued in this chapter that people who make this argument are wrong—not because the interests of gays and lesbians hoping to marry are unworthy of our concern, but because the interests of all the children in our society are *more* worthy of our concern. When I look at the United States today, I see many problems, but to me, children are the group in our society who are most vulnerable. They are the ones most at risk, the ones whose needs most demand our response. When I had lunch in 2003 with Evan Wolfson, the executive director of Freedom to Marry and the main architect of the legal struggle for gay marriage, I tried to raise the issue of children's rights. He could hardly have been less interested, telling me simply (as I mentioned in this book's introduction) that he believes that children are "adaptable."

Yes, children are adaptable. But what exactly do we as a society want our children to adapt to? To growing up without the mother and father who made them? To being told that whoever happens to be taking care of them at the time is their "parent"? To not knowing their biological origins? To accepting without complaint whatever the grownups decide to do? To the shrinking of their human rights? To listening to a lot of didactic happy-talk about families coming in all shapes and sizes?

Evan sees people who are suffering and wants to help them. As a leader of a grassroots movement, he has spent many years working for a certain kind of social change. For Evan, it's also personal. He is gay—one of the "them" in this matter. He is fighting partly for himself, and that accounts for much of his passion.

I have three children, so it's personal for me, too. I am fighting partly for them, for the society they will be adults in, for the future.

Evan is confident that his side, the side of new freedoms, is going to win. He may be right. New freedoms are hard to argue against, even in the name of children, and if you want to try something difficult, try telling freedom-loving Americans that what they really need is a stronger "social institution."

But there we are. What do you think, kind reader? The wheel's in spin. Nothing is inevitable. Both sides have a case. Which answer do you think *should* prevail?

8

Determining Marriage's Fate

This thing called "marriage" becomes almost like a third person in the relationship, and that's not the kind of relationship I want.
—Tede Matthews, 1992[1]

It is not your love that sustains the marriage, but from now on, the marriage that sustains your love.
—Dietrich Bonhoeffer, 1943[2]

If this book had a subtitle, it would be "An Argument about Institutions." Pretty sexy, huh? Actually, institutions *can* be sexy. Reading a poem to a woman in an effort to woo her. Wearing come-hither jewelry on an important occasion. Taking a vow when you marry "to have and to hold" one another forever. None of these instances of human sexual communication, none of these ways of inviting or promising, would be meaningful or even possible without social institutions.

Without institutions, human sexuality itself would be one-dimensional (some occasional bumping and grinding) and, compared with what we have now, pretty boring. Indeed, without viable institutions, *all* forms of human sociality would be raw, primitive, and ultimately arbitrary and dangerous, a harkening back to the state of nature, or what the philosopher Thomas Hobbes called "No Society ... And the life of man solitary, poore, nasty, brutish, and short."[3]

In her fascinating book *How Institutions Think,* the anthropologist Mary Douglas investigates what she calls the "social control of cognition," or the degree to which our thinking depends upon our institutions.[4] Human beings are inextricably social. We only live in groups. We need to communicate with one another. We need to share our ideas and preferences. We try to agree on what we need, what we should remember, and how to cooperate. We want to know what we can expect from others and what others expect from us. Almost as much as we want food and shelter, we want to make promises, and to have those promises understood, and to have others be able to make promises to us.

We do these things by creating institutions. In this sense, institutions are the way society influences how individuals think. Institutions are the way we pool our thoughts and therefore make possible shared categories of thought. Douglas points out that "for discourse to be possible at all, the basic categories have to be agreed on. Nothing else but institutions can define sameness."[5]

By making possible and distilling *social* or shared thought, institutions do much of our classifying. They do much of our remembering and forgetting. In these and other ways, our institutions largely tell us who we are. As Douglas puts it, they "confer identity."[6]

Perhaps most of all, "legitimated institutions make the big decisions." If the question is which detail to accent, or which short-term tactics to employ, individuals are less likely to think socially, or to think via their institutions. But whenever the questions are what Douglas calls life and death—what is just, what is sacred, what is a citizen, what is a spouse—our institutions necessarily step in to cue and guide us. "For better or worse," Douglas, says, "individuals really do share their thoughts and they do to some extent harmonize their preferences, and they have no other way to make the big decisions except within the scope of institutions they build."[7]

The main question in the United States regarding the future of marriage is not whether we will adopt gay marriage. The main question is whether the *social institution* of marriage will become weaker or stronger.

The whole story is encapsulated in the two quotations at the beginning of this chapter. They frame perfectly the question that we as a society face. When Tede Matthews observes that "this thing called 'marriage' becomes almost like a third person in the relationship," he is exactly right. He is saying what Mary Douglas is saying. The "marriage"—that "third person in the relationship," that seemingly external voice demanding to be heard and occasionally issuing orders—is the social institution!

Tede Matthews wants none of it. He rejects the presence of this outside influence, which is another way of saying that he rejects the institution of marriage. Apparently he is speaking only for himself, and it's good that he knows what he wants. But what if he wanted to change the world? We can't know for sure, but if he were a sociologist or a family law professional intent on bringing about fundamental social change, he might have told the interviewer instead that he favors the deinstitutionalization of marriage. No more interference from that third person in anyone's relationship!

Now let's look at it from another perspective. When Dietrich Bonhoeffer says, "It is not your love that sustains the marriage, but from now on, the marriage that sustains your love," he is making a wonderfully precise distinction between an emotion and an institution. The love leads to marriage, and when the lovers marry, they want both their love and their marriage to last. But "from now on," from their wedding day on, their love does not make the marriage last. *The marriage makes their love last.* The feeling does not sustain the institution, but if all goes well—if both the couple and the institution do their jobs—it will work the other way around. Analytically, Bonhoeffer largely agrees with Tede Matthews. For Bonhoeffer, too, the marriage is "like a third person in the relationship." The marriage is something over and surrounding the love of the spouses. And yet for Bonhoeffer it's precisely that third person, the *institution,* that can elevate everything and help the love endure.

Same question. Same analytic framework. Completely opposite conclusions.

As we've seen, more than a few opinion leaders in the United States today agree with Tede Matthews, not with Dietrich Bonhoeffer. They favor the love part, but not the institution part. For this reason, they are working as hard and creatively as they can to weaken marriage. Almost all of them agree that adopting same-sex marriage would be an important step toward their goal, but gay marriage is not the big prize. The big prize is deinstitutionalization.

In Chapter Six, we saw that Judith Stacey and plenty of others reject outright each of marriage's customary forms—the form of opposites, the form of two, and the form of sex—and that they are deeply suspicious of the degree to which marriage creates authoritative public meaning. They have concluded that marriage is too strong in our society, and so they want to knock it off its perch. To use Mary Douglas's terminology, they dislike the degree to which we Americans let the institution of marriage "control our cognition," or do our thinking for us, especially regarding "the big decisions."

We can all probably agree that there are times when even worthy institutions do become overbearing. I grew up in the South, graduating from high school in 1973. During my teenage years, football ruled. Football seemed about as important as religion, and religion was *very* important. My grandmother in Birmingham, Alabama, had two framed pictures in her living room. One was of Jesus. The other was of Paul "Bear" Bryant, the University of Alabama football coach. *That's* how important football was. I played football. I went to the games and followed the teams. But looking back, I think that football was socially more important than it should have been. It overshadowed too many other valuable things. In that time and place, football as a social institution was too strong.

But when I look at marriage as a social institution in the United States in the early years of the twenty-first century, I do not see an institution grown imperious and overbearing. I do not see an institution that is pushing people around, locking them into rigid patterns that do not serve their interests or society's. On the contrary. The marriage-is-too-strong argument probably had some validity in the 1950s, but today we plainly see a vitally important institution that is weak and, at least in some respects, steadily getting weaker.

So let's do a quick health exam: What are the most essential "body parts" of marriage today as a social institution? How healthy are they? Is the overall diagnosis terminal? Or does the patient still have a fighting chance?

Second, what exactly is deinstitutionalization today made of? What are its main features, and how do they relate to one another and add up to a whole? If we say that we are against deinstitutionalization, what precisely are we against? Does arresting deinstitutionalization necessarily mean stopping gay marriage?

Finally, is healthier marriage in the United States possible? What would improvement look like? Can we as a society strengthen and reinstitutionalize marriage? Should we try? If we wanted to try, how would we begin?

Grappling with these questions can help us discern marriage's possible future, but that future is by no means preordained. I hope that answering these questions as carefully as possible will better equip all of us as free citizens to participate in determining what the fate of marriage will be.

Leading Marriage Indicators

Because we agree that the health of our economy is an important matter, bearing directly upon our individual and collective well-being, U.S. policy makers insist on knowing with some precision how the economy is doing at any point in time. The experts have generally agreed on what the key indicators are—the fundamental measurements that reveal the most about our economic health. We as a society tend to keep careful track of these leading economic indicators. We pay close attention to whether and how they are changing, so that we can accurately estimate not only where we stand today, but also whether the overall direction of the economy is encouraging or alarming. To provide us with the information necessary to make these judgments, each month the Joint Economic Committee of the U.S. Congress issues a public report called *Economic Indicators*.

Today we should do something similar regarding marriage. If we care what happens to the institution, we can determine easily enough what the key indicators are. As a society we should pay close attention to whether and how these numbers are changing. We should discuss them as frequently and intensely as we discuss leading economic indicators, and work together to do everything we realistically can to improve these core measurements of marriage's health in our society.

Historically we have never done this work, but today we need to. Marriage in the United States is clearly in trouble, yet it remains our foundational and arguably most important social institution. It is certainly our most pro-child social institution. Surely most of us could agree that strengthening marriage is at least as important for us Americans today as getting richer. To help stimulate a much-needed public conversation, here is a proposed U.S. Marriage Index. I hope that it, or something like it, can catch on, and over time become widely used and cited.

Table 1
U.S. Marriage Index

	1970	1980	1990	2000
Percent of Adults Married	71.7	65.5	61.9	59.5
Percent of First Marriages Intact	73.3	67.7	62.5	58.5
Percent of Births to Married Parents	89.3	81.6	72.0	66.8
Percent of Children Living with Their Own Married Parents	68.7	64.0	60.8	59.7
Percent of Children Living with Two Married Parents	85.2	76.7	72.5	68.1
Index of Marriage's Institutional Vitality[8]	**77.6**	**71.1**	**65.9**	**62.5**

Let's analyze these key indicators. The first is the percentage of adults who are married. Marriage is certainly not for everyone, and across time and cultures, many people who do not marry make impressive contributions to society. Yet because we are fundamentally a pair-bonding species, in most societies, including our own, marriage is generally normative and the overwhelming majority of adults do marry. Knowing the proportion of adults in the population who are married is the most basic and obvious indicator of marriage's institutional vitality. After all, if you want to measure the institutional strength of the Church or the Socialist Party, certainly the best way to start is by asking what proportion of people go to church or join the party. The same is true regarding marriage.

Scholars measure this phenomenon in several different ways. For example, they can ask: What proportion of today's adults are likely to marry at least once during their lives? Or they can ask: In any given year, how many marriages occur for every one thousand unmarried adults? Or they can ask: During how much of the total adult life span is today's typical adult likely to be married? My own preferred measurement, because it is simple and clear, is to ask: What proportion of adults are currently married? Each of these different ways of measuring can yield valuable insights. But for all of them, the bottom line is basically the same: in recent decades, Americans have become less likely to marry.

Several social trends help to account for this shift. One is that Americans are waiting longer to marry. The median age at first marriage is currently about 26 for females and 27 for males (up from about 20 for females and 23 for males in 1960). This trend itself is probably a mixed blessing. Considerable evidence suggests that *very* early marriages (such as teen marriages) are at greater risk of instability and divorce. On the other hand, there is little evidence to suggest that people typically gain much in the way of stability or happiness by waiting later than their middle 20s to marry, and some evidence suggests that those who marry at age 30 or later tend to be more unhappy in their marriages and more likely to divorce.[9]

Another obvious trend that has pushed down the proportion of married adults is divorce. (U.S. divorce rates peaked in the early 1980s.) Another major cause, especially in more recent years, is the steady rise of nonmarital cohabitation. Yet another factor appears to be a small decrease in the likelihood of divorced persons to remarry. One probable aspect and cause of less marriage in the United States in recent decades is some increase in the (still fairly small) proportion of Americans who will never marry.[10] Overall, if our concern is marriage as a social institution, clearly the steadily decreasing proportion of Americans who are married reveals a significant erosion of the institution's reach and vitality.

The second key indicator is the proportion of first marriages still intact. Marriage advocates focus on this indicator for two reasons. At least in form, these marriages tend to reflect what is most hopeful about marriage. In a high-divorce culture, they are commitments sustained, promises kept. Also, first marriages still intact are important to marriage advocates because second and third marriages are significantly more likely to end in divorce.[11] The steadily declining share of first marriages that are intact is distressing evidence of institutional failure and fragility.

The third leading marriage indicator is the proportion of U.S. children born to married parents. Marriage is the great gift that parents and society give to children. A child born outside of marriage is not doomed to failure, of course; many such children do very well. Nor is my parents' marriage certificate a surefire guarantee of my happiness and flourishing. But if the social science research of this generation tells us anything with reasonable certainty, it tells us that marriage typically benefits children and that high rates of unwed childbearing constitute a direct threat to child well-being.[12]

As we've seen, for marriage to be a vital, authoritative social institution, it need not necessarily exercise a monopoly on sexual intercourse. (Remember our friends the Trobrianders?) But it *does* of necessity need to exercise an effective monopoly on childbearing. In any society, the gradual lowering of the percentage of children born to married couples demonstrates an erosion of marriage's institutional coherence.

The remaining indicators also concern the living arrangements of American children. Our fourth indicator—the percentage of children living with their own two married biological parents—measures the prevalence of the family structure that, according to a large and growing body of social science evidence, tends to be best for children. The deep purpose of marriage in human societies is to establish precisely this family structure. Of our five leading indicators, this one is the most diagnostic and probably the most important.

The fifth indicator also measures the prevalence of children being raised by married parents, but this one includes stepparents as well as biological parents. The scholarly evidence on the well-being of children in blended families is mixed; indeed, some studies suggest that these children, despite the economic advantages that frequently accrue from living with two married parents, often do no better overall, and on some key outcome measurements actually do worse, than children in one-parent homes.[13] Yet remarriage is still marriage, and it does provide important benefits for large and growing numbers of children and spouses in the United States. Consequently it seems appropriate to include this measurement as well among our list of leading marriage indicators, in part as a complement and supplement to the fourth and (in my view) more crucial one.

Our Marriage Index is designed to measure both current status and direction over time. Note that each indicator is framed positively (how many are married?) rather than negatively (how many are divorced?). For all five indicators, higher numbers indicate better outcomes for individuals and society than do lower numbers. Consequently, for each year we can fold all five of the specific indicators into one bottom line—a single composite number indicating the overall institutional vitality of marriage in that year.

In recent decades, all five indicators have worsened significantly. The greatest deterioration is in the percentage of births to married parents, which dropped from 89.3 in 1970 to 66.8 in 2000, representing a decline of 22.5 points, or about 25 percent. Preliminary data on unwed births in the United States for the year 2004 suggest that this indicator has continued to decline since 2000.[14]

The smallest amount of deterioration, however, is in the single most important indicator: the percentage of children living with their two biological married parents. That figure changed from 68.7 percent in 1970 to 59.7 percent in 2000, a drop of nine points, or about 13 percent over three decades. This not-so-bad figure partly reflects some genuinely good news: a modest decline of divorce among married parents since the early 1980s.[15] The overall change in this crucial indicator is disappointing but not precipitous. There is plenty left to work with. Today in the United States, about six of every ten children under age 18 are living with their two biological parents who are married to each other. That's an important fact.

Chapter Six referred to a much-discussed article by Pastor Donald Sensing arguing sadly that any talk of strengthening marriage in the United States is "specious" because "there's little left to save." Andrew Sullivan offered this article as a case for accepting gay marriage, reasoning that if marriage as a pro-child institution is already dead and gone, why "draw the line now" at same-sex couples?[16]

The next time you hear someone make this argument, kind reader, remember that 60 percent of U.S. children, a significant majority, are still living with their two natural parents who are married to each other. While this represents a decline of 13 percent in thirty years, it does not mean that it's "too late" to think about improving marriage in the United States since there is "little left to save," or that the only realistic next step is to give everyone equal access to the rubble.

Let's look at our other indicators. In 2000, about 60 percent of U.S. adults were married. About 59 percent of first marriages were still intact. About 68 percent of all U.S. children were living with two married parents.

Our composite number representing marriage's overall institutional vitality for the year 2000 is 62.5, reflecting a drop of about 15 points, or 19 percent, since 1970. This is not great news, but the game is hardly over. Living with married parents, usually one's two biological parents, is still normative for U.S. children. Despite the beating that it has taken in recent decades, marriage remains our main social template for bearing and raising children. A modest but growing number of our fellow citizens are searching as creatively as they can, and with some early successes, for ways to improve and strengthen marriage in our society.[17]

For these reasons, among others, grandly announcing that marriage today is institutionally beyond saving is both frivolous and irresponsible. It is intellectually frivolous because the data simply do not support such a conclusion. And it is morally irresponsible because, especially in a free society, it is wrong to preach that we can do nothing to change what cries out for change, or that we must become servile and passive in the face of demographic trends threatening our key social institution.

Leading Marriage Values

To augment the findings in our Marriage Index, and to explore further whether or not it is realistic today for Americans to seek to protect marriage as an authoritative, pro-child social institution, let's look at some international opinion data. The International Social Survey Programme (ISSP) interviewed adults in 24 countries in 1994 and 35 countries in 2002 on a range of topics, including marriage and family life. The results are intriguing.

Let's focus on the six questions from this survey that are most directly relevant to our inquiry into the institutional vitality of marriage. Respondents were asked whether they agreed or disagreed with the following statements.

1. *"Married people are generally happier than unmarried people."*
In 2002, researchers posed this question to adults in 35 countries. In the United States, 41 percent of respondents generally agreed with the statement, 26.5 percent generally disagreed, and the rest stated no opinion. Thirteen countries scored higher than the U.S. in the "agree" categories (led by the Philippines at 60.4 percent and Russia at 61.4 percent) while 21 countries scored lower (led by Norway at 16.7 percent and Sweden at 15.7 percent). So the U.S. ranks near the top of the middle third in the diverse group of countries surveyed on this question.[18]

2. *"People who want children ought to get married."*
In the United States, 65.3 percent agreed, while 25.9 percent disagreed. Only seven countries agreed more strongly (including the Philippines and Cyprus, both at about 76 percent), while 27 countries agreed less (including Belgium at 31.5 percent and the Netherlands at 25.3 percent). So on this crucial question, the U.S. ranks near the middle of the top third among the countries surveyed.[19]

3. *"One parent can bring up a child as well as two parents together."*
Amazingly, 42.3 percent of U.S. respondents agreed with this statement. By what possible logic, other than wishful thinking or not wanting to hurt anyone's feelings, could one reasonably conclude that, regarding one of life's most time-consuming and challenging tasks, it doesn't really matter whether one person is doing it alone, or two together? Would you offer the same opinion about the two pilots in the cockpit of the airplane on your transcontinental flight, or the two lifeguards on the beach watching your children swim in the ocean?[20]

More amazingly still, respondents in sixteen countries around the world were even more likely to agree with this statement, including more than 60 percent in Brazil, Chile, Denmark, Taiwan, and the Philippines. On the other hand, eighteen countries agreed with this statement less than did the United States, led by Cyprus (15.3 percent), the Slovak Republic (22.6 percent) and Latvia (23.6 percent). The U.S. on this question stands almost exactly in the middle of the countries surveyed.[21]

4. *"It is all right for a couple to live together without intending to get married."*
In the United States, 46.5 percent agreed with this statement. Only five of the 35 countries agreed less: Japan (42.5 percent), the Slovak Republic (33.1 percent), Cyprus (32.7 percent), Taiwan (27.8 percent), and the Philippines (19.3 percent). In the other 29 countries, agreement was higher, and in most cases much higher. In five countries—the Netherlands, Sweden, Denmark, Portugal, and Belgium—levels of agreement with this statement topped 80 percent. In Denmark, 92.6 percent of respondents agreed. On this question, the U.S. ranks near the middle of the bottom third of countries surveyed.[22]

5. *"Divorce is usually the best solution when a couple can't seem to work out their marriage problems."*
In the United States, 43 percent agreed. To me that's a high number, but it's actually the third lowest among the countries surveyed, exceeded in anti-divorce scruple only by Japan (34.8 percent) and the Philippines (36.6 percent). The other 31 countries registered higher levels of agreement; and in most cases the level of agreement was much higher. For example, in four countries—what was formerly East Germany, Austria, Spain, and Brazil—more than 80 percent of respondents agreed with this statement. On this question, the U.S. ranks near the bottom of the countries surveyed.[23]

Another recent survey of a nationally representative sample of U.S. adults sheds additional light on current American attitudes regarding divorce. About 43 percent of respondents agree (while 56 percent disagree) that "In the absence of violence and extreme conflict, parents who have an unsatisfactory marriage should stay together until their children are grown." About 88 percent agree that "Couples who marry should make a lifelong commitment to one another, to be broken only under extreme circumstances." More than 90 percent agree that "Divorce is a serious national problem in the United

States today." About 59 percent agree (and 41 percent disagree) that "Society would be better off if divorces were harder to get."[24]

6. "The main purpose of marriage these days is to have children."
In the 1994 survey, interviewers asked adults in 24 countries whether they agreed with this statement. To me, this question is confusing and a bit misleading. The researchers deleted it from their 2002 survey, and I agree with their decision to do so, even though I am a child advocate as well as a marriage nut. If this book has only one idea, it's that marriage is intrinsically connected to raising children. Yet I doubt that even *I* would tell an interviewer that I agree that "the main purpose of marriage these days is to have children." Leave aside the issue of whether that sly term "these days" inappropriately suggests to the respondent that the interviewer is already convinced that marriage "these days" is different from marriage in previous days. The deeper problem is that the question itself sounds ill fitting and somehow off-track—even to someone who spends much time "these days" thinking about the links between marriage and children.

Consider an analogy: Public libraries constitute a valuable social institution. A basic, widely acknowledged good of the library as an institution is the spreading of knowledge. On a more utilitarian and individual level, an important goal of the library is to make it convenient and inexpensive for individuals to read the books they choose. The two are closely related, but they are not exactly the same thing, and therefore they are stated somewhat differently. Now, do you agree or disagree that "The main purpose of joining the library these days is the spreading of knowledge"? I would probably answer, "I joined the library to check out books!" After all, conveniently gaining access to the books is my immediate goal; it's the main practical benefit I get as a result of joining the library. But such an answer does not change the fact that probably the library's most fundamental reason for being as a social institution is the spreading of knowledge.

Securing for the child a recognized mother and father is a fundamental good of marriage. But it is odd for an interviewer to raise the broad question of "why marry?" without also mentioning the specific and quite important matter of sharing one's life with a spouse! That is probably the most obvious and immediate goal of individuals considering marriage. If someone were to ask me, what is the main purpose (or goal) of marriage these days, my answer would be something like: To find a spouse with whom to make a shared life and a family.

But despite this flaw in the question itself, the results merit our consideration for two reasons. First, only 13 percent of U.S. respondents agreed with the statement. Moreover, only two countries had lower levels of agreement: New Zealand (12.8 percent) and Canada (10.4 percent). So on this question, the United States apparently stands near one end of the spectrum of international opinion. The other 21 countries expressed stronger endorsements of this statement, with agreement levels of roughly 50 percent or higher in Hungary, the Czech Republic, Poland, Bulgaria, Russia, the Philippines, and Israel.[25] So millions of people around the world, apparently with what philosophers call the goods of marriage firmly in mind, do tell interviewers they agree that the main purpose of marriage these days is to have children.

Regarding U.S. attitudes on this topic, consider also the answers to a question—in my view a much better question—recently posed to a nationally representative sample of adults: "Which of the following is in your opinion the more important characteristic of a good marriage." About 13 percent chose "Promotes the happiness and well-being of the married individuals." About 10 percent chose "Produces children who are well-adjusted and who will become good citizens." And, in a remarkable display of commonsense wisdom about marriage, about three-quarters of all respondents (74 percent) said that "The two are about equally important."[26]

Overall, I am encouraged and also a bit surprised by these results. Compared with many other countries, public support for marriage as a social institution is fairly robust in the United States. The very low proportion of Americans who agree that "the main purpose of marriage these days is to have children" is certainly consistent with the trend toward deinstitutionalization, and may also at least partly reflect the popularity of the idea that the essential definition of marriage is a close relationship between two people.

Regarding the other five marriage-related statements, U.S. respondents showed surprising levels of support for marriage as an institution, at least in comparison with the other countries surveyed, and in particular in comparison with countries in western and northern Europe. On two of the statements—married people are happier, and one parent can be as good as two—American respondents express enough pro-marriage-as-an-institution sentiment to place the United States roughly in the middle of the spectrum of international opinion. On the remaining three statements—people who want children should marry, cohabitation without intending to marry is all right, and divorce is usually the best answer for a troubled marriage—American answers place the United States at or near the top of the international range in stated support for marriage as an institution. That fact is heartening.

For our purposes, probably the most important—I think the most diagnostic—statement in the survey is "People who want to have children ought to get married." When most people in a society stop believing in this idea, that society has stopped believing in marriage as a social institution. Marriage can survive with a certain amount of popular doubt about the value of the institution. It can survive with widespread sex before marriage, widespread cohabitation before marriage, and even a fair amount of divorce. These trends are certainly not good for marriage, but marriage can endure them and probably survive. Marriage cannot survive in a society that no longer embraces the idea that people who want to have children should get married.

In the Netherlands, three of every four people reject this idea. In the United States, two of every three people endorse it.[27] This one fact tells me that in the United States, despite our setbacks and many serious challenges, we still have a fighting chance to protect and renew marriage as a pro-child social institution.

The Parts of the Whole

The ideas and social trends pointing toward the deinstitutionalization of marriage in the United States are formidable. They can be divided into four main parts:

1. The spread of unwed childbearing and the decline of the idea that people who want to have children ought to get married.

2. The spread of divorce and the decline of the ideal of marital permanence.
3. The spread of same-sex marriage and the rise of the idea that marriage should be redefined as a private close relationship between two people.
4. The spread of third-party participants in reproduction and the decline of the idea that children have a birthright to their own two natural parents, a mother and a father.

There are other possible candidates for this list, including the decline of the marital fertility rate, uncertainty and flux in gender roles, and the rise of nonmarital cohabitation. But the four phenomena above are the most important. They are the ones driving marriage most forcibly toward deinstitutionalization.

Moreover, as ideas about what is good or acceptable, they all hang together and reinforce one another. They are a syndrome. They are based on shared philosophical presuppositions and related demographic factors. Wherever one is strong, the others are likely also to be strong. Conversely, an individual or society that opposes one of them will probably tend to oppose the others as well. That is why those who are overtly hostile to marriage as an institution typically support gay marriage, and why the very arguments that for years have been used most frequently to attack marriage, and to push for its further deinstitutionalization, are now being used to advocate for same-sex marriage.

These correlations can be shown in statistical form with data from the survey conducted in 35 countries by the International Social Survey Programme in 2002. Responses to the five key questions on marriage as an institution are divided into four tables according to the current policy on same-sex unions in the countries surveyed. The fifth table below (Table 6) compares the weighted averages for each group. (Note that high levels of agreement on the first two statements reflect support for marriage as an institution, while lower levels of agreement on the latter three statements tend to reflect pro-marriage attitudes.)

The overall pattern is fairly clear. By far the weakest support for marriage (lower agreement on the first two statements; higher agreement on the last two) is in the seven surveyed countries that

Table 2

Percentage of Populations Agreeing with Statements about Marriage in Surveyed Countries Recognizing Same-Sex Marriage

	Married people are happier	People who want children should marry	One parent can be as good as two together	Cohabiting without intending to marry is all right	Divorce is usually the best solution to marriage problems
Belgium	16.9	31.5	39.7	85.2	66.8
Denmark	23.6	50.6	62.1	92.6	69.2
Finland	26.5	47.6	30.4	79.0	63.2
Netherlands	22.7	25.3	40.0	89.6	74.2
Norway	16.7	42.3	38.5	79.0	55.8
Spain	24.8	35.7	46.9	76.3	81.4
Sweden	15.7	30.9	40.9	86.9	54.4
Average	**21.0**	**37.7**	**42.6**	**84.1**	**66.4**
Weighted Average*	**21.5**	**37.8**	**43.2**	**83.1**	**68.4**

have same-sex marriage. The twelve countries that do not recognize same-sex marriage but do have marriage-like civil unions show significantly more support for marriage. The two countries with regionally limited recognition of gay unions (Australia and the United States) do better still on these support-for-marriage measurements, as do those thirteen surveyed countries without gay marriage and without marriage-like civil unions.

In some instances, the differences between the groups of countries are quite large. For example, people in countries with gay marriage are less than half as likely as people in countries without gay unions to say that married people are happier. Perhaps most importantly, they are *significantly* less likely—37.8 percent compared with 60.3 percent—to say that people who want children ought to get married. They are also significantly more likely—83.1 percent compared with 49.7 percent—to say that cohabiting without intending

*"Average" does not take into account the differences in sample size among the surveyed countries. "Weighted Average" does take these differences into account. Table 6 displays weighted averages only.

Table 3
Percentage of Populations Agreeing with Statements about Marriage in Surveyed Countries Recognizing Same-Sex Civil Unions

	Married people are happier	People who want children should marry	One parent can be as good as two together	Cohabiting without intending to marry is all right	Divorce is usually the best solution to marriage problems
Brazil	50.2	62.7	59.8	68.9	86.1
Czech Republic	40.5	56.1	41.5	57.6	63.1
France	21.5	37.4	28.6	79.4	60.4
Germany*	37.4	52.9	47.4	75.7	75.7
Great Britain	25.1	53.0	41.2	69.6	62.4
Hungary	52.7	45.6	27.3	74.3	58.4
Israel	50.6	65.0	29.9	52.9	66.9
New Zealand	24.5	52.0	29.0	63.7	52.5
Northern Ireland	34.6	57.4	45.2	56.7	64.5
Portugal	26.0	48.1	38.6	81.3	78.3
Slovenia	42.2	35.6	29.7	68.3	66.2
Switzerland	29.1	43.8	47.2	86.3	67.6
Average	**36.2**	**50.8**	**38.8**	**69.9**	**66.8**
Weighted Average	**36.0**	**51.2**	**39.7**	**69.9**	**67.6**

to marry is all right, and are somewhat more likely to say that divorce is usually the best solution to marriage problems. Compared with Australia and the United States, the two countries with regional recognition only, these countries are significantly more likely to say that divorce is usually the best solution. The only question for which no real pattern is apparent is the one asking whether one parent can raise a child as well as two together.[28]

*For this 2002 survey, the ISSP researchers treated the former East Germany and the former West Germany as separate countries. For these tabulations, I combine them into one country (Germany). Accordingly, the total number of countries surveyed in Tables 2–6 is 34, as compared with 35 in the 2004 ISSP publication.

Table 4
Percentage of Populations Agreeing with Statements about Marriage in Surveyed Countries in Which Some Regions Recognize Same-Sex Marriage

	Married people are happier	People who want children should marry	One parent can be as good as two together	Cohabiting without intending to marry is all right	Divorce is usually the best solution to marriage problems
Australia	44.2	65.9	31.0	65.4	52.5
United States	41.0	65.3	42.3	46.5	43.0
Average	**42.6**	**65.6**	**36.7**	**56.0**	**47.8**
Weighted Average	**42.7**	**65.6**	**36.3**	**56.6**	**48.1**

Along similar lines, the World Values Survey, based in Stockholm and conducted by scholars from around the world, periodically interviews nationally representative samples of the populace of some eighty countries on all six inhabited continents on a range of issues, including marriage and the family. Its results are therefore more representative of the global community than the International Social Survey Programme questionnaire. While the latter contained six questions directly relevant to marriage as an institution, the World Values Survey contains only three—but they are terrific questions! And because every study has limitations and no one study can be definitive, it's always wise to see whether results derived from one study are confirmed or disconfirmed by results from a similar study conducted by different scholars.

Here again, the countries surveyed are divided into four groups according to policy on same-sex unions, and a summary table (Table 11) compares the weighted averages.

The results from this World Values Survey are remarkably similar to those from the International Social Survey Programme. The weakest support for marriage as an institution is in those countries with same-sex marriage. Countries with same-sex civil unions show more support, and countries with only regional recognition show still more support. By significant margins, the most support for marriage is in countries without same-sex unions.

Table 5
Percentage of Populations Agreeing with Statements about Marriage in Surveyed Countries That Do Not Recognize Same-Sex Unions

	Married people are happier	People who want children should marry	One parent can be as good as two together	Cohabiting without intending to marry is all right	Divorce is usually the best solution to marriage problems
Austria	36.0	44.1	51.9	76.8	83.5
Bulgaria	57.8	65.6	26.4	49.3	66.4
Chile	31.1	45.7	62.2	67.3	76.8
Cyprus	54.8	75.5	15.3	32.7	67.6
Ireland	32.6	54.3	45.8	62.0	61.4
Japan	35.6	62.2	57.3	42.5	33.8
Latvia	46.6	58.9	23.6	48.9	61.6
Mexico	33.5	45.3	47.5	52.7	72.8
Philippines	60.4	75.6	64.9	20.3	36.6
Poland	51.7	70.9	59.9	60.5	63.9
Russia	61.4	56.9	42.1	55.6	54.0
Slovakian Republic	45.8	70.1	22.6	33.1	55.4
Taiwan	37.4	76.0	60.9	27.8	44.0
Average	**45.0**	**61.6**	**44.6**	**48.4**	**59.8**
Weighted Average	**43.5**	**60.3**	**46.7**	**49.7**	**60.6**

These correlations do not prove that gay marriage *causes* marriage to get weaker. I am not trying to prove causation. I am only trying to prove correlation. But correlation is important. Correlations show that certain things tend naturally to cluster together.[29]

For example, show me some teenagers who smoke, and I can be confident that these same teenagers are also more likely to drink than other teenagers. Why? Because these behaviors tend to hang together, especially among teenagers.[30] We cannot say with statistical exactness if one behavior *causes* the other, or if either of them, or both together, *cause* these teens to engage in other risky behaviors, such as skipping school, not getting enough sleep, or forming

Table 6
Summary of Attitudes about Marriage in Surveyed Countries, by Legal Status of Same-Sex Marriage[31]

	Married people are happier	People who want children should marry	One parent can be as good as two together	Cohabiting without intending to marry is all right	Divorce is usually the best solution to marriage problems
Countries with Same-Sex Marriage	21.5	37.8	43.2	83.1	68.4
Countries with Civil Unions	36.0	51.2	39.7	69.9	67.6
Countries with Regional Recognition	42.7	65.6	36.3	56.6	48.1
Countries without Same-Sex Unions	43.5	60.3	46.7	49.7	60.6

friendships with peers who get into trouble. Precisely because these things are connected and tend to reinforce one another, it is virtually impossible for the researcher to pull out just one behavior or attitude from the cluster and then gauge the degree to which it alone is causing or is likely to cause some personal or (what is even harder to measure) social change. *All we can say with certainty is that these things typically go together.* To the degree possible, we hope that our children can avoid *all* of them, the entire syndrome—drinking, smoking, skipping school, missing sleep, making friends with other children who do these things—in part because we know that any one of them increases exposure to the others.

It's the same with marriage. A rise in unwed childbearing and a decline in the belief that people who want to have children should get married. High divorce rates and less belief in marital permanence. The embrace of gay marriage and of the belief that marriage itself is a personal private relationship. The acceptance of collaborative reproduction and of the casual effacing of the child's double origin. *These things go together.*

Table 7
Percentage of Populations Agreeing with Statements about Marriage in Surveyed Countries Recognizing Same-Sex Marriage

	A child needs a home with both a father and a mother to grow up happily	It is all right for a woman to want a child but not a stable relationship with a man*	Marriage is an outdated institution
Belgium	81.1	51.6	30.6
Canada	71.6	45.2	22.3
Denmark	66.9	52.3	15.0
Finland	60.4	53.6	18.0
Iceland	70.9	81.9	8.3
Netherlands	66.3	49.8	25.0
Norway[32]	85.3	23.5	13.5
South Africa	89.5	36.4	33.9
Spain	84.5	79.2	24.6
Sweden	60.1	31.7	20.4
Average	**73.7**	**50.5**	**21.2**
Weighted Average	**76.6**	**48.3**	**23.6**

We cannot tease out and demonstrate statistically what is causing what, or what is likely in the future to cause what. But we do know that these trends fit together and form a natural pattern. If you tend to accept any one or two of them, you probably tend to accept the others as well. And as a strategic matter, if you are fighting for any one of them, you should—you almost certainly already do—support all of them, since a victory for any of them clearly advances all the others as well. Judith Stacey and her anti-marriage colleagues from Chapter Six were not making any of this up. *These things do go together.*

Therefore, to the degree that it makes any sense to oppose gay marriage, it makes sense *only* if one also opposes with equal

*For this question, respondents were given the option of answering "approve," "disapprove," or "depends." The percentages given here are for "approve."

Table 8
Percentage of Populations Agreeing with Statements about Marriage in Surveyed Countries Recognizing Same-Sex Civil Unions

	A child needs a home with both a father and a mother to grow up happily	It is all right for a woman to want a child but not a stable relationship with a man	Marriage is an outdated institution
Brazil[33]	87.2	52.0	29.5
Croatia	89.0	66.0	8.3
Czech Republic	86.0	39.3	11.4
France	86.1	49.5	36.3
Germany	90.7	30.3	18.1
Great Britain	66.8	30.8	25.9
Hungary	95.4	38.4	17.1
Luxembourg	85.4	45.8	32.8
New Zealand	77.3	15.3	16.1
Northern Ireland	69.7	31.2	22.9
Portugal	74.8	35.8	24.8
Slovenia	88.0	55.8	27.4
Switzerland[34]	88.5	37.5	24.1
Average	**83.5**	**40.6**	**22.7**
Weighted Average	**84.3**	**40.7**	**22.4**

clarity and intensity the other main trends pushing our society toward post-institutional marriage. After all, the big idea is not stopping gay marriage. The big idea is stopping the erosion of society's most pro-child institution. Gay marriage is only one facet of the larger threat to that institution.

Shall We Reinstitutionalize Marriage?

In the academic world, the smart money is on deinstitutionalization. Andrew J. Cherlin, a prominent family sociologist from Johns Hopkins University who supports same-sex marriage and also

Table 9
Percentage of Populations Agreeing with Statements about Marriage in Surveyed Countries in Which Some Regions Recognize Same-Sex Marriage

	A child needs a home with both a father and a mother to grow up happily	It is all right for a woman to want a child but not a stable relationship with a man	Marriage is an outdated institution
Argentina	91.3	61.4	19.3
Australia[35]	70.7	36.6	18.5
Italy	92.4	27.6	17.0
United States	64.4	41.8	10.1
Average	**79.7**	**41.9**	**16.2**
Weighted Average	**80.2**	**39.5**	**16.6**

agrees forthrightly that gay marriage contributes substantially to deinstitutionalization, rates the odds of any future shift toward a more "institutionalized form of marriage" in the United States as "very unlikely."[36] The historian Stephanie Coontz is much more blunt: "Forget the fantasy of solving the challenges of modern personal life by reinstitutionalizing marriage."[37] That comment gets my attention, for several reasons. First, I've noticed over time that nearly every sentence that Stephanie Coontz writes contains at least one piece of confusion. In this sentence, it's the notion that she must disabuse her readers of the belief that strengthening marriage is a way of "solving the challenges of modern personal life." I certainly harbor no such illusion, and I do not know a single person who does.

Stephanie Coontz has made a career out of arguing that her own philosophical preferences and the laws of historical inevitability are one and the same. In *The Way We Never Were: American Families and the Nostalgia Trap*, she consults history and announces that anyone who believes that families in the past were at times more stable than they are now, or that it might be a good idea to try to lower our current rates of divorce and unwed childbearing, suffers from a mental disability called "nostalgia." In *The Way We Really Are: Coming to Terms with America's Changing Families*, she again

Table 10

Percentage of Populations Agreeing with Statements about Marriage in Surveyed Countries That Do Not Recognize Same-Sex Unions

	A child needs a home with both a father and a mother to grow up happily	It is all right for a woman to want a child but not a stable relationship with a man	Marriage is an outdated institution
Albania	**98.9**	**11.6**	**8.6**
Algeria	97.5	6.2	12.7
Armenia[38]	97.9	36.9	14.1
Austria	87.8	38.2	20.1
Azerbaijan[39]	91.6	24.0	18.3
Bangladesh	99.0	3.7	5.1
Belarus	94.5	60.6	17.0
Bosnia & Herzegovina	94.7	47.8	13.9
Bulgaria	97.1	46.4	17.9
Chile	83.2	73.1	31.4
China	95.4	1.8	14.3
Colombia	86.3	75.7	25.3
Dominican Republic[40]	85.3	48.2	10.8
Egypt	98.5	4.9	4.1
El Salvador	94.2	28.4	14.9
Estonia	95.7	28.7	15.8
Georgia[41]	98.0	41.1	15.3
Greece	96.1	30.7	15.7
India	95.5	9.9	19.6
Indonesia	88.8	4.2	3.2
Iran	86.0	3.3	20.3
Ireland	67.5	32.3	22.3
Japan	90.1	22.9	10.4
Jordan	98.1	2.2	12.4
Kyrgyzstan[42]	97.6	29.6	32.9
Latvia	93.1	55.4	16.4
Lithuania	79.5	61.1	20.5

Table 10 *(continued)*

	A child needs a home with both a father and a mother to grow up happily	It is all right for a woman to want a child but not a stable relationship with a man	Marriage is an outdated institution
Macedonia	97.0	52.5	18.3
Malta	92.9	15.6	6.7
Mexico	87.4	47.0	20.6
Moldova	96.7	37.3	31.6
Montenegro	96.7	37.0	12.3
Morocco	98.3	2.6	5.2
Nigeria	96.6	18.0	15.4
Pakistan	98.1	0.1	1.4
Peru	93.6	49.1	20.0
Philippines	96.6	14.5	17.3
Poland	96.9	41.8	9.3
Puerto Rico	75.9	56.6	12.7
Romania	94.7	48.7	12.5
Russia	94.8	53.6	21.7
Saudi Arabia[43]	95.3	3.5	16.6
Serbia	89.4	53.9	17.8
Singapore	93.7	18.4	20.8
Slovakian Republic	95.2	23.3	11.5
South Korea	97.0	21.9	15.6
Tanzania	96.7	14.9	8.3
Turkey	97.2	6.75	7.4
Uganda	96.2	18.9	19.8
Ukraine	97.1	40.1	18.0
Uruguay[44]	89.8	66.7	21.0
Venezuela	88.8	64.8	25.4
Vietnam	97.2	16.0	8.8
Zimbabwe	98.4	7.4	11.0
Average	**93.3**	**30.7**	**15.6**
Weighted Average	**93.8**	**28.5**	**15.2**

Table 11
Summary of Attitudes about Marriage in Surveyed Countries, by Legal Status of Same-Sex Marriage[45]

	A child needs a home with both a father and a mother to grow up happily	It is all right for a woman to want a child but not a stable relationship with a man	Marriage is an outdated institution
Countries with Same-Sex Marriage	76.6	48.3	23.6
Countries with Same-Sex Unions	84.3	40.7	22.4
Countries with Regional Recognition	80.2	39.5	16.6
Countries without Same-Sex Unions	93.8	28.5	15.2

consults history and announces that nothing, absolutely nothing, can be done to slow or reverse the trend of family fragmentation. Recently, in *Marriage, a History,* she reports further researches telling her that marriage has already changed, deeply and irreversibly, from a structured social institution to a private relationship. The subtitle of the book says it all: "How Love Conquered Marriage." All of which proves, by the way—according to History, that is—that gay marriage and marriage are now a wonderful fit.[46]

Throughout her books and articles, whatever idea Coontz does not like—whatever idea she believes that History has ruled out of bounds—is likened to a cancelled television series, especially *Leave It to Beaver* ("*Leave It to Beaver* was not a documentary") and, for some reason, *Ozzie and Harriet*. She concludes one recent article with these words: "That series has been cancelled."[47]

Stephanie Coontz is also a prominent activist. In 1996, along with Judith Stacey, she cofounded the Council on Contemporary Families, a group largely devoted to defending the upswing in divorce and unwed childbearing, or at least castigating anyone who speaks against either of these trends. So when this same Stephanie Coontz declares yet again, with such emphasis, that, according to History, we must "forget the fantasy" of "reinstitutionalizing marriage," that comment does get my attention. It tells me that a serious, concerted effort to reinstitutionalize marriage at this moment in our history may be just what the doctor ordered.

So here is a proposed five-part agenda for reinstitutionalizing marriage in the United States over the next decade:

1. Push the success rate for first marriages up from about 60 percent to 75 percent.

Already, our national divorce rate is modestly declining. Today, the odds that a new first marriage will avoid divorce appear to be about 60 percent.[48] What if, through more and better marriage education and other positive social changes, we pushed it up over the next decade to 75 percent? That would certainly constitute significant progress toward reinstitutionalization. It would also strengthen our society and, according to virtually all the evidence we have, improve the life prospects and well-being of many of our citizens, including children. Does that sound like a wild fantasy? Does History require us to forget about such a goal entirely?

2. Push the rate of unwed childbearing down from about 36 percent to below 30 percent.

During the mid and late 1990s, our national rate of unwed childbearing basically stopped rising. Now, unfortunately, it appears to be increasing again. Currently about 36 percent of U.S. children are born outside of marriage. If we viewed it as an important national goal, we might search for reasonable ways over the next decade to stop that number once again from increasing, and maybe even begin to push it down a bit. With real effort, we might get it down to 28 or 30 percent. That would mean a great deal to a great many children and their parents. Is it true that only a fantasist could imagine such progress?

3. Make no further changes regarding the legal redefinition of marriage.

Right now, gay marriage is permitted in only one state, Massachusetts. (It is legal there not because the citizenry or the legislature support it—majorities across the board oppose it—but because the state supreme judicial court effectively imposed it judicially). What if things remained pretty much that way in the United States for the next decade? Ten years of no further change in the basic definition of marriage—is that beyond our power to imagine?

4. Increase public scrutiny and regulation of the fertility industry.
A great many nations of the world, even including much of Europe, are far stricter than the United States in prohibiting surrogate or contract pregnancy (paying someone to have a baby for you) and in regulating what we in the United States have come unashamedly to call the fertility industry, especially practices and procedures involving third-party participation in procreation, such as selling or donating sperm or eggs. What if, in the coming few years, we Americans managed to change our laws to become a bit more like Europe in this crucial area? To do so would strengthen children's rights in the United States and constitute a limited but clear cultural message in favor of marriage as an institution and against the degradation and commodification of childbearing. Is such a change beyond the realm of possibility?

5. Have a national conversation about what marriage is.
It will not surprise you to learn that Stephanie Coontz's favored, according-to-what-History-requires definition of marriage is "a private relationship between two individuals."[49] Apparently more than a few Americans agree, and especially the most vocal of our opinion leaders. Might it be possible for us to have a serious conversation about this dubious conclusion?

Taken together, are these changes too crazy even to imagine? Should we be sternly reprimanded by History and sent to bed without supper for even thinking such thoughts? I don't believe so. I think most Americans would support these goals. By almost any measurement, realizing them would make our society better. They are certainly not radical. In fact, compared with the cutting-edge agenda of the deinstitutionalizers—three or four parents for little Billy, tossing the inherited meaning of marriage out the window without so much as a by-your-leave, and doing everything but cheerleading (and sometimes even that) for divorce and unwed childbearing—this short-term agenda for reinstitutionalization seems positively mild.

If we as a society were to achieve these five goals, or at least come close, during the next decade or so, we would likely discover that these positive changes are synergistic and mutually reinforcing. Why? Because they *correlate with one another.* They hang together. They are based on shared philosophical presuppositions and related demographic factors. Just as the trends driving deinstitutionalization tend to work together in a downward spiral, these small pieces of progress toward reinstitutionalization would probably work together as well in an upward trajectory.

Some of our writers may be presently changing channels, but this series has not been cancelled. As we saw in Table 1, currently our society's overall Marriage Index rating—our composite measurement of marriage's institutional vitality—stands at about 62.5, down from 77.6 in 1970. In the 1970s, the index fell 6.5 points. In the 1980s, it fell another 5.2 points, and in the 1990s, another 3.4 points. So the rate of overall decline appears to be steadily slowing down. Is it impossible to imagine that we could stop the decline altogether in the next decade and begin to push the index in a positive direction? To me and many of my colleagues in the grassroots marriage movement, and also I think to many other Americans, it is not impossible to imagine.

The most important single indicator—the proportion of children living with their own two married parents—is the one showing the smallest decline. If that number were to go up in the coming decade or so by only 4.3 percentage points, the United States on this crucial measurement would be as strong as in 1980. Such incremental bits of progress would not "solve the challenges of modern personal life." (Whoever has that formula should put it in a bottle.) But it would measurably improve the health of our society and the happiness and well-being of many adults and children.

What would be the specific results of such a shift? Several respected family scholars recently sought a statistical answer to a hypothetical question. If family structure in the United States were as strong today as it was in 1970—in our terms, if today's Marriage Index stood at 77.6 instead of 62.5—what difference would it make in the area of child poverty? Summarizing the scholarly literature, Isabel V. Sawhill of the Brookings Institution writes: "With some exceptions, these studies generally find that most, and in some cases all, of the increase in child poverty over the past thirty to forty years can be explained by changes in family structure."[50] Sawhill also summarizes her own research in this area: "If enough marriages had taken place to return the incidence of single parenting to 1970 levels, and the incomes of the men and women were combined, the poverty rate among children in 1998 would have fallen by about a third."[51]

In 1996, Robert I. Lerman of the Urban Institute reached a similar conclusion:

> The results [of the study] show that the 1971–1989 trend away from marriage among parents accounted for nearly half of the increase in income inequality among children and for the entire rise in child poverty rates.... Thus, despite the lower earnings of today's unmarried men, raising the proportion of mothers who are married would substantially reduce child poverty in the U.S.[52]

This effect is not simply because there may be two earners, but also because there is something specifically about *marriage* that tends to boost earnings and reduce poverty. Lerman's recent studies show that married-couple families are significantly less likely to experience poverty than *any* other family type, including those with at least two potential earners. Even after controlling for other relevant variables, this and similar research suggests that marriage plays an independent role in raising income and reducing poverty.[53]

Recently, Paul R. Amato of Pennsylvania State University applied statistical analysis to a broader hypothetical question: If the proportion of U.S. children living with their two biological parents were as high today as it was in 1980, what would be the likely impact on a range of social problems affecting adolescent well-being? Alternatively, what if the proportion were as high today as it was in 1970? According to our Marriage Index, the proportion of children living with their own two married parents would need to rise only 4.3 percentage points to reach the level of 1980, and a total of 9 percentage points to return to the level of 1970. Here are the social problems of adolescents that Amato looked into:

School failure	With U.S. family structure as strong today as it was in 1980, each year about 300,000 fewer adolescents would fail a grade at school.

	At the 1970 level of strength, about 643,000 fewer adolescents each year would fail a grade.
School suspension	1980 level: 485,000 fewer school suspensions each year. 1970 level: 1,040,000 fewer.
Needs psychotherapy	1980 level: 248,000 fewer adolescents each year need therapy. 1970 level: 531,000 fewer.
Delinquent behavior	1980 level: 216,000 fewer adolescent delinquents each year. 1970 level: 464,000 fewer.
Involved in violence	1980 level: 211,000 fewer involved in violence each year. 1970 level: 453,000 fewer.
Smokes cigarettes	1980 level: 240,000 fewer adolescent smokers each year. 1970 level: 515,000 fewer.
Considers suicide	1980 level: 83,000 fewer adolescents each year consider suicide. 1970 level: 179,000 fewer.
Attempts suicide	1980 level: 29,000 fewer adolescents each year attempt suicide. 1970 level: 62,000 fewer.[54]

I think these and similar improvements are not only possible, but positively worth fighting for.

Announcing that, according to History, we are powerless to do anything about what most of us plainly view as serious challenges is pure flapdoodle. There *is* no mysterious force out there telling us what is inevitable. There *are* no historical laws controlling us. Our past sets certain conditions for us, but ultimately we are free people. The wheel is always in spin. We can learn from experience. We can decide together to go in new directions, or even in old directions.

In the 1940s, when many demographers worried about low U.S. birth rates, probably no one predicted the massive baby boom of the 1950s and early 1960s. In the 1970s, very few people predicted the imminent collapse of communism as an imperium and a world political movement. Quite the contrary. Especially regarding the big questions, the future is not known to us, because the future is finally an event in shared freedom.

That's why optimism is typically a weak idea, but hope is the most powerful idea around. The Czech playwright and political leader Vaclav Havel wisely points out that optimism is believing that doing a certain thing will turn out well in the future, whereas hope is believing that doing a certain thing makes sense, regardless of how it finally turns out. Optimism comes from reading the tea leaves, trying to figure the odds, making predictions. Hope comes from what Havel calls "elsewhere." Havel opted for hope, and the world is much better off as a result.[55] Ultimately it is the only serious moral stance.

To implement and build on the five-part agenda outlined above, here are a few specific, concrete ideas for reinstitutionalizing marriage in the United States:

- End marriage penalties for low-income Americans by guaranteeing that any low-income couple who suffers a financial loss due to the decision to marry (usually through the loss of benefits) is legally entitled to a payment or tax credit from the federal government equal to the amount of the loss.
- Pass new laws offering financial and other incentives, such as reduced marriage license fees, tax credits, and shorter waiting periods, to couples who participate in premarital education.
- Increase public and private sector funding for comprehensive, multisector, community-based initiatives aimed at strengthening marriage and improving outcomes for children.
- Make marriage education and other marriage support services more accessible to low-income couples and communities.
- Encourage churches and other houses of worship to incorporate marriage mentoring as a regular part of congregational life.
- Do not legally redefine marriage as a private relationship between two people.
- Learn more about marriage formation and marriage success in communities of color.
- Add high-quality marriage and relationship education to the public school curriculum.

- Teach young people in schools and elsewhere that unwed childbearing is wrong.
- Create communities of therapists who are pro-marriage and who are improving educational models for working with distressed couples.
- Seek to reduce unnecessary divorce by combining longer waiting periods for divorce with stronger provisions for family courts to refer couples to marriage education.
- Expand children's rights to include the right to a natural biological heritage (a father's sperm and a mother's egg) and the right to know their biological origins.
- Create a blue-ribbon Commission on Marriage charged with leading a civil, serious public conversation about the meaning and possible future of marriage in the United States and establishing national goals for strengthening marriage.

These ideas only scratch the surface. Recently, with William Doherty of the University of Minnesota, I co-chaired a two-year initiative to survey marriage leaders and experts across the country, listening to their priorities and gathering their ideas for strengthening marriage. That process yielded 93 specific recommendations, a number of which I have included in my baker's dozen above.[56]

If we wish to make progress toward reinstitutionalizing marriage, there is no shortage of ways and means. The main questions we face are not practical or technical. They do not center on feasibility. They center on philosophy—on whether we as a society, when all is said and done, believe that reinstitutionalization is a worthy goal. To me, and to many of my colleagues, it is a worthy goal. Why?

Because a society in which marriage does not thrive is not a thriving society.

Because the gift of the self through marriage is one of the finest things that humans are made for.

Because a child deserves a mother and a father who love the child and love each other.

Because the goal is not only desirable, it is possible.

Because we owe it to ourselves to do all that we can to improve marriage's fate.

Appendix

Topics in the Anthropology of Kinship

Patrocentrism and Preformation

THE THEORY OF PATROCENTRISM—the view that the father is the essential originator of children—influenced scholarly writing and scientific investigation for many centuries. According to the sixteenth-century physician Lemnius of Zirizea, the uterus is the "till'd ground for to sow the seeds on."[1] The eighteenth-century French scientist Compte Buffon employed a different metaphor: "the male semen is the sculptor, the menstrual blood is the block of marble, and the fetus is the figure which is fashioned out of this combination."[2]

In his fascinating book from 1930, *Early Theories of Sexual Generation,* F. J. Cole details the history of the doctrine of "preformation," which played an important role in European scientific thought about reproduction from the late seventeenth century to the beginning of the nineteenth century. Preformation, in brief, is the view that the preborn animal does not develop through a process of successive differentiation, but instead exists readymade from the beginning and develops only by (basically) getting larger. Some preformation theorists believed that the animal-in-miniature exists in the egg; these were the proponents of "ovism." Others asserted that the readymade animal exists in the male semen; they were the proponents of "animalculism." The significant improvement of microscopes in the late seventeenth century, which led to the discovery of male spermatozoa, provided a big boost to the proponents of animalculism—their drawings of human male spermatozoa resemble very tiny human beings. (Ovists spent lots of time studying chicken eggs; the mammalian ovum was not discovered by European scientists until 1827.) In his book, Cole wonders why animalculism, which seems at least in retrospect to have begged as many scientific questions as it purported to answer, persisted as an important scientific view for as long as it did. He answers: "The widespread support which animalculism received may be partly explained as the result of subconscious bias. Such a view endorsed the superior status of the male sex, through which alone the distinctive characters of a species were preserved and inherited."[3]

In some respects, this concept of the father as the fundamental originator of children has become so familiar to us that it seems natural—if not like the air we breath, then at least like an inheritance that we can easily either ignore or take for granted. Yet this attitude prevents us from appreciating the historically particular and quite radical—not to mention empirically inaccurate—nature of the claim. In particular, I believe that this entire issue has been underappreciated by scholars focusing on marriage and family life. Those who *have* examined it tend to be feminists.[4]

Bilateral Filiation

The universal phenomenon that anthropologists including A. R. Radcliffe-Brown and Meyer Fortes have termed bilateral filiation can be illustrated with countless examples. In the spirit of our Trobriand analysis, we'll approach the topic by examining traditional understandings of pregnancy in several societies in New Guinea, Melanesia, Polynesia, Asia, and Africa. Let's marvel at their diversity, while also looking where we can for the universal, or what we might call their underlying truth and beauty.

Like the Trobrianders, the people of Bellona Island, one of the Solomon Islands in Polynesia (not far from the Trobriands), traditionally have believed that sexual intercourse is not the cause of conception. Pregnancy occurs when a spirit-baby, who has been living in the abode of the gods beyond the eastern horizon, is implanted in the womb of a woman. This happy event occurs when *her husband's* deities and deceased ancestors are pleased with the marriage and therefore decide to bring the spirit-baby to the wife. In cases where a woman after she marries does not become pregnant, it is customary for her husband to offer prayers to his ancestors and deities. The Bellonese believe that these prayers usually produce the pregnancy that the couple desires. Bellonese women do not pray for children.

These beliefs (modern biology aside) are powerfully suggestive of some fundamental truths. The first is the power of the mother-child bond. The Bellonese often call a child "the fruit of a woman." The mother's procreative power is obvious and inside her already—she doesn't need to pray for it. The second and related truth is that every child needs a father. For the Bellonese, and for all or nearly all human groups, every child by rights should affiliate with its father as well as its mother. Toward this end, the Bellonese, who do not recognize a *biological* bond between a husband and his wife's child, seem to go out of their way to underscore as part of their basic worldview the *spiritual* bond between a husband and the child that is borne by his wife. Note also that this father-creating, father-defining bond is made possible, both practically and theoretically, by one thing only: marriage.[5]

The island of Tikopia is another of the Solomon Islands in Polynesia. If we compare the Tikopia understanding of conception with its counterpart in neighboring Bellona, we see essentially the *opposite* pattern regarding gender; but if we are looking for the universal, we see essentially the *same* underlying phenomenon. Among the patrilineal Tikopia, the traditional belief is that the male semen enters the woman's womb and coagulates into the substance from which the child is made. Thus the mother, apart from her role as incubator and haven for the fetus, does not contribute *materially* to the initial conception of the child. In this respect, she is similar to the Bellonese father. But she does, also like the Bellonese father, contribute to the child *spiritually*, for "within the womb the Atua Fafine, the female deity, forms the baby out of the coagulated semen."[6]

The Northern Mandak people of central New Ireland in Papua New Guinea, like the Trobrianders, trace their blood lines on a matrilineal basis. Yet their view of procreation, as reported in the 1970s, appears to have much in common physiologically with the male seed model, for the anthropologist reports that "it is the male-given substance [semen] alone which contributes the blood, skin, and internal organs of the fetus," while the mother's role is "to nourish and protect the male-provided substance." At the same time, however, the Northern Mandak place an extremely high cultural value on the concept of maternal nurturance. In this Melanesian society, a person's "primary and essential sustenance is derived from female procreative functions," in part because "throughout gestation the infant is fed in the womb entirely from maternal sources." The result is that every Northern Mandak child is viewed as coming in different and complementary ways from both her mother and her father.[7]

Among the Orokaiva of Papua New Guinea, all pregnancies traditionally involve the entry into the woman's body of the spirit of a deceased ancestor. In the case of a male child, it is believed that sexual intercourse *in addition to* the entry of the spirit produces the baby. In the case of a female child, it is believed that the spirit alone does the trick, without any assistance from sexual intercourse. Yet in both cases—as is true in the Trobriands as well—sexual intercourse during pregnancy is believed to contribute to the health and vitality of the soon-to-be-born child. In the case of female children, it is believed that the spirit who enters the woman is from her lineage, and for this reason, the wife and her kin provide the name for the newborn daughter. In the case of male children, a medicine man is called in to determine which set of ancestors, his or hers, provided the spirit that helped to constitute the baby. If the answer is "hers," the wife and her kin name the little boy. If the answer is "his," the husband and his kin do the naming. On this basis, it appears that about half the male babies of the Orokaiva are inspirited matrilineally and about half patrilineally. As long as the man and woman are married, he is legally the father of all the children she bears.

The Orokaiva traditionally teach that men have a special strength and power (*ivo*) that women do not possess and which, when transmitted to a wife's womb during intercourse, helps to produce a male child. (The Orokaiva kinship system is based on patrilineal descent; only male offspring can carry on the lineage.) Daughters, by contrast, are believed—at least by the overwhelmingly male informants who talk to anthropologists!—to be constituted solely from the purportedly weaker blood of the mother. In its overall patriarchal bias, this notion of *ivo* is remarkably similar to some of the early Western theories of procreation described in Chapter Three.[8]

Among the Mae-Enga of New Guinea, conception *begins* when the male semen mixes with the (even more powerful) female menstrual blood in the woman's womb. Four months later, the developing fetus acquires an individual personality, its personal essence, by virtue of being entered and animated by a spirit. This spirit, it turns out, has been implanted in the fetus by the totality of the *father's* deceased ancestors. For the Mae-Enga, then, while the child's physical body comes primarily from the mother—her blood, they say, makes the child's skin and flesh—the child's personality comes essentially from the father's ancestral ghosts. Corporal vitality is largely "maternal." Spiritual vitality is largely "paternal."

From this belief flow many consequences. One is that when a man is physically injured (when the mother-part of him is hurt), he must customarily provide gifts to his maternal kin, since it is assumed that ghosts from his father's side either harmed him or did not adequately protect him. For this failure originating from his father's side of things, the man owes compensation to his mother's family. For example, if a man's hair "is cut or disarranged against his wishes, he is shamed by this invasion of his individuality and owes compensation to his maternal kin." The Mae-Enga kinship system is based on many reciprocal duties and expectations—there are times when maternal kin must give to paternal kin—but on the whole, according to a major study, the maternal kin typically end up on top as a result of these ongoing exchanges. After all, most people get sick or are injured at some time and everyone eventually dies, and each time this happens, the mother's family is owed compensation for the physical harm that has befallen her child.

Again, the details differ, but in this society as well we see the two fundamental principles working together. The first is that every child is a mother's child. If the child physically suffers, something that the *mother* gave the child has been harmed, and attention must be paid. The second principle is that every child is a father's child. A father should protect his child, and when that child suffers, there is a sense in which this father particularly, and fathers more generally, are responsible, and attention must be paid. If there is a clearer example in the anthropological literature of the fundamental idea that every child deserves both a mother and a father, I have not encountered it.[9]

For the Bimin-Kuskusmin of Papua New Guinea, "proper procreation is embedded in a recognized context of social categories and relations articulated in the institution of marriage." Without marriage, parenthood is improper and the child born of such an improper union is therefore at physical risk, largely because the child will not have received *finiik* spirits—the special spirits that animate and empower the preborn child, beginning at conception, and that come to the child from deceased paternal and maternal ancestors, in response to ritual requests from the wife and the husband. To achieve full personhood, then, every Bimin-Kuskusmin child needs spiritual gifts from his mother's relatives *and* his father's relatives. Similarly, cases of male adultery within marriage are believed to provoke the wrath of ancestors, which in turn can harm the development of the man's preborn child, disrupting both physical health and spiritual capacity. For the Bimin-Kuskusmin, then, marriage provides the child not only with two responsible parents, but also with two lineages, each of which is essential to well-being.[10]

According to the Kachin people of North Burma (in the early 1940s), who trace their descent patrilineally and commonly live in somewhat extended family groups (*htinggaw*) of close patrilineal kin, a person's physical appearance—as well as character or reputation—comes not at all from the father and his people, but from the mother and her relatives, because the mother feeds her child in her womb and at her breast. So far, this is an almost exact inversion of Trobriand thinking on this issue. At the same time, however, a Kachin child is believed to acquire its soul (*minla*) at the moment of birth and from its immediate physical surroundings, and for this reason it is important for the child to be born in its *father's* house.

E. R. Leach characterizes marriage among the Kachin, which involves gift exchanges and a ceremony called *num shalai*, as fundamentally an institution to "legitimize the status of the offspring." A Kachin husband is the legal and responsible father of all children born to his wife, even in cases in which he is clearly not the biological genitor. Or if an unmarried couple that has a child later gets married, the child's basic legal protections are thereby assured and the husband becomes the child's legal and recognized father, but at the same time, such a child will always suffer from a lower status or rank than a child born to the same couple after they are married. The essential cultural narrative could hardly be clearer. For every Kachin child, a mother and a father, properly through marriage.[11]

In the early twentieth century, E. E. Evans-Pritchard studied the Azande people of central Africa. The Azande are patrilineal; each child is a member of the father's clan. As the Azande see it, the male semen contains the child's soul—the word for semen (*nzira* or *mbisimo gude*) literally means "the soul of the child." It is this "spiritual" soul which, at the time of death, goes to the land of ghosts, at the head of streams. But each Azande also has a second or "body" soul which, at the time of death, changes into a totem animal of a clan. This soul comes from the mother; specifically, it comes from the mucus (*nzira*) that the woman emits during sexual intercourse. Evans-Pritchard writes: "Thus two souls, one of the man and one of the woman, are necessary for the birth of a child and if either partner lacks these souls marriage will be unfruitful." And again: "both man and woman contribute to produce a child through the union of their souls." As a result, each child is fundamentally affiliated with both its father and its mother, despite the presence of what we might call a patriarchal bias. As Evans-Pritchard puts it, "There is always a balance and a bias in such matters in every community in the world."[12]

Each of the ten diverse societies examined in *African Systems of Kinship and Marriage* provides evidence of the importance in human groups of bilateral affiliation and the rule of a legal mother and a legal father for every child. Consider the Swazi people of southwest Africa. According to the anthropologist Hilda Kuper, the "starting-point of the Swazi kinship system"—mother, father, and child—"depends as in all societies on a recognition of a social relationship" between the two parents. That relationship is marriage.

Reports Kuper: "The Swazi say 'A child is one blood with its father and its mother', but if a man has refused to perform the recognized marriage ceremony the children will belong to the mother's kin." Such a situation is viewed as highly undesirable: "Swazi consider the production of legitimate children a social obligation of adult men and women."

What happens in the doubly unhappy event of a Swazi man without children dying, and leaving behind a lover whom he has not married? Among the Swazi, the most important marriage gift to the bride's family is cattle. This gift is specifically connected to—it is intended to ensure—the legal and ritual affiliation of her future children with her husband and his clan. In the case of the dead childless man and his surviving lover, "it is the duty of his father or his father's heir to give cattle for her and provide a 'thigh' from the kinship group to raise children for the deceased." In this unusual case, the importance to the society of legitimated parenthood, fatherhood, and patrilineal filiation continues even after a would-be biological father has died.[13]

These case studies, which could be multiplied almost without end, clearly underscore the universality or at least near-universality of human bilateral affiliation and therefore of marriage and social fatherhood as foundational human institutions. At the same time—back to the Trobrianders and the matriarchal bias—it is also true, at least in principle, that marriage and fatherhood are somewhat weaker and more precarious in matrilineal kinship systems than they are in patrilineal systems.[14]

Polygyny and Polyandry

Some scholars in their definitions of marriage have amended or altered the phrase "a woman and a man" in order to take account of the existence in a great many societies of polygyny, in which marriage rules permit the male to be married to two or more women at the same time, as well as the existence in a very few societies of polyandry, in which marriage rules permit the female to be married to two or more men at the same time. I have not made such an alteration in my suggested definition of marriage for two reasons.

First and most importantly, these forms of what might be termed compound marriage do not violate the basic principle of "a woman and a man." For example, in societies that permit polygyny, a man with three wives marries each of his wives separately, never as a group. Legally, economically, and practically, he has a distinct marital relationship with each of his wives. Under the existing marriage rules of his society, he has gotten married three different times, while each of his wives has gotten married only once. Each child of a polygynous marriage is legally as well as in other respects the child of one mother and one father. I personally disapprove of polygyny (mainly because it both promotes and reflects social inequality, and is inconsistent with full human flourishing for women). But conceptually, a polygynous marriage conforms to the principal that each marriage unites one woman with one man.

Polyandry is a similar case. It is extremely rare in human societies—it seems to exist or have existed only in some areas of Tibet, Sri Lanka, and southern India—and typically involves two or more brothers each married to the same woman. While in some respects a more ambiguous and (regarding a universal conceptualization of marriage) harder-to-define institution, polyandry still fundamentally constitutes, in my view and in the view of many others, an example of a compound, not group, form of marriage. In Tibet, for example, where polyandry is permitted, authority in the polyandrous household is typically exercised solely by the eldest brother—a fact that can often cause a younger brother to leave a polyandrous union and start a monogamous one. Similarly, it is often (though not always) the eldest brother alone who participates formally in the marriage ceremony, and the eldest brother alone whom all the children, even those biologically fathered by a younger brother, call "father." Alternatively, in some forms of polyandrous marriage, including in southern India, legal and social fatherhood for each child is assumed by one of the brothers, not on the basis of seniority or the presumption of biological paternity, but instead by virtue of a ritual act. It is also commonly (though again not always) the case that the brothers/co-husbands in a polyandrous marriage cohabit with the wife successively, not jointly.

As an institution, polyandry seems to be related to external social conditions such as restricted social mobility, scarce economic resources, sex ratio imbalances, and structural problems facing male siblings regarding the inheritance of land. In this respect, we might view polyandry largely as a kind of hybrid institution, typically grafting the enduring power of the sibling bond onto the basic template of marriage, in the service of a social goal—in this case, it appears, usually shared sibling control of the family's land—that is generally extraneous to marriage's fundamental purposes.[15]

The second reason for the wording "a woman and a man" is that monogamy—only one woman married to only one man—is not only the universal prototype of human marriage, it also describes the actual marriage experience of the overwhelming majority of human beings who marry today or who have ever married in history. Polyandry is extremely rare. On the other hand, most human groups legally permit polygyny, though in practice it is primarily entered into by the society's richest and most politically powerful males (and the women whom they marry). After all, if most or even a sizeable minority of men in any given society were actually married to two or more women at the same time, there would likely be a dramatic and possibly chaos-producing shortage of wives! But such is seldom the case. In many societies, rich and powerful men have arranged matters such that they are legally permitted to have more than one wife. But for most others, marriage in practice is monogamous, conforming to the rule of two: only one husband married to only one wife.

Polyamory

As a "what's new" topic for people who favor deinstitutionalizing marriage, polyamory is hot these days. Among many of these anti-marriage activists, same-sex marriage is taken for granted. It feels blasé, like yesterday's big new idea. Polyamory is still transgressive. It still shocks the uninitiated. Polyamory is tomorrow's big new idea, being worked out today by creative theorists in academic conferences, advanced support groups, and little journals.

One such theorist is Drucilla Cornell of Rutgers University. In a politically liberal society, she writes, the state "should have no right to privilege or impose one form of family structure or sexuality over another." Advocates of same-sex marriage make this point constantly. But watch where Cornell goes with it. In a liberal society there can be "no state-enforced single relationship—not monogamy, heterosexuality, polygamy, or polyandry." She asks: Should four women be able to contract a legally recognized group marriage with one another? Yes, Cornell concludes, they should. All sorts of diverse intimate relationships, so long as they are entered into voluntarily, are equally valid and therefore equally deserving of being legally recognized as marriages. What are the implications of this concept for public policy? In Cornell's view, the bottom line is that "we need to advocate for different forms of plural marriage." She waxes poetic: "Love, in the end, demands that we stretch our imagination to see new possibilities for kinship and learn from those that already exist."[16]

Another theorist in this camp is Elizabeth F. Emens of the University of Chicago Law School. She writes that

> the existence of some number of people choosing to live polyamorous lives should prompt all of us to think harder about this issue. It should prompt us to think about our own choices and about the ways that our norms and laws urge upon us one model rather than pressing us to make informed, affirmative choices about what might best suit our needs and desires. At a moment when same-sex couples rush to the altar, I suggest that we take this opportunity to question the desirability and justice of monogamy's law.[17]

Finally, don't look now, but endorsements and positive portrayals of both compound (polygamous and polyandrous) marriages and group or polyamorous marriages are even now making their first (and not particularly blushing) appearances in mainstream public discourse and popular entertainment, in the United States and elsewhere. A 2004 feature in the *Milwaukee Journal Sentinel* reports that the campaign for same-sex marriage in the United States "is laying the groundwork for polyamorists to acquire legal status for their three-, four- and more-way relationships." A columnist for the *Southern Voice* in 2005 asks: "Are we not polyamorists? Once we win equal marriage, we may have to fight to arrange our marriages the way we like." In Canada, two recently commissioned government studies have recommended decriminalizing polygamy.

A new U.S. television drama debuting in 2006 on HBO is *Big Love*, about a nice guy with three wives. The show's writers, Mark V. Olsen and Will Scheffer, say that they want to be "nonjudgmental and humane" about polygamy and suggest that this family form is "an ideal way to look at marriage and family." In 1999 the U.S. Unitarian Universalist Church recognized a group called "Unitarian Universalists for Polyamorous Awareness," which works to make their church "the first poly-welcoming mainstream religious denomination." (Among the main U.S. Christian denominations, Unitarians have the highest proportion of college graduates, the highest proportion of members with postgraduate degrees, and the highest per capita income.) In 2006, a four-day "Heartland Polyamory Conference" was held in Indiana, complete with workshops on "poly parenting."

Something very close to a socially recognized group marriage took place amidst much fanfare in the Netherlands in 2005. The legal basis of the three-way wedding was a private cohabitation contract. The group tying the knot consisted of a man who says he is heterosexual and two women who say they are bisexual.

Which raises an interesting legal and moral question for the advocates of same-sex marriage, such as Jonathan Rauch, who vigorously insist that *two* is the true and only number, and who instantly cry foul (slippery-slope argument!) when anyone suggests that jettisoning the first and arguably most foundational of marriage's rules—the rule of opposites—would make both of the other main rules—the rule of two, the rule of sex—more vulnerable to assault and more seemingly arbitrary. Here is the problem: If a person's sexual orientation becomes, as same-sex marriage advocates insist that it must and will become, a legitimate foundation for organizing the structure of that person's marriage—that is, if orientation as such becomes a publicly and legally endorsed basis on which a person can decide whether and whom to marry—*why not* permit a bisexual woman to marry one man and one woman? Is she less worthy of respect and public recognition than, say, a lesbian or a gay man? Are her life goals and her social-sexual needs less legitimate? Are we really prepared to say that, from now on regarding marriage, the rule of opposites is irrelevant, excessively restrictive, and discriminatory, whereas the rule of two stands sacrosanct and untouchable? I seriously doubt it. So does Judith Stacey. So do many of her allies in the struggle for same-sex marriage. So do the emerging leaders in the U.S. bisexual community who seriously aim to win legal recognition for polyamorous marriage in the United States in coming years.

After all, if same-sex marriage becomes normative, on what moral basis could a fair-minded person possibly oppose bisexual, polyamorous marriage? Particularly when bisexual persons will be making exactly the same claim as homosexual persons about the need for marriage as a legal institution to accommodate and respect sexual orientation?

Institutionally, marriage has always been mute and formally indifferent when confronted with subjective and often quite complex questions of individual sexual orientation. The marital institution does not ask a person about her or his orientation. It bars no one from marrying on the basis of orientation, and it evicts no one from the institution on the basis of orientation. But if we as a society cross that Rubicon—if sexual desire becomes a valid legal principle for structuring a marriage—it is hard to imagine the moral metric by which bisexual spousal groups would be excluded from this newly orientation-sensitive institution.[18]

The Disappearance of Kinship?

E. R. Leach's notion that marriage can be reduced analytically to a "bundle of rights" is something of a transitional argument in the recent history of anthropology, just as Leach himself emerges in hindsight as a transitional figure in the field, with one foot still firmly planted in the classical or modern era, and the other lifted off the ground and clearly aimed in the direction of postmodernism. (His influential *Rethinking Anthropology* was published in 1961.)[19] As late as 1967, Robin Fox in his book *Kinship and Marriage* could still report: "Kinship is to anthropology what logic is to philosophy or the nude is to art; it is the basic discipline of the subject." But that was about to change. In anthropology, the days of the nude—or what Fox at the time also described as anthropology's central concern with the "basic facts" of "birth, copulation, and death"—were numbered.[20]

By 1974, Rodney Needham, explicitly seeking to "resume Leach's iconoclasm," could blithely announce that *kinship itself* can be reduced analytically to "the allocation of rights"—rights which, it turns out, "are not of any specific kind" and certainly "have no intrinsic connexion with the facts, or the cultural idioms, of procreation." Therefore, when all is said and done, "there is no such thing as kinship; and it follows that there can be no such thing as kinship theory." As to marriage, forget that one, too. Marriage is merely "an odd-job word" that is "worse than misleading in comparison and of no real use at all in analysis."[21]

During the 1970s and early 1980s, these and similar ideas became astonishingly popular among anthropologists, as the classic modernist concerns with kinship structures and institutions across societies fell quickly out of favor and were largely replaced by postmodernist concerns related to feminism, Marxism, and symbolic or interpretive anthropology. A remarkable intellectual transformation took place. In fairly short order, kinship terms linked to biology and genealogy were out. Kinship terms as pure social constructions were in. The study of social institutions and structures was out. The study of symbols and underlying experiences of power and powerlessness was in. Conventional sexuality was out. Transgressive sexuality was in. Empathic and detailed description was out. Dense theorizing was in.

And what is the fate today of those classic concerns with marriage and family life that once animated the work of so many distinguished social anthropologists, a number of whom I have cited in this book? Those concerns have all but vanished. In 2001, the anthropologist Linda Stone, reviewing the previous two decades, concluded that "nearly a whole generation of anthropologists largely forgot about kinship as a distinct domain. A telling development was that undergraduate courses on kinship were often deleted from the curriculum in departments of anthropology." From the early 1970s to the mid 1990s, not a single textbook on kinship was published in the United States. The authors of an anthropology textbook published in 2000 remarked, "Today, anthropologists demonstrate such a decided *lack* of interest in the topic of kinship that it is tempting to declare that it is no longer a key concept."[22] In this transformation, some important criticisms and insights have emerged, but much has been lost or ignored, especially for those who still notice—notwithstanding the warnings of Needham and others to the contrary—that marriage exists everywhere in the world, that it is a social institution, and that this social institution is interesting and important.[23]

The same transformation with respect to marriage occurred in other fields as well. In the 1970s and early 1980s, sociologists studying marriage and the family increasingly, and often with great stridency, denounced marriage as a retrograde institution that needed to be either eliminated or fundamentally altered. Similarly, family law scholars during this period increasingly concurred that the proper goal of marriage law is not to recognize or protect marriage, but instead to deinstitutionalize it by eliminating distinctions in law between marriage and other close relationships. In all three cases—anthropology, sociology, and family law—the erstwhile custodians of the institution suddenly and often quite fiercely turned against the institution itself. Why these changes occurred is a complex story. They have affected, mostly for the worse, an entire generation of scholarship. Only in very recent years have these ideas themselves begun to be viewed by some leading researchers as rigid and outdated, while the study of marriage and of social institutions more generally has started to make something of a comeback.[24]

Acknowledgments

A PERSON WRITING A BOOK usually has a question that is disturbing his or her peace, demanding that attention be paid. The question that nagged me into writing this book is how we can revitalize marriage as a pro-child social institution. I've been struggling with this question more or less continuously since the late 1980s. But today it seems newly relevant and particularly urgent. Our current national controversy over same-sex marriage, which first emerged in the late 1990s and shows no signs of abating, not only invites but also *requires* us to pay renewed attention to fundamental questions about the role of marriage in our society. Today's gay marriage debate is an invaluable opportunity for Americans to have a serious national discussion about marriage's meaning and future. This book is my contribution to that discussion.

Many friends and colleagues have helped me to grapple with my question. For reading drafts of chapters and generously offering their comments, I am deeply grateful to Raina Sacks Blankenhorn, Dan Cere, Maggie Gallagher, Robert George, David Gilmore, David Gutmann, Heather Higgins, James Turner Johnson, Stanley Kurtz, Elizabeth Lurie, Elizabeth Marquardt, John M. Miller, David Popenoe, Barbara Dafoe Whitehead, W. Bradford Wilcox, and Peter Wood.

Writing a book takes time, and some of the time I needed, I took from my family. For putting up with that, and for being supportive in more ways than I can say, I am so grateful to my wife, Raina, and our children, Raymond, Allie, and Sophie. I am grateful *to* them and *for* them.

I appreciate the willingness of my friends at Encounter Books to take a chance on this book. My argument in this book (to speak with moderation!) runs a bit against the grain of conventional wisdom in the publishing industry and among opinion leaders. Yet my two editors, Peter Collier and Roger Kimball—both of them fine and accomplished writers themselves—encouraged me throughout and have been important colleagues.

I am also very thankful to my colleagues at the Institute for American Values, where I have spent nearly twenty years of my working life and where I hope and plan to spend the rest. My bosses on the Institute's Board of Directors generously gave me time, resources, and encouragement. Without their help and without the aid of the Institute's financial contributors, this book would never have been possible. My staff colleagues Elizabeth Marquardt, Sara Butler Nardo, Charity Navarrete, Bonnie Robbins, Alex Roberts, Deb Strubel, Josephine Tramontano, and Brad Wilcox have been wonderfully supportive. At the Institute, we are an ensemble, not a chorus. Some of these coworkers disagree with at least parts of this book. Yet notwithstanding this fact, and in part due to it, all of them have been terrific and much-valued colleagues.

Arthur and Joann Rasmussen have my deepest admiration and respect. They have been cherished friends to me and my family, wise and selfless leaders of the Institute for American Values, and generous supporters of many people and institutions seeking to improve our society. I wrote the final pages of this book in their home in the mountains in Walton, New York, on some unforgettably beautiful spring days.

I want to thank my Institute colleague Deb Strubel and Carol Staswick of Encounter Books for their important editorial advice and assistance.

I am honored to dedicate this book to my friend and teacher John W. Miller, who was the first person to urge me to write it. He gave me the great gift of teaching me why and how to study the world's oldest marriage laws, and has been a wonderful guide and mentor at every stage. He and his wife, Louise, are a truly inspiring example of what marriage can be.

Notes

Introduction

[1] G. K. Chesterton, *What's Wrong with the World* (1910; San Francisco: Ignatius Press, 1994), pp. 193–94.

[2] See Isaiah Berlin, "Two Conceptions of Liberty," in Berlin, *Four Essays on Liberty* (Oxford, U.K.: Oxford University Press, 1969); William A. Galston, *Liberal Pluralism: The Implications of Value Pluralism for Political Theory and Practice* (Cambridge, U.K.: Cambridge University Press, 2002).

[3] John Locke, *Two Treatises of Government* (1698; Cambridge, U.K.: Cambridge University Press, 1965), p. 319.

[4] In 2004 in the U.S., an estimated 35.7 percent of all births were to unmarried women. See Brady E. Hamilton et al., *Preliminary Births for 2004*, Health E–Stats (Hyattsville, Md.: National Center for Health Statistics, October 28, 2005), Table 1.

[5] Amara Bachu, *Trends in Marital Status of U.S. Women at First Birth: 1930 to 1994*, Population Division Working Paper no. 20 (Washington, D.C.: U.S. Bureau of the Census, March 1998), Table 1.

[6] William J. Goode, *World Changes in Divorce Patterns* (New Haven: Yale University Press, 1993), pp. 135–40, 153–54; Ailsa Burns, "Mother-Headed Families: An International Perspective and the Case of Australia," *Social Policy Report* 6, no. 1 (Spring 1992), pp. 6–7.

[7] Matthew Bramlett and William Mosher, "First Marriage Dissolution, Divorce, and Remarriage: United States," *Advance Data*, no. 323 (Hyattsville, Md.: National Center for Health Statistics, May 31, 2001); Rose M. Krieger and Jason M. Fields, "Number, Timing, and Duration of Marriages and Divorces: 1996," *Current Population Reports* P70–80 (Washington, D.C.: U.S. Census Bureau, February 2002), pp. 17–18.

[8] Bramlett and Mosher, "First Marriage Dissolution, Divorce, and Remarriage: United States."

[9] Larry L. Bumpass and James A. Sweet, "Children's Experience in Single-Parent Families: Implications of Cohabitation and Marital Transitions," *Family Planning Perspectives* 21, no. 6 (November–December 1989), pp. 259–60; Frank F. Furstenberg Jr. and Andrew J.

Cherlin, *Divided Families: What Happens to Children When Parents Part* (Cambridge, Mass.: Harvard University Press, 1991), p. 11.

[10] "To Fulfill These Rights," Remarks of President Lyndon B. Johnson at Howard University, Washington, D.C., June 4, 1965.

[11] *The Marriage Movement: A Statement of Principles* (New York: Institute for American Values, 2000), p. 4; *What Next for the Marriage Movement?* (New York: Institute for American Values, 2004), p. 5.

[12] Joshua R. Goldstein, "The Leveling of Divorce in the United States," *Demography* 36, no. 3 (August 1999), pp. 409–14.

[13] Brady E. Hamilton et al., *Preliminary Births for 2004,* Health E–Stats (Hyattsville, Md.: National Center for Health Statistics, October 28, 2005), Figure 2.

[14] Ibid., p. 5. See also *Facts at a Glance, 2005,* Publication 2005–02 (Washington, D.C.: Child Trends, March 2005).

[15] General Social Surveys, 1973–2002, National Opinion Research Center, University of Chicago. See also Paul R. Amato et al., "Continuity and Change in Marital Quality between 1980 and 2000," *Journal of Marriage and the Family* 65 (2003), pp. 1–22.

[16] Allen Dupree and Wendell Primus, *Declining Share of Children Lived with Single Mothers in the Late 1990s* (Washington, D.C.: Center on Budget and Policy Priorities, June 15, 2001).

[17] Sharon Vandivere, Kristen Anderson Moore, and Martha Zaslow, *Children's Family Environments: Findings from the National Survey of America's Families* (Washington, D.C.: Urban Institute, 2001); Gregory Acs and Sandi Nelson, *Changes in Family Structure and Child Well-Being: Evidence from the 2002 National Survey of America's Families* (Washington, D.C.: Urban Institute, August 15, 2003).

[18] Alex Kotlowitz, "It Takes a Wedding," *New York Times,* November 13, 2002.

[19] Jane Eisner, "After 35 Years, Marriage Found Its Spot on Society's Center Stage," *St. Paul Pioneer Press,* January 2, 2003.

[20] John le Carré, *The Incongruous Spy* (New York: Walker & Co., 1962), p. 77.

[21] Stephanie Coontz, *Marriage, a History: From Obedience to Intimacy, or How Love Conquered Marriage* (New York: Viking, 2005).

[22] George Elliot Howard, *A History of Matrimonial Institutions* (1904; New York: Humanities Press, 1964); Willystine Goodsell, *A History of the Family As a Social and Educational Institution* (New York: Macmillan, 1915); Edward Westermarck, *The History of Human Marriage,* 3 vols. (New York: Allerton Book Co., 1922).

[23] Stephanie Coontz seldom engages systematically with any one issue or body of evidence. Few individual topics get more than one or two sentences in a row. For example, her discussion of illegitimacy in matrilineal societies is assessed in Chapter Five, n. 58.

Chapter 1 ▪ What Is Marriage?

[1] Gregg Easterbrook, "Easterblogg," *New Republic Online*, posted November 21, 2003.

[2] David Brooks, "The Power of Marriage," *New York Times*, November 22, 2003.

[3] Richard Cohen, "This May Be Good for Marriage," *Washington Post*, November 20, 2003.

[4] Barbara J. Risman, quoted in Barbara Barrett, "Does Marriage Need Government's Help?" *Raleigh News and Observer*, January 19, 2004.

[5] E. J. Graff, "What Marriage Means," *Advocate*, February 29, 2000. See also E. J. Graff, *What Is Marriage For? The Strange History of Our Most Intimate Institution* (Boston: Beacon Press, 2000).

[6] Andrew Sullivan, "The Daily Dish," *AndrewSullivan.com*, posted November 29, 2003.

[7] Brief of the Professors of the History of Marriage, Families, and the Law as Amici Curiae in Support of Plaintiffs-Appellants, *Lewis v. Harris*, Supreme Court of New Jersey, Docket 58389 (Newark, October 6, 2005), pp. 1–2, 16.

[8] Nathaniel Frank, "Joining the Debate but Missing the Point," *New York Times*, February 29, 2004.

[9] "The Case for Gay Marriage," *Economist*, February 26, 2004.

[10] Dawn Barron, "Marriage Is a Civil Contract That Unites Two Individuals," *Olympian* (Olympia, Wash.), March 26, 2004.

[11] Rich Schmaltz, "Gay Marriage—What's All the Fuss?" *Cincinnati Enquirer*, August 4, 2004.

[12] Crispin Sartwell, "'Marriage Amendment' a Threat to Constitution," *Philadelphia Inquirer*, February 25, 2004.

[13] *Principles of the Law of Family Dissolution: Analysis and Recommendations* (Newark, N.J.: Matthew Bender & Co., 2002), p. 63.

[14] Opinion of the Justices, in *Goodridge v. Department of Public Health*, Massachusetts Supreme Judicial Court (Boston: November 18, 2003), pp. 2, 6–7.

[15] Memorandum Opinion and Order on Cross Motions for Summary Judgment, no. 04–2–04964–4 SEA, in *Andersen v. King County*, Superior Court of the State of Washington for King County (Seattle: August 4, 2004), pp. 5, 13.

[16] Justice Doris Ling-Cohan, Opinion in *Hernandez et al. v. City of New York,* Supreme Court of the State of New York (New York: February 4, 2005), pp. 11, 59–60.

[17] Law Commission of Canada, *Beyond Conjugality: Recognizing and Supporting Close Personal Adult Relationships* (Ottawa: 2001), pp. 129, xviii.

[18] Opinion of the Justices, no. SJC-08860, in *Goodridge v. Department of Public Health,* Massachusetts Supreme Judicial Court (Boston: November 18, 2003), p. 10.

[19] Helen E. Fisher, *Anatomy of Love: The Natural History of Monogamy, Adultery, and Divorce* (New York: W. W. Norton, 1992), p. 102.

[20] Bertrand Russell, *Marriage and Morals* (London: George Allen & Unwin Ltd., 1929), pp. 125, 189. See also p. 64.

[21] Opinion of the Justices, no. SJC-08860, in *Goodridge v. Department of Public Health,* p. 7.

[22] Opinions of the Justices to the Senate, no. SJC-09163, Massachusetts Supreme Judicial Court (Boston: February 3, 2004), p. 9.

[23] Arland Thornton, "Changing Attitudes toward Family Issues in the United States," *Journal of Marriage and the Family* 51, no. 4 (1989), pp. 873–93.

[24] See Norval D. Glenn, "Values, Attitudes, and the State of American Marriage," in *Promises to Keep: Decline and Renewal of Marriage in America,* ed. David Popenoe, Jean Bethke Elshtain, and David Blankenhorn (Lanham, Md.: Rowman & Littlefield, 1996), pp. 15–33.

Chapter 2 ▪ Prehistory

[1] Claude Masset, "Prehistory of the Family," in *A History of the Family,* vol. 1, *Distant Worlds, Ancient Worlds,* ed. Andre Burguiere et al. (Cambridge, Mass.: Harvard University Press, 1996), p. 71.

[2] Aristotle, *Ethics,* trans. J. A. K. Thompson (New York: Penguin Classics, 1965), bk. 8, no. xii (p. 280).

[3] *The Politics of Aristotle,* trans. Ernest Barker (London: Oxford University Press, 1958), bk. 1, ch. 2 (p. 3).

[4] Plutarch, "On Affection for Offspring," in *Moralia* VI, trans. W. C. Helmbold (Cambridge, Mass.: Harvard University Press, 1939), pp. 349, 351.

[5] Lucretius, *The Nature of the Universe,* trans. R. E. Latham (Baltimore: Penguin Books, 1964), pp. 199–200, 202.

[6] Ibid., 168. See also Aristotle, *Generation of Animals,* trans. A. L. Peck (Cambridge, Mass.: Harvard University Press, 1942), bk. 4, chs. 1–3

(pp. 395–417); "The Seed," in *Hippocratic Writings*, ed. G. E. R. Lloyd (New York: Penguin Books, 1983), pp. 317–23.

[7] Thomas Hobbes, *Leviathan* (1651; New York: Penguin Books, 1985), pp. 186, 254.

[8] John Locke, *Two Treatises of Government* (1698; Cambridge, U.K.: Cambridge University Press, 1965), p. 179.

[9] Ibid., pp. 206–7.

[10] Ibid., pp. 318–19.

[11] Ibid., pp. 214, 310, 319–20.

[12] Ibid., pp. 321–22. Locke's understanding of marriage, while formulated in a vocabulary more civic and political than overtly religious or confessional, is nevertheless remarkably consistent with the most important strands of religious thought about marriage in seventeenth-century Britain.

Recall Locke's argument that marriage was, for humans, "the first Society," and is the foundation of society as a whole. About three decades earlier, in 1667, John Milton in *Paradise Lost* (IV: 750–752) had written:

> Hail, wedded Love, mysterious law, true source
> Of human offspring, sole propriety
> In Paradise of all things common else!

In *Marriage Duties*, published in 1620 by the Puritan divine Thomas Gataker, a popular teacher and preacher of his generation, we similarly learn that marriage is important because "this societie is the first that ever was in the world," and that marriage "is the fountaine from which the rest flow." So when Locke, nearly eighty years later, called marriage "the first Society," he was drawing upon a well-established argument. As James Turner Johnson puts it: "To say that marriage is the foundation of all social life would be possible for all sorts of Englishmen in the early seventeenth century." See James Turner Johnson, *A Society Ordained by God: English Puritan Marriage Doctrine in the First Half of the Seventeenth Century* (Nashville: Abingdon Press, 1970), p. 103. The Gataker quotation is cited in Johnson, p. 94.

While this book's mode of exposition is essentially anthropological and historical, and therefore also secular, this excerpt from seventeenth-century British thought illustrates a larger theme. At most times and in most places in Western history, religiously informed ways of defining marriage, at least with respect to the institution's underlying "natural" foundations and purposes, clearly resemble and in most respects closely parallel secular and scholarly formulations;

moreover, there is essential agreement across the board about what, in essence, marriage is. It is also worth noting that the marriage idea from seventeenth-century Britain, in both its secular and religious iterations, crossed the Atlantic during that same century in order to serve as the foundation of the marriage culture of the United States.

To my knowledge, the best short overview of the conceptions and purposes of marriage in the Western Christian tradition is John Witte Jr., "The Goods and Goals of Marriage," *Notre Dame Law Review* 76, no. 3 (April 2001), pp. 1019–71.

[13] Sigmund Freud, *Totem and Taboo* (1913; New York: W. W. Norton, 1950), pp. 141, 149.

[14] Ibid., pp. 51, 141. See also Freud, *Civilization and Its Discontents* (1930; New York: W. W. Norton, 1961), pp. 70–80.

[15] Frederick Engels, *The Origin of the Family, Private Property, and the State* (1884; New York: Pathfinder Press, 1972), pp. 46, 50. See also J. J. Bachenof, *Myth, Religion, and Mother Right: Selected Writings of J. J. Bachenof* (Princeton, N.J.: Princeton University Press, 1973).

[16] Engels, *The Origin of the Family*, pp. 68–69.

[17] Ibid., pp. 74, 79.

[18] Ibid., p. 68.

[19] Claude Lévi-Strauss, *The View from Afar* (New York: Basic Books, 1985), pp. 40–41. Lévi-Strauss further concludes that what he calls the "conjugal family," based on monogamous marriage, "appears to be a practically universal phenomenon, present in every type of society."

[20] Claude Lévi-Strauss, "Introduction," in *A History of the Family*, vol. 1, *Distant Worlds, Ancient Worlds*, ed. Burguiere et al., p. 5.

[21] Helen E. Fisher, *Anatomy of Love: The Natural History of Monogamy, Adultery, and Divorce* (New York: W. W. Norton, 1992), p. 150.

[22] Pierre van den Berghe, *Human Family Systems: An Evolutionary View* (Prospect Heights, Ill.: Waveland Press, 1990), pp. 36–37; Peter J. Wilson, *Man the Promising Primate: The Conditions of Human Evolution*, 2nd ed. (New Haven: Yale University Press, 1983), p. 48; Donald Symons, *The Evolution of Human Sexuality* (New York: Oxford University Press, 1979), p. 130.

[23] Peter J. Wilson, *Man the Promising Primate*, p. 55.

[24] Edward O. Wilson, *On Human Nature* (Cambridge: Harvard University Press, 1978), p. 141; Van den Berghe, *Human Family Systems: An Evolutionary View*, pp. 40–45.

[25] Claude Masset, "Prehistory of the Family," in *A History of the Family*, vol. 1, *Distant Worlds, Ancient Worlds*, ed. Burguiere et al., p. 82. See also Symons, *The Evolution of Human Sexuality*, pp. 96–141.

[26] Peter J. Wilson, *Man the Promising Primate,* pp. 57, 67.

[27] Symons, *The Evolution of Human Sexuality,* pp. 76, 86; Helen Fisher, *The Sex Contract: The Evolution of Human Behavior* (New York: William Morrow, 1982), pp. 94–100.

[28] Paul W. Turke, "Concealed Ovulation, Menstrual Synchrony, and Paternal Investment," in *Biosocial Perspectives on the Family,* ed. Erik E. Filsinger (Newbury Park, Calif.: Sage Publications, 1988), pp. 119–36, esp. 124–25.

[29] Symons, *The Evolution of Human Sexuality,* p. 76.

[30] Peter J. Wilson, *Man the Promising Primate,* pp. 45–47.

[31] Ibid., p. 46.

[32] Sarah Blaffer Hrdy, *Mother Nature: A History of Mothers, Infants, and Natural Selection* (New York: Pantheon, 1999), pp. 383–93.

[33] Commission on Children at Risk, *Hardwired to Connect: The New Scientific Case for Authoritative Communities* (New York: Institute for American Values, 2003), pp. 16–32.

[34] Ibid., pp. 16–17.

[35] Rebecca A. Turner et al., "Preliminary Research on Plasma Oxytocin in Normal Cycling Women: Investigating Emotional and Interpersonal Distress," *Psychiatry: Interpersonal and Biological Processes* 62, no. 1 (Summer 1999), pp. 77–114; Lisa M. Diamond, "What Does Sexual Orientation Orient? A Biobehavioral Model Distinguishing Romantic Love and Sexual Desire," *Psychological Review* 110, no. 1 (2003), pp. 173–92.

[36] Andreas Bartels and Semir Zeki, "The Neural Correlates of Maternal and Romantic Love," *NeuroImage* 21 (2004), pp. 1155–66.

[37] Claude Lévi-Strauss, *The View from Afar* (New York: Basic Books, 1985), p. 40.

[38] Peter B. Gray et al., "Marriage and Fatherhood Are Associated with Lower Testosterone in Males," *Evolution and Human Behavior* 23 (2002): 193–201; Allan Mazur and Joel Michalek, "Marriage, Divorce, and Male Testosterone," *Social Forces* 77, no. 1 (1998), pp. 315–30.

[39] See Helen Fisher, *Why We Love: The Nature and Chemistry of Romantic Love* (New York: Henry Holt, 2004).

[40] Edward Westermarck, *The Future of Marriage in Western Civilization* (New York: Macmillan, 1936), p. 5. See also Westermarck, *History of Human Marriage,* vol. 1 (New York: Allerton Book Co., 1922), pp. 26–77.

[41] Alexander Marshack, *The Roots of Civilization* (New York: McGraw-Hill, 1972), pp. 305–39.

[42] Marija Gimbutas, *The Civilization of the Goddess: The World of Old Europe* (New York: HarperCollins, 1991), p. 342.
[43] Ibid., p. 222.
[44] Ibid., pp. 249, 342–49.
[45] Ibid., pp. 283, 331.
[46] Gerda Lerner, *The Creation of Patriarchy* (New York: Oxford University Press, 1986), pp. 30–31.

Chapter 3 ▪ The River Valleys

[1] John W. Miller, *Calling God "Father": Essays on the Bible, Fatherhood, and Culture* (New York: Paulist Press, 1999), pp. 18–22.
[2] Gerda Lerner, *The Creation of Patriarchy* (New York: Oxford University Press, 1986), pp. 125–31. See also James Frazer, *The Golden Bough: A Study in Magic and Religion* (1922; Ware, U.K.: Wordsworth Editions, 1993), p. 331.
[3] Herodotus, *The Histories*, trans. A. D. Godley (Cambridge, Mass.: Harvard University Press, 1966), bk 1: 199 (pp. 251–52) and bk 1: 196 (p. 249).
[4] See the King James Bible, 2 Kings 18:4; 2 Kings 23:7; Jeremiah 7:18; and Hosea 4:12–14. For discussions of this issue, see David R. Mace, *Hebrew Marriage* (London: Epworth Press, 1953), pp. 232–39; John W. Miller, *Meet the Prophets* (New York: Paulist Press, 1987), pp. 65–75, 81–83.
[5] Marten Stol, "Private Life in Ancient Mesopotamia," in *Civilizations of the Ancient Near East*, ed. Jack M. Sasson (Peabody, Mass.: Hendrickson Publishers, 2000), p. 493.
[6] Karen Rhea Nemet-Nejat, *Daily Life in Ancient Mesopotamia* (Peabody, Mass.: Hendrickson Publishers, 2002), p. 137; J. N. Postgate, *Early Mesopotamia: Society and Economy at the Dawn of History* (New York: Routledge, 1992), p. 106.
[7] See the introductions in *The Epic of Gilgamesh: A New Translation*, trans. Andrew George (New York: Penguin Classics, 1999); *The Epic of Gilgamesh*, ed. N. K. Sandars (New York: Penguin Classics, 1960).
[8] All Gilgamesh quotations are from the Sandars version of *The Epic of Gilgamesh*, pp. 62–63, 65, 67–69, 85–86, 88, 91, 102. The last quotation is similar to later words in the Hebrew scriptures, Ecclesiastes 9:8–9.
[9] Stol, "Private Life in Ancient Mesopotamia," p. 490.
[10] Gwendolyn Leick, *Mesopotamia: The Invention of the City* (New York: Penguin Books, 2001), pp. 13–14.
[11] Prologue to "Laws of Lipit-Ishtar," in Martha T. Roth, *Law Collections from Mesopotamia and Asia Minor* (Atlanta: Scholars Press, 1997), p. 25.

[12] Marija Gimbutas, *The Civilization of the Goddess: The World of Old Europe* (New York: HarperCollins, 1991), p. 342.

[13] "Lipit-Ishtar Lawcode," trans. S. N. Kramer, law no. 27, in *Ancient Near Eastern Texts*, ed. James B. Pritchard (Princeton, N.J.: Princeton University Press, 1950), p. 160.

[14] "Laws of Eshnunna," no. 27 and no. 28 (partial), in Roth, *Law Collections from Mesopotamia and Asia Minor*, p. 63.

[15] Postgate, *Early Mesopotamia*, p. 103.

[16] Ibid.; and Stol, "Private Life in Ancient Mesopotamia," p. 489.

[17] Stol, "Private Life in Ancient Mesopotamia," p. 489.

[18] Postgate, *Early Mesopotamia*, pp. 103–4.

[19] "The Laws of Eshnunna," trans. Albert Goetz, in *Ancient Near Eastern Texts*, ed. Pritchard, p. 163. The original text of this law is defective, and as a result, while the basic meaning and intent of the law are not in dispute, the exact translation is. See Roth, *Law Collections from Mesopotamia and Asia Minor*, p. 70; and Hans Jochen Boecker, *Law and the Administration of Justice in the Old Testament and Ancient Near East* (Minneapolis: Augsburg Publishing House, 1980), p. 62.

[20] Stol, "Private Life in Ancient Mesopotamia," p. 489; and Jean-Jacques Glassner, "From Sumer to Babylon," in *A History of the Family*, vol. 1, *Distant Worlds, Ancient Worlds*, ed. Burguiere et al. (Cambridge, Mass.: Harvard University Press, 1996), pp. 107–8.

[21] In this section I have summarized the main points of law provisions 128 through 164 of the Code of Hammurabi, relying on both the translation by Theophile J. Meek in *Ancient Near Eastern Texts*, ed. Pritchard, pp. 171–73; and the one in Roth, *Law Collections from Mesopotamia and Asia Minor*, pp. 105–12.

[22] Annie Forgeau, "The Pharaonic Order," in *A History of the Family*, vol. 1, *Distant Worlds, Ancient Worlds*, ed. Burguiere et al., p. 130.

[23] Says Colossians 3:21 (King James Version): "Fathers, provoke not your children to anger, lest they be discouraged." And Ephesians 6:4: "And, ye fathers, provoke not your children to wrath: but bring them up in the nurture and admonition of the Lord." Apart from the more general and of course quite frequent instruction to obey God, I believe that these may be the only two statements in the Bible that constitute specific instructions to fathers on how to treat their children. This fact suggests to me that the Bible, while sometimes criticized for its hard sayings, not to mention its patriarchal bias, is in fact quite sensitive to the exact father-child problem that Ptah-Hotep is discussing, and that it suggests, by way of solution, pretty much the opposite of Ptah-Hotep's approach.

[24] "The Instructions of the Vizier Ptah-Hotep," trans. John A. Wilson, in *Ancient Near Eastern Texts,* ed. Pritchard, pp. 413–14.

[25] "The Instructions of Ani," trans. John A. Wilson, in *Ancient Near Eastern Texts,* ed. Pritchard, p. 421.

[26] "The Instructions of the Vizier Ptah-Hotep," pp. 468–69.

[27] Samuel N. Kramer, *The Sumerians: Their History, Culture, and Character* (Chicago: University of Chicago Press, 1963), pp. 115–16, 160–62. See also Jean Bottero, *Religion in Ancient Mesopotamia* (Chicago: University of Chicago Press, 2001), pp. 94–95.

[28] Herodotus, *The Histories,* trans. Godley, bk. 2: 121, 126, 135 (pp. 413–23, 429, 437–39).

[29] The refrain of this hymn is "The city's built on pleasure!" Benjamin R. Foster, *From Distant Days: Myths, Tales, and Poetry of Ancient Mesopotamia* (Bethesda, Md.: CDL Press, 1995), p. 349. See also Bottero, *Religion in Ancient Mesopotamia,* p. 67.

[30] *The Epic of Gilgamesh,* ed. Sandars, p. 86.

[31] Kramer, *The Sumerians,* pp. 291–99; David Bakan, *And They Took Themselves Wives: The Emergence of Patriarchy in Western Civilization* (San Francisco: Harper & Row, 1979), p. 32.

[32] For definitions of "social institution" that are consistent with, and help to inform, the way that I am using the term, see Talcott Parsons, *The Social System* (New York: Free Press, 1951), pp. 39–40; David Popenoe, *Sociology* (Englewood Cliffs, N.J.: Prentice Hall, 1995), p. 83.

[33] Charles Frankel, *The Case for Modern Man* (New York: Harper & Brothers, 1955), p. 203.

[34] "The Creation Epic," trans. E. A. Speiser, in *Ancient Near Eastern Texts,* ed. Pritchard, pp. 60–72.

[35] Bottero, *Religion in Ancient Mesopotamia,* pp. 74–75; Leick, *Mesopotamia: The Invention of the City,* pp. 19–21, 252; Kramer, *The Sumerians,* pp. 122, 148.

[36] See, for example, Genesis 15:4, 18.

[37] Bakan, *And They Took Themselves Wives,* pp. 12, 70, 138.

[38] "Enki and Ninhursag: A Paradise Myth," trans. S. N. Kramer, in *Ancient Near Eastern Texts,* ed. Pritchard, pp. 37–41, especially lines 250–268. See also Kramer, *The Sumerians,* pp. 147–49.

[39] Lerner, *The Creation of Patriarchy,* p. 149.

[40] Mace, *Hebrew Marriage,* pp. 206, 263.

[41] Bottero, *Religion in Ancient Mesopotamia,* p. 66.

[42] *The Law Code of Manu,* trans. Patrick Olivelle (New York: Oxford University Press, 2004), p. 157. See also the Dharmasutra of Vasistha

17:6–11, in *Dharmasutras*, trans. Olivelle (New York: Oxford University Press, 1999), p. 293.

[43] *The Meaning of the Glorious Koran*, trans. Mohammed Marmaduke Pickthall (New York: Meridian Books, 1997), 23:13, 80:18–19, 86:5–7.

[44] Plato, *Timaeus*, trans. Donald J. Zeyl (Indianapolis: Hackett, 2000), pp. 86–87. See also "The Seed," in *Hippocratic Writings*, ed. G. E. R. Lloyd (New York: Penguin Books, 1983), pp. 317–23.

[45] Aristotle, *Generation of Animals*, trans. A. L. Peck (Cambridge, Mass.: Harvard University Press, 1942), bk. 1, chs. 22, 119; bk. 4, chs. 3, 403; bk. 4, chs. 4, 443; bk. 2, chs. 4, 185; bk. 1, chs. 11, 113; bk. 2, chs. 4, 193; bk. 2, chs. 1, 133; bk. 4, chs. 6, 461; bk. 5, chs. 3, 525.

[46] *Aeschylus 1: Oresteia*, trans. Richmond Lattimore (Chicago: University of Chicago Press, 1953), pp. 140, 148, 158. See also R. P. Winnington-Ingram, "Clytemnestra and the Vote of Athena," *Journal of Hellenistic Studies* 68 (1948), pp. 130–47. For analyses of this play in relationship to reproductive theory more generally in the ancient Near East and elsewhere, see Erich Fromm, "The Theory of Mother Right and Social Psychology," in Fromm, *The Crisis of Psychoanalysis* (Greenwich, Conn.: Fawcett Publications, 1970), pp. 114–16; Grace Harris, "Furies, Witches, and Mothers," in *The Character of Kinship*, ed. Jack Goody (London: Cambridge University Press, 1973), pp. 145–59; Lerner, *The Creation of Patriarchy*, pp. 205–11; and John W. Miller, *Calling God "Father": Essays on the Bible, Fatherhood, and Culture* (New York: Paulist Press, 1999), pp. 18–22.

[47] See Appendix, "Patrocentrism and Preformation," pp. 247–48.

Chapter 4 ▪ Trobriand Islands

[1] This debate is extensive. See Ernest Jones, "Mother-Right and the Sexual Ignorance of Savages," *International Journal of Psycho-Analysis* 6, Part 2 (April 1925), pp. 109–30; Alex C. Rentoul, "Physiological Paternity and the Trobrianders," *Man*, vol. 31 (August 1931), pp. 152–54; F. G. Lounsbury, "Another View of Trobriand Kinship Categories," *American Anthropologist*, n.s. 67, no. 5, Part 2 (October 1965), pp. 142–85; Edmund Leach, "Virgin Birth," *Proceedings of the Royal Anthropological Institute of Great Britain and Ireland*, no. 1966 (1966), pp. 39–49; Melford E. Spiro, "Virgin Birth, Parthenogenesis, and Physiological Paternity: An Essay in Cultural Interpretation," *Man*, n.s. 3, no. 2 (June 1968), pp. 242–61; Spiro, "Virgin Birth," *Man*, n.s. 7, no. 2 (June 1972), pp. 315–16; H. A. Powell, "Territory, Hierarchy and Kinship in Kiriwina," *Man*, n.s. 4, no. 4 (December 1969), pp. 580–604; Susan Montague, "Trobriand Kinship and the Virgin

Birth Controversy," *Man*, n.s. 6, no. 3 (September 1971), pp. 353–68; J. A. Barnes, "Genetrix: Genitor: Nature: Culture," in *The Character of Kinship*, ed. Jack Goody (Cambridge, U.K.: Cambridge University Press, 1973), pp. 61–73; Carol Delaney, "The Meaning of Paternity and the Virgin Birth Debate," *Man*, n.s. 21, no. 3 (1986), pp. 493–513; Andre Van Dokkum, "Belief Systems about Virgin Birth: Structure and Mutual Comparability," *Current Anthropology* 38, no. 1 (February 1997), pp. 99–104; Dokkum, "On 'Virgin Birth' and a Paradox of Procreation," *Current Anthropology* 41, no. 3 (June 2000), pp. 429–30. An important early book that, along with the Malinowski corpus, helped to frame much of the subsequent debate on this issue is Ashley Montagu, *Coming into Being among the Australian Aborigines: The Procreative Beliefs of the Australian Aborigines*, 2nd ed. (1937; London: Routledge & Keegan Paul, 1974).

2 Bronislaw Malinowski, *Sex, Culture, and Myth* (New York: Harcourt, Brace & World, 1962), p. 68.

3 Bronislaw Malinowski, *The Sexual Life of Savages in North-Western Melanesia* (1929; Boston: Beacon Press, 1987), p. 3.

4 Susan Montague, "Trobriand Kinship and the Virgin Birth Controversy," *Man*, n.s. 6, no. 3 (September 1971), p. 360.

5 Bronislaw Malinowski, *Crime and Custom in Savage Society* (1926; Paterson, N.J.: Littlefield, Adams & Co., 1959), pp. 35–36.

6 Malinowski, *Sexual Life*, pp. 103, 69.

7 Bronislaw Malinowski, *Coral Gardens and Their Magic: A Study of the Methods of Tilling the Soil and of Agricultural Rites in the Trobriand Islands* (1935; New York: Dover Publications, 1978).

8 Malinowski, *Sexual Life*, pp. 78, 103–4.

9 H. A. Powell, "Genealogy, Residence and Kinship in Kiriwina," *Man*, n.s. 4, no. 2 (June 1969), p. 197; Powell, review of *Women of Value, Men of Renown* by Annette B. Weiner, in *American Anthropologist*, n.s. 82, no. 3 (September 1980), p. 701.

10 Malinowski, *Coral Gardens*, pp. 207–17.

11 Malinowski, *Sexual Life*, pp. 24–26, 42.

12 Ibid., p. 15.

13 Ibid., p. 227.

14 Ibid., p. 121; Annette B. Weiner, *Women of Value, Men of Renown: New Perspectives in Trobriand Exchange* (Austin: University of Texas Press), pp. 190–91.

15 Malinowski, *Sexual Life*, p. 122.

16 Girls try hard to avoid being seen entering or leaving their boyfriends' bachelors' house, and strictly avoid eating food with or in

front of their boyfriends, since eating together in Trobriand culture is a sign of a much more serious, about-to-be-married relationship. See Malinowski, *Sexual Life*, pp. 57–64, 80–81; Weiner, *Women of Value*, pp. 169–73, 187. See also Norval Glenn and Elizabeth Marquardt, *Hooking Up, Hanging Out, and Hoping for Mr. Right: College Women on Dating and Mating Today* (New York: Institute for American Values, 2001).

17 Marguerite S. Robinson, "Complementary Filiation and Marriage in the Trobriand Islands: A Re-Examination of Malinowski's Material," in *Marriage in Tribal Societies*, ed. Meyer Fortes (Cambridge, U.K.: Cambridge University Press, 1972), pp. 123, 128.

18 Ibid., pp. 130–32. The sequence of marriage gift exchanges is also described in Malinowski, *Sexual Life*, pp. 76–80.

19 Annette B. Weiner, *The Trobrianders of Papua New Guinea* (New York: Holt, Rinehart & Winston, 1988), p. 78.

20 Weiner, *Women of Value*, pp. 183–84.

21 Robinson, "Complementary Filiation and Marriage," p. 138.

22 Weiner, *Women of Value*, pp. 189–90.

23 Malinowski, *Sexual Life*, p. 65.

24 Malinowski, *Crime and Custom*, p. 34.

25 Ibid..; Robinson, "Complementary Filiation and Marriage," pp. 149–50; Annette B. Weiner, "Reproduction: A Replacement for Reciprocity," *American Ethnologist* 7, no. 1 (1980), p. 81.

26 Malinowski, *Sexual Life*, pp. 17–18. On the meaning of *kopo'i*, see also Weiner, *The Trobrianders*, p. 56.

27 Stanley N. Kurtz, "A Trobriand Complex," *Ethos* 21, no. 1 (1993), p. 99.

28 Malinowski, *Crime and Custom*, p. 101; and Malinowski, *Argonauts of the Western Pacific* (1922; Long Grove, Ill.: Waveland Press, 1984), pp. 71–72.

29 Malinowski, *Sexual Life*, p. 7.

30 Weiner, *Women of Value*, p. 125.

31 Malinowski, *Sexual Life*, pp. 165–68.

32 Ibid., p. 166.

33 Ibid., pp. 174–76.

34 Weiner, *Women of Value*, pp. 123–29; Weiner, *The Trobrianders*, pp. 5–61; Malinowski, *Sexual Life*, pp. 171, 175–76.

35 See A. R. Radcliffe-Brown, "Patrilineal and Matrilineal Succession," in Radcliffe-Brown, *Structure and Function in Primitive Society* (Glencoe, Ill.: Free Press, 1952), pp. 32–48. See also Meyer Fortes, "The Structure of Unilineal Descent Groups," *American Anthropologist*, n.s. 55, no. 1 (January–March 1953), pp. 17–41; Fortes, "Descent, Filiation and

Affinity: A Rejoinder to Dr. Leach," Part I in *Man* 59 (November 1959), pp. 193–97, and Part II in *Man* 59 (December 1959), pp. 206–12; and Edmund Leach, "Complementary Filiation and Bilateral Kinship," in *The Character of Kinship*, ed. Jack Goody (Cambridge, U.K.: Cambridge University Press, 1973), pp. 53–58. Also see Appendix, "Bilateral Filiation," pp. 248–54.

36 Malinowski, *Crime and Custom*, pp. 106–11; and *Sexual Life*, 177–78; and Robinson, "Complementary Filiation and Marriage," pp. 123, 150–51.

37 Malinowski, *Crime and Custom*, p. 109.

38 Robinson, "Complementary Filiation and Marriage," p. 155.

39 Malinowski, *Sex, Culture, and Myth*, pp. 62–63. See also Malinowski, *Sexual Life*, p. 172.

40 Malinowski, *Sex and Repression in Savage Society* (1927; London: Routledge, 2001), pp. 169–70. In *Coral Gardens* (p. 208), Malinowski simply writes that the principle of legitimacy "decrees that all children must have a father."

41 Malinowski, *Sexual Life*, pp. 165–66.

42 Talcott Parsons, "The Incest Taboo in Relation to Social Structure and the Socialization of the Child," *British Journal of Sociology* 5, no. 2 (June 1954), p. 102. Regarding the structure and erotic economy of the nuclear family, Parsons also concludes (p. 104) that "in view of the wide variety of human customs in so many respects, its relative uniformity is impressive and deserves to be counted as one of the most important universals of human society."

43 Radcliffe-Brown, *Structure and Function*, p. 38.

44 Meyer Fortes, "Malinowski and the Study of Kinship," in *Man and Culture: An Evaluation of the Work of Bronislaw Malinowski*, ed. Raymond Firth (London: Routledge & Keegan Paul, 1960), p. 187.

45 Meyer Fortes, "Filiation Reconsidered," in Fortes, *Kinship and the Social Order* (Chicago: Aldine Publishing Co., 1969), pp. 251–52, 261–62, 264. For these reasons, Fortes also (p. 253) defines filiation as "the relationship created by the fact of being the legitimate child of one's parents."

In 1965, the anthropologist Margaret Mead made this same basic point with admirable succinctness. She reports that all human societies "insist that women must have husbands, so that children may have fathers." That's the key idea. She continues: "There are no people anywhere, whatever their race and however simple and primitive their way of life, who do not have the idea of legitimacy; there are no people who do not, in the simplest sense, differentiate between a child with a recognized father and a child without one." Margaret Mead and Ken Hyman, *Family* (New York: Macmillan, 1965), p. 45.

Chapter 5 ■ What Marriage Is

1 James A. Brundage, *Law, Sex, and Christian Society in Medieval Europe* (Chicago: University of Chicago Press, 1987), pp. 89–93, 138–40; Philip Lyndon Reynolds, *Marriage in the Western Church: The Christianization of Marriage during the Patristic and Early Medieval Periods* (Boston: Brill Academic Publishers, 2001), pp. 32, 258, 328. See also Levin L. Schucking, *The Puritan Family* (New York: Schocken Books, 1970), pp. 21–23.

2 See Appendix, "Polygyny and Polyandry," pp. 254–56.

3 Robin Fox, *Kinship and Marriage: An Anthropological Perspective* (Baltimore: Penguin Books, 1967), p. 27.

4 Ladislav Holy, *Anthropological Perspectives on Kinship* (London: Pluto Press, 1996), p. 124.

5 Jack R. Goody, "Marriage Prestations, Inheritance and Descent in Pre Industrial Societies," *Journal of Comparative Family Studies* 1, no. 1 (Autumn 1970), p. 37.

6 Pierre L. van den Berghe, *Human Family Systems: An Evolutionary View* (Prospect Heights, Ill.: Waveland Press, 1979), pp. 45, 47.

7 Suzanne G. Frayser, *Varieties of Sexual Experience: An Anthropological Perspective on Human Sexuality* (New Haven, Conn.: HRAF Press, 1985), p. 248.

8 Laura Betzig, "Causes of Conjugal Dissolution: A Cross-Cultural Study," *Current Anthropology* 30, no. 5 (December 1989), pp. 654–76. The quotation is from p. 668.

9 George Murdock, *Social Structure* (New York: Macmillan, 1949), p. 1.

10 Edward Westermarck, *The Future of Marriage in Western Civilization* (New York: Macmillan, 1936), p. 21.

11 Quoted in Brundage, *Law, Sex, and Christian Society*, p. 136.

12 E. R. Leach, "Polyandry, Inheritance and the Definition of Marriage: With Particular Reference to Sinhalese Customary Law," in *Rethinking Anthropology* (London: Athlone Press, 1961), pp. 105–13.

13 Ibid., p. 183. See also Appendix, "The Disappearance of Kinship?" pp. 259–61.

14 Douglass C. North, "Economic Performance through Time," *American Economic Review* 84, no. 3 (June 1994), pp. 360–61. See also Lance E. Davis and Douglass C. North, *Institutional Change and American Economic Growth* (Cambridge, U.K.: Cambridge University Press, 1971).

15 A. R. Radcliffe-Brown, *Structure and Function in Primitive Society* (Glencoe, Ill.: Free Press, 1952), pp. 10–11.

[16] *Dharmasutras: The Law Codes of Ancient India*, trans. Patrick Olivelle (Oxford, U.K.: Oxford University Press, 1999), pp. 86, 367.

[17] *The Law Code of Manu*, trans. Patrick Olivelle (Oxford, U.K.: Oxford University Press, 2004), pp. 75, 161.

[18] *Dharmasutras*, p. 55.

[19] Joan Frigole Reixach, "Procreation and Its Implications for Gender, Marriage, and Family in European Rural Ethnography," *Anthropological Quarterly* 71, no. 1 (January 1998), p. 37.

[20] Radcliffe-Brown, *Structure and Function in Primitive Society*, pp. 30–31. Radcliffe-Brown also writes: "Marriage is a social arrangement by which a child is given a legitimate position in the society, determined by parenthood in the social sense." See A. R. Radcliffe-Brown, Introduction to *African Systems of Kinship and Marriage*, ed. Radcliffe-Brown and Daryll Forde (London: Oxford University Press, 1950), p. 4.

[21] *Notes and Queries on Anthropology*, 6th ed. (London: Routledge & Keegan Paul, 1951), p. 71.

[22] Kathleen Gough, "Nayar: Central Kerala," in *Matrilineal Kinship*, ed. David M. Schneider and Kathleen Gough (Berkeley: University of California Press, 1961), p. 363.

[23] Van den Berghe, *Human Family Systems: An Evolutionary View*, p. 46.

[24] Alan Barnard, "Rules and Prohibitions: The Form and Content of Human Kinship," in *Companion Encyclopedia of Anthropology*, ed. Tim Ingold (London: Routledge, 1994), p. 798. See also Conrad Phillip Kottak, *Anthropology: The Exploration of Human Diversity* (New York: Random House, 1974), p. 281.

[25] For a summary of this research, see Linda J. Waite and Maggie Gallagher, *The Case for Marriage: Why Married People Are Happier, Healthier, and Better Off Financially* (New York: Doubleday, 2000), pp. 97–123. See also a publication co-authored by a diverse panel of thirteen leading family scholars, *Why Marriage Matters: Twenty-one Conclusions from the Social Sciences* (New York: Institute for American Values, 2002), pp. 9–11.

[26] Bronislaw Malinowski, *The Sexual Life of Savages in North-Western Melanesia* (1929; Boston: Beacon Press, 1987), pp. 416–21.

[27] A. R. Radcliffe-Brown, Introduction to *African Systems of Kinship and Marriage*, ed. Radcliffe-Brown and Daryll Forde, pp. 42–46; Arthur Phillips, ed., *Survey of African Marriage and Family Life* (London: Oxford University Press, 1953), pp. xv, 2–4.

[28] See Claude Lévi-Strauss, *The Elementary Structures of Kinship* (Boston: Beacon Press, 1969; first published in French, 1949). See also Lévi-Strauss, "The Family," in *Man, Culture, and Society*, ed. Harold L. Shapiro (New York: Oxford University Press, 1956), pp. 261–85.

[29] I am grateful to Stanley N. Kurtz for discussing this issue with me. See his valuable book, *All the Mothers Are One: Hindu India and the Cultural Reshaping of Psychoanalysis* (New York: Columbia University Press, 1992).

[30] The most important example is E. Kathleen Gough, "The Nayars and the Definition of Marriage," *Journal of the Royal Anthropological Institute of Great Britain and Ireland* 89, no. 1 (January–June 1959), pp. 23–34. Gough proposes to alter the definition of marriage in order to make the Nayars fit. I understand her concern, and I agree that marriage is fundamentally connected to the legitimization of children, but I think her proposal a mistake. As others have argued, and as I try to suggest in this chapter, instead of torturing the definition of marriage to make the Nayars fit, it's probably better simply to admit that, for obvious historical reasons, the Nayar mating system is a dramatic exception to the rule. For a Nayar-friendly definition of marriage, Gough (p. 32) suggests the following: "Marriage is a relationship established between a woman and one or more other persons, which provides that a child born to the woman under circumstances not prohibited by the rules of the relationship, is accorded full birth-status rights common to normal members of his society or social stratum."

[31] *The Law Code of Manu*, pp. 19–20.

[32] Gough, "Nayar: Central Kerala," p. 357.

[33] Ibid., pp. 360–63.

[34] Cited in ibid., p. 370.

[35] Gough, "The Nayars and the Definition of Marriage," p. 24.

[36] Gough, "Nayar: Central Kerala," p. 329. See also Linda Stone, *Kinship and Gender: An Introduction* (Boulder, Col.: Westview Press, 1997), pp. 137–42.

[37] Fox, *Kinship and Marriage*, pp. 100–3; Lévi-Strauss, "The Family," pp. 262–63; Radcliffe-Brown, *Structure and Function in Primitive Society*, pp. 6–41.

[38] Gough, "Nayar: Central Kerala," p. 372, also p. 383.

[39] For discussion of this phenomenon outside Nuerland, see Melville J. Herskovits, "A Note on 'Woman Marriage' in Dahomey," *Africa* 10, no. 3 (1937), pp. 335–41; Laura Bohannan, "Dohomean Marriage: A Revaluation," *Africa* 19, no. 4 (1949), pp. 273–87; Eileen Jensen Krige, "Woman-Marriage, with Special Reference to the Lovedu—Its Significance for the Definition of Marriage," *Africa* 44 (1974), pp. 11–37.

[40] E. E. Evans-Pritchard, *Kinship and Marriage among the Nuer* (Oxford, U.K.: Oxford University Press, 1951), pp. 71–74.

41 Ibid., pp. 58–98. His discussion of the role of bridewealth in Nuer marriage and Nuer society is extensive and masterful.

42 Ibid., p. 108.

43 Ibid., p. 109. Basically the same practice occurs in other societies as well. For example, in the Hebrew scriptures we learn that Er, the son of Judah and the brother of Onan, has died: "And Judah said unto Onan, Go unto thy brother's wife, and marry her, and raise up seed to thy brother." King James Bible, Genesis 38:8. See also "The Levirate Marriage," in David R. Mace, *Hebrew Marriage: A Sociological Study* (London: Epworth Press, 1953), pp. 95–118.

44 Ibid.

45 Ibid., pp. 120, 122.

46 Gilbert H. Herdt, "Ritualized Homosexual Behavior: An Introduction," in *Ritualized Homosexuality in Melanesia*, ed. Herdt (Berkeley: University of California Press, 1984), pp. 6–7.

47 E. E. Evans-Pritchard, "Sexual Inversion among the Azande," *American Anthropologist*, n.s. 72, no. 6 (December 1970), p. 1429.

48 Ibid., pp. 1430–31.

49 Herdt, "Ritualized Homosexual Behavior," pp. 6, 65–66.

50 Linda S. Stone, "Gay Marriage and Anthropology," *Anthropology News*, May 2004.

51 Ibid.

52 Denis Foster Johnston, *An Analysis of Sources of Information on the Population of the Navaho*, Smithsonian Institution Bureau of American Ethnology, Bulletin 197 (Washington, D.C.: U.S. Government Printing Office, 1966), pp. 1, 7, 14, 30, 44–45; Gary Witherspoon, "A New Look at Navajo Social Organization," *American Anthropologist*, n.s. 72, no. 1 (February 1970), pp. 60–65. See also Louise Lamphere, "Ceremonial Co-Operation and Networks: A Reanalysis of the Navajo Outfit," *Man*, n.s. 5, no. 1 (March 1970), pp. 39–59.

53 Dorothea Leighton and Clyde Kluckhohn, *Children of the People* (Cambridge, Mass.: Harvard University Press, 1947), p. 76.

54 Ibid., p. 46.

55 Stone, *Kinship and Gender*, p. 127.

56 Leighton and Kluckhohn, *Children of the People*, p. 80.

57 David F. Aberle, "Navaho," in *Matrilineal Kinship*, ed. Schneider and Gough, p. 128.

58 It is also hard to reconcile with Stephanie Coontz's perfunctory assertion that "the concept of illegitimacy is completely foreign to matrilineal societies, such as the Navajo people of North America, in which descent and inheritance pass through the female line." This

constitutes her entire discussion of illegitimacy in matrilineal societies in her book *Marriage, a History: From Obedience to Intimacy, or How Love Conquered Marriage* (New York: Viking, 2005), p. 29.

Coontz is wrong on the Navajo in particular and wrong in her larger claim about the concept of illegitimacy, as can be seen in the seminal field research of Bronislaw Malinowski on the matrilineal peoples of the Trobriand Islands (see Chapter Four). Based on this research, Malinowski developed a general anthropological principal that he called the *rule of legitimacy,* holding that in all human societies, matrilineal as well as patrilineal, people clearly distinguish between legitimate (born to married parents) and illegitimate (born to an unmarried mother) births, and view the mother-child unit alone, without a socially recognized father, as sociologically incomplete and therefore not desirable.

What is the basis of Coontz's wildly inaccurate assertion? It is hard to be sure, since she rarely bothers with detail and almost never explains her terms, but she seems to believe that "the concept of illegitimacy" centers fundamentally on *inheritance.* She repeatedly stresses that connection; and this (utterly confused) idea might explain why she would write that "the concept of illegitimacy is completely foreign to matrilineal societies." After all, virtually by definition, children in matrilineal societies legally inherit through their mothers! More broadly, Coontz's apparent belief that the concept of legitimacy is reducible to conflicts over inheritance is consistent with her general (basically Marxist) belief that historically *marriage itself* is fundamentally reducible to conflicts over property.

But I am only guessing. This particular assertion by Coontz remains a mystery. Someone writing about anthropological research on marriage and yet not really knowing what "illegitimacy" means is like someone writing about art history and yet not really knowing what "nude" means.

59 Aberle, "Navaho," p. 128.

60 Ibid., pp. 96, 129.

61 Leighton and Kluckhohn, *Children of the People,* pp. 13, 19–22, 27, 30–32.

62 Ibid., pp. 54, 59, 247.

63 Gary Witherspoon, *Navajo Kinship and Marriage* (Chicago: University of Chicago Press, 1975), pp. 32–33.

64 Witherspoon, "A New Look at Navajo Social Organization," p. 59.

65 Malinowski, *The Sexual Life of Savages in North-Western Melanesia,* pp. 165–66.

[66] Mike Anton, "Marriage a Malleable Institution throughout History," *Los Angeles Times*, March 31, 2004.

[67] Evan Wolfson, *Why Marriage Matters: America, Equality, and Gay People's Right to Marry* (New York: Simon & Schuster, 2004), pp. 3, 6, 60.

[68] Ibid., pp. 88–89.

[69] David Popenoe, "Can the Nuclear Family Be Revived?" *Society* 35, no. 5 (July–August, 1999), republished in Popenoe, *War over the Family* (New Brunswick, N.J.: Transaction Publishers, 2005), p. 207.

[70] "The Scholarly Consensus on Marriage," Center for Marriage and Families Fact Sheet no. 2 (New York: Institute for American Values, 2006).

[71] David Popenoe and Barbara Dafoe Whitehead, *The State of Our Unions: The Social Health of Marriage in America, 2005* (Piscataway, N.J.: Rutgers University National Marriage Project, 2005), p. 24.

[72] Popenoe, "Can the Nuclear Family Be Revived?" p. 207.

[73] Kristin Anderson Moore et al., *Marriage from a Child's Perspective: How Does Family Structure Affect Children, and What Can We Do about It?* (Washington, D.C.: Child Trends, Research Brief, June 2002), pp. 1–2, 6. For the same point, see also Patrick Heuveline, Jeffrey M. Timberlake, and Frank F. Furstenberg Jr., "Shifting Childrearing to Single Mothers: Results from 17 Western Countries," *Population and Development Review* 29, no. 1 (March 2003), p. 48.

[74] For a short and in my view brilliant explanation of why kin relationships can never be reduced to economic relationships, see David M. Schneider, "The Nature of Kinship," *Man* 64 (November–December 1964), pp. 180–81.

[75] Two books document this history in considerable detail: Reynolds, *Marriage in the Western Church;* and Brundage, *Law, Sex, and Christian Society in Medieval Europe.* See also the opening chapter of John Witte Jr., *From Sacrament to Contract: Marriage, Religion, and Law in the Western Tradition* (Louisville, Ky.: Westminster John Knox Press, 1997). I am grateful to John Witte and James Turner Johnson for discussing these issues with me.

[76] Reynolds, *Marriage in the Western Church*, pp. 370–85.

Chapter 6 ▪ Deinstitutionalize Marriage?

[1] See www.unmarried.org.

[2] "The Alternatives to Marriage Project Welcomes Same-Sex Marriage in Massachusetts—and Looks Ahead," press release, May 16, 2004, Alternatives to Marriage Project, Albany, N.Y. See also Dorian Solot and Marshall Miller, *Unmarried to Each Other: The Essential Guide to*

Living Together as an Unmarried Couple (New York: Marlowe & Co., 2002).

[3] Jonathan Rauch, *Gay Marriage: Why It Is Good for Gays, Good for Straights, and Good for America* (New York: Times Books, 2004), pp. 89–90, 93.

[4] Ibid., p. 24.

[5] Judith Stacey, *Patriarchy and Socialist Revolution in China* (Berkeley: University of California Press, 1983), p. 1.

[6] Judith Stacey, "When Patriarchy Kowtows: The Significance of the Chinese Family Revolution for Feminist Theory," in *Capitalist Patriarchy and the Case for Socialist Feminism*, ed. Zillah Eisenstein (New York: Monthly Review Press, 1979), pp. 299–348.

[7] Judith Stacey, *Brave New Families* (New York: Basic Books, 1990).

[8] Judith Stacey, *In the Name of the Family: Rethinking Family Values in the Postmodern Age* (Boston: Beacon Press, 1996), esp. ch. 3.

[9] The founding statement of the Council on Families is *Marriage in America: A Report to the Nation* (New York: Institute for American Values, 1995). See also David Popenoe, Jean Bethke Elshtain, and David Blankenhorn, eds., *Promises to Keep: Decline and Renewal of Marriage in America* (Lanham, Md.: Rowman & Littlefield, 1996). A cofounder (with Stacey) of the Council on Contemporary Families, Arlene Skolnick, criticizes our work in "Family Values: The Sequel," *American Prospect* (May–June 1997), pp. 86–94. One of Stacey's most recent criticisms of our work is in Melanie Heath and Judith Stacey, "Transatlantic Family Travail," *American Journal of Sociology* 108, no. 3 (November 2002), pp. 658–68.

[10] Stacey was an expert witness in the *Halpern* case in Ontario, Canada, which was the major court case regarding the adoption of same-sex marriage in Canada. See "Reply Factum of the Applicant Couples," *Halpern v. Canada (A.G.)*, Ontario Superior Court of Justice (Toronto: Epstein Cole LLP, October 2001), para. 80–82.

[11] Judith Stacey, "Lesbian and Gay Families Are Songbirds in the Mine," paper for the Fourth Annual BlueCross BlueShield of Massachusetts Invitational Journalism-Work/Family Conference (Waltham, Mass.: Community, Families, and Work Program, Women's Studies Research Center, Brandeis University, August 26, 2003), p. 1.

[12] See Victoria Clarke and Sara-Jane Finlay, "'For Better or Worse?': Lesbian and Gay Marriage," *Feminism and Psychology* 14, no. 1 (2004), pp. 17–23.

[13] See Suzanna Danuta Walters, "Take My Domestic Partner, Please: Gays and Marriage in the Era of the Visible," in *Queer Families, Queer*

Politics: Challenging Culture and the State, ed. Mary Bernstein and Renate Reimann (New York: Columbia University Press, 2001), pp. 338–57.

[14] Stacey, *In the Name of the Family*, pp. 122–23, 127.

[15] Ibid., p. 127.

[16] Judith Stacey's aversion to any notion of institutionality as regards human sexual bonding is bone-deep, extending even to the level of formal academic definitions. Almost all scholars believe that marriage and the family are in fact social institutions that can be described and defined. Stacey doesn't. She tells us that "anthropological and historical studies" have convinced her that "the family is not an institution, but an ideological, symbolic construct that has a history and a politics." One is tempted, as a matter of logic, to reply that the definition of "institution" is not inconsistent with, and certainly not conceptually opposed to or separate from, something—let's call it a structure or "construct"—that contains "ideological" and "symbolic" dimensions and that also has "a history and a politics." So her proposed distinction really doesn't work at all. See Stacey, "Good Riddance to 'The Family': A Reply to David Popenoe," *Journal of Marriage and the Family* 55, no. 3 (August 1993), p. 545.

This rejection of any hint of institutionality also explains Stacey's furious attack on the phrase "the family"—as in "Good Riddance to 'The Family'" and "The Family Is Dead, Long Live Our Families." In Stacey-speak, the phrase "the family," since it is singular, suggests an institution, which is very bad, whereas the plural form, "families," is more suggestive of private intimate bonds operating outside of the constraints of institutions. I report this fact because, to the uninitiated, slogans such as "The Family Is Dead, Long Live Our Families" can appear somewhat impenetrable.

The root-and-branch rejection of institutions—virtually *all* institutions—is closely linked to the philosophical Marxism from which Stacey's worldview largely derives. The sociologist Anton Zijderveld brilliantly describes the sense in which Marxism represents a yearning for "a society without institutions, for human praxis without limiting structures, freedom without alienation, human action without institutional rules and norms." Anton C. Zijderveld, *The Abstract Society* (Garden City, N.Y.: Doubleday, 1970), p. 32.

[17] Stacey, *Lesbian and Gay Families Are the Songbirds in the Mine;* Stacey, *In the Name of the Family*, pp. 123–24, 128. She also writes: "I have come to believe that legitimizing gay and lesbian marriages would promote a democratic, pluralistic expansion of the meaning, practice, and

politics of family life in the United States. This could help to supplant the destructive sanctity of *the family* with respect for diverse and vibrant *families*." *In the Name of the Family*, p. 126.
Stacey expresses more ambivalence about same-sex marriage's deinstitutionalizing potential in "Legal Recognition of Same-Sex Couples: The Impact on Children and Families," *Quinnipiac Law Review* 23 (2004), pp. 529–40.

[18] Stacey, *In the Name of the Family*, pp. 122–23, 128.

[19] Evan Wolfson, "Crossing the Threshold: Equal Marriage Rights for Lesbians and Gay Men and the Intra-Community Critique," *Review of Law and Social Change* 21, no. 3 (1994), p. 579.

[20] Ibid., p. 589.

[21] Ibid., pp. 599–80.

[22] Rauch, *Gay Marriage*, p. 90.

[23] Ellen Willis, contribution to "Can Marriage Be Saved? A Forum," *Nation*, July 5, 2004, pp. 16–17.

[24] Maria Bevacqua, "Feminist Theory and the Question of Lesbian and Gay Marriage," *Feminism and Psychology* 14, no. 1 (2004), pp. 36, 39.

[25] See Appendix, "Polyamory," pp. 256–59.

[26] David L. Chambers, "What If? The Legal Consequences of Marriage and the Legal Needs of Lesbian and Gay Male Couples," *Michigan Law Review* 95, no. 447 (November 1996), pp. 448, 490–91. Chambers has also proposed, for "lovers and the best of friends," establishing "a state-sanctioned status other than marriage that would be available to any unmarried pair with a close relationship—whether cohabiting or not, whether romantically involved or not, whether same-sex or opposite-sex, whether related by blood or not." Chambers would call this new status "designated friends." He proposes this new legal category in addition to (not instead of) same-sex marriage. See Chambers, "For the Best of Friends and for Lovers of All Sorts, a Status Other Than Marriage," *Notre Dame Law Review* 76, no. 5 (2001), pp. 1348, 1352.

[27] Jonathan Rauch, "Gay Marriage Is Risky, but Banning It Is Riskier," *National Journal*, May 15, 2004.

[28] Kevin Bourassa, "Love and the Lexicon of Marriage," *Feminism and Psychology* 14, no. 1 (2004), p. 57. See also Kevin Bourassa and Joe Varnell, *Just Married: Gay Marriage and the Expansion of Human Rights* (Madison: University of Wisconsin Press, 2002).

[29] *Halpern v. Canada (A.G.)*, Court Docket C39172 and C39174, Court of Appeal for Ontario (Toronto: June 10, 2003), para. 5.

[30] Jennifer Vanasco, "Not Just a Right—a Rite," *Chicago Free Press*, August 25, 2004.

[31] John Corvino, "Civil Discourse on Civil Unions," *Between the Lines*, January 20, 2005.

[32] Michael Warner, *The Trouble with Normal: Sex, Politics, and the Ethics of Queer Life* (Cambridge, Mass.: Harvard University Press, 2000), p. 32.

[33] Irene Javors with Renate Reimann, "Building Common Ground: Strategies for Grassroots Organizing on Same-Sex Marriage," in *Queer Families, Queer Politics*, ed. Bernstein and Reimann, pp. 296, 304.

[34] Ibid., pp. 294, 296, 303. These same themes emerge in Ellen Lewin, "Weddings without Marriage: Making Sense of Lesbian and Gay Commitment Rituals," in *Queer Families, Queer Politics*, ed. Bernstein and Reimann, pp. 44–52.

[35] Paul Varnell, "Gay Marriage: Ready, Set ...," *Windy City Times*, March 12, 1998.

[36] See Kathleen E. Hull, "The Political Limits of the Rights Frame: The Case of Same-Sex Marriage in Hawaii," *Sociological Perspectives* 44, no. 2 (2001), pp. 207–32. See also Gretchen A. Stiers, *From This Day Forward: Commitment, Marriage, and Family in Lesbian and Gay Relationships* (New York: St. Martin's Press, 1999), pp. 165, 184.

[37] William N. Eskridge Jr., *The Case for Same-Sex Marriage: From Sexual Liberty to Civilized Commitment* (New York: Free Press, 1996), pp. 8–9.

[38] Pamela J. Smock and Wendy D. Manning, "Living Together Unmarried in the United States: Demographic Perspectives and Implications for Family Policy," *Law and Policy* 26, no. 1 (January 2004), pp. 87–117. See also Larry L. Bumpass and Hsien-Hen Lu, "Trends in Cohabitation and Implications for Children's Family Context in the United States," *Population Studies* 54 (2000), pp. 29–41; Scott M. Stanley, "What Is It with Men and Commitment, Anyway?" *Threshold* 83 (March 2005), pp. 4–11; Steven Nock, *Marriage in Men's Lives* (New York: Oxford University Press, 1998); Barbara Dafoe Whitehead and David Popenoe, "The Marrying Kind: Which Men Marry and Why," in *The State of Our Unions 2004* (Piscataway, N.J.: Rutgers University National Marriage Project, June 2004), pp. 6–14.

[39] See William J. Doherty et al., *Why Marriage Matters: Twenty-one Conclusions from the Social Sciences* (New York: Institute for American Values, 2002); Linda J. Waite and Maggie Gallagher, *The Case for Marriage: Why Married People Are Happier, Healthier, and Better Off Financially* (Doubleday: New York, 2001).

[40] Even Judith Stacey, to her admitted discomfort, and even though she later clarified that she doesn't believe it, found herself making exactly

this pro-marriage point—what an irony!—in her role as an expert witness in a same-sex marriage court case in 2001. See Stacey, "Marital Suitors Court Social Science Spin-sters," *Social Problems* 51, no. 1 (February 2004), p. 137. Interestingly, in this same essay (pp. 139–40) Stacey comes quite close to arguing that a politically committed scholar—especially one practicing "public sociology"—is justified in suppressing research findings that contradict the scholar's political agenda.

41 See Chambers, "What If? The Legal Consequences of Marriage and the Legal Needs of Lesbian and Gay Couples." See also Joshua Baker, *1000 Federal Benefits of Marriage? An Analysis of the 1997 GAO Report* (Washington, D.C.: Institute for Marriage and Public Policy, May 26, 2004). For a ranking of the popularity of the argument about benefits within the universe of public arguments in favor of same-sex marriage, see Stiers, *From This Day Forward,* p. 165.

42 Andrew Sullivan, "Frum on Marriage," from "The Daily Dish," *AndrewSullivan.com,* posted February 28, 2005.

43 Reply Factum of the Applicant Couples, *Halpern v. Canada (A.G.),* Ontario Superior Court of Justice (Toronto: Epstein Cole LLP, October 2001), para. 10.

44 Ibid., para. 24, 75, 77.

45 See transcript of "Gay Marriage Debate within the Gay Community," *Talk of the Nation,* National Public Radio, February 16, 2004.

46 Stiers, *From This Day Forward,* p. 109. Stiers also (p. 186) writes: "Thus the legalization of gay marriages has a radical potential to alter religious, social, and legal definitions of what a marriage is supposed to be."

47 Jeffrey Weeks, Brian Heaphy, and Catherine Donovan, *Same Sex Intimacies: Families of Choice and Other Life Experiments* (London: Routledge, 2001), p. 47.

48 Ibid., p. 108.

49 Mary Bernstein, "Gender, Queer Family Policies, and the Limits of Law," in *Queer Families, Queer Politics,* ed. Bernstein and Reimann, p. 433.

50 Andrew Sullivan, *Virtually Normal: An Argument about Homosexuality* (New York: Alfred A. Knopf, 1995), p. 179.

51 Eskridge, *The Case for Same-Sex Marriage,* p. 11.

52 Dale Carpenter, "Gay Marriage and Procreation," *Bay Area Reporter,* March 18, 2004.

53 Amici Curiae Brief of the Professors of the History of Marriage, Families, and the Law, in *Goodridge v. Department of Public Health,* Massa-

chusetts Supreme Judicial Court no. SJC-08860 (Boston: Goodwin Proctor, LLP, November 8, 2002), p. 38.

[54] Opinion of the Justices, in *Goodridge v. Department of Public Health*, Massachusetts Supreme Judicial Court (Boston: November 18, 2003), p. 10.

[55] One small example from the historiography of marriage may help us to regain our bearings, and perhaps realize how far into unreality the discussion of this topic has descended. In 1970, long before same-sex marriage was even a glimmer on the horizon, the religion scholar James Turner Johnson of Rutgers, for reasons that need not detain us here, felt obliged to explain why, over the course of many generations in seventeenth-century Britain, there appear to have been exactly *no* Anglican sermons focusing on "the duty of procreation" in marriage. If procreation was indeed central to marriage—and the Anglican Prayer Book of the time explicitly states of marriage, "First, It was ordained for the procreation of children"—why did the ministers *never* preach about it? Exhort their flocks to strive energetically to reach this important goal? Make sure that no one was confused or uninformed about what to do? As Johnson explains, "there are no Anglican homilies on the duty of procreation" because "the biological model" underlying the duty in question points to "the simplicity of achievement of the primary end, procreation." Well put!

Yes, marriage as an institution *is* centrally about bearing and raising children. So why did none of the ministers of the Church of England ever feel the need to warn, threaten, cajole, remind, or try legally to pressure the married members of their congregations to have sexual intercourse resulting in the birth of children? For the same reasons that they never considered it necessary to interrogate engaged couples about their willingness to produce offspring, or threaten them with harsh penalties, such as cancelling their marriage, if they refused as a condition of marriage to bear children. It was for the same reasons that we don't have laws requiring birds to sing or fish to swim. We can be certain that those seventeenth-century ministers never imagined that they were creating some kind of legal loophole that could be used generations later in defense of the absolutely astonishing proposition that marriage is not intrinsically connected to bearing and raising children. See James Turner Johnson, *A Society Ordained by God: English Puritan Marriage Doctrine in the First Half of the Seventeenth Century* (Nashville: Abingdon Press, 1970), p. 22.

[56] Civil Marriage Act (Bill C-38), House of Commons of Canada (Ottawa, Ontario), 1st Session, 38th Parliament, 53 Elizabeth II, 2004–2005.

[57] Chambers, "What If? The Legal Consequences of Marriage and the Legal Needs of Lesbian and Gay Male Couples," p. 316.

[58] In 2005 the Law Commission of New Zealand, in a report called *New Issues in Legal Parenthood*, recommended a series of legal changes permitting groups of collaborating adults—sperm donors, egg donors, and parental couples and individuals—to make agreements such that some New Zealand children will have three or more legal parents. See Law Commission of New Zealand, *New Issues in Legal Parenthood*, Report no. 88 (Wellington, New Zealand, April 2005).

[59] The feminist philosopher Sylviane Agacinski brilliantly reflects on what she calls the "double origin" of each child—the fact that every child comes from one mother and one father, who, through their sexual union, bridge the basic divide in the human species. Agacinski refuses all propositions, including the proposition of gay marriage, that would deny this fact and (from the child's point of view) this birthright. For example, she tells an interviewer: "I think there is no absolute right to a child, since the right implies an increasingly artificial fabrication of children. In the interests of the child, one cannot efface its double origin." In *Parity of the Sexes*, Agacinski examines the consequences of disconnecting legal from natural parenthood and of insisting that marriage is no longer based on male-female reunion. For example, she points out that

> if we suspend [i.e., seek to deny] sexual duality, there is no longer any reason why there must be two and only two parents. Why not three fathers, or four mothers? The binary model for the couple is not produced by love or pleasure, but by sexuation, that is, genital differentiation. There are not two parents because they love each other, but because heterogeneity of the race is necessary and sufficient for creating life. On the other hand, sexual practices and amorous ties do not necessarily involve either mixed partners, or even a couple's relationship.

Commenting on the "odd" idea that marriage as an institution is intrinsically concerned, either way, with issues of sexual orientation, Agacinski writes that "marriage was not instituted to legalize heterosexuality, but to regulate filiation."

See Sylviane Agacinski, *Parity of the Sexes* (New York: Columbia University Press, 2001), pp. xiii–xiv. Agacinski's interview comments cited here are from "Questions autour de la filiation," *Ex aequo* (July 1998), as translated from the French by Judith Butler and appearing in Butler, *Undoing Gender* (New York: Routledge, 2004), p. 118.

[60] "Romney Links Gay Marriage, U.S. Prestige," *Boston Globe,* February 26, 2005.

[61] "Not Fair, Governor," editorial, *Boston Globe,* March 3, 2005.

[62] Wolfson, "Crossing the Threshold," pp. 576–77.

[63] Summing up a large body of research, the respected scholar Sara McLanahan in 1994 put it this way: "Children who grow up in a household with only one biological parent are worse off, on average, than children who grow up in a household with both of their biological parents, regardless of the parents' race or educational background, regardless of whether the parents are married when the child is born, and regardless of whether the parent remarries." See Sara McLanahan and Gary Sandefur, *Growing Up with a Single Parent: What Hurts, What Helps* (Cambridge, Mass.: Harvard University Press, 1994), p. 1.

In a more recent survey, published in 2005, the prominent family sociologist Paul R. Amato makes basically the same point: "Research clearly demonstrates the children growing up with two continuously married parents are less likely than other children to experience a wide range of cognitive, emotional, and social problems, not only during childhood, but also in adulthood. Although it is not possible to demonstrate that family structure is the cause of these differences, studies that have used a variety of sophisticated statistical methods, including controls for genetic factors, suggest that this is the case. This distinction is even stronger of we focus on children growing up with two happily married biological parents." For these reasons, Amato recommends new and stronger U.S. public policies aiming to "increase the share of children growing up with two continuously married biological parents." See Paul R. Amato, "The Impact of Family Formation Change on the Cognitive, Social, and Emotional Well-Being of the Next Generation," *The Future of Children* 15, no. 2 (Fall 2005), pp. 89–90.

[64] "2-Parent Families Rise after Change in Welfare Laws," *New York Times,* August 12, 2001.

[65] For example, in its 2003 *Goodridge* decision, the Massachusetts Supreme Judicial Court issues this accusation:

> The "marriage is procreation" argument singles out the one unbridgeable difference between same-sex and opposite-sex couples, and transforms that difference into the essence of legal marriage.... In doing so, the State's action confers an official stamp of approval on the destructive stereotype that same-sex relationships are inherently unstable and inferior to opposite-sex relationships and are not worthy of respect.

Note that the justices are openly indulging in an accusation of bad faith: People who argue that marriage is intrinsically connected to bearing and raising children are "singling out" this one issue for no valid reason other than to perpetuate hateful stereotypes about homosexuals. This argument not only betrays a stunning ignorance about the purposes of marriage and the family as human institutions, it is also obviously intended by the justices as a means of silencing, rather than seriously engaging, other points of view. Shame on them. See Opinion of the Justices, *Goodridge v. Department of Public Health*, pp. 10–11.

66 See www.familyevolutions.com.

67 Alan M. Dershowitz, "To Fix Gay Marriage, Government Should Quit the Marriage Business," *Los Angeles Times*, December 3, 2003.

68 Alisa Solomon, "State to Church: I Want a Divorce," *Village Voice*, March 3–9, 2004.

69 Jo Ann Citron, "Will It Be Marriage or Civil Union?" *Gay and Lesbian Review* 11, no. 2 (2004), pp. 10–12.

70 Dershowitz, "To Fix Gay Marriage, Government Should Quit the Marriage Business."

71 David Moats, "Civil Rites," *San Jose Mercury News*, February 22, 2004.

72 Steve Swayne, "Civil Unions: 'Different and Better,'" *Bay Windows* (Boston), May 4, 2000.

73 Steve Swayne, "Church, State, and Marriage," *Rutland Herald*, May 4, 2004. See also Swayne, "Separate State-Sanctioned Unions from Religious Marriages," *Valley News* (Vermont), June 21, 2003; and Swayne, "Gay Couples Are Holding Together," *Rutland Herald*, June 16, 2004.

74 For evidence of how religious practice and affiliation in the U.S. typically tends to improve parenting and enrich and strengthen marital relationships, see W. Bradford Wilcox, *Soft Patriarchs, New Men: How Christianity Shapes Fathers and Husbands* (Chicago: University of Chicago Press, 2004); and Wilcox, "For the Sake of the Children? Family-Related Discourse and Practice in the Mainline," in *The Quiet Hand of God: Faith-Based Activism and the Public Role of Mainline Protestantism*, ed. Robert Wuthnow and John H. Evans (Berkeley: University of California Press, 2002), pp. 287–316.

75 Bourassa, "Love and the Lexicon of Marriage," pp. 58, 61.

76 Andrew Sullivan, Introduction to *Same-Sex Marriage: Pro and Con*, ed. Sullivan (New York: Vintage Books, 1997), p. xviii.

In *Virtually Normal* (p. 179), Sullivan offers a definition of marriage: "a social and public recognition of a private commitment" and "the highest recognition of personal integrity." In addition, the "center" of the marriage contract is "an emotional, financial, and psychological bond between two people." In his introduction to *Same-Sex Marriage,* Sullivan elaborates on these points. He writes (pp. xix–xx) that while marriage used to be "a means of bringing up children," today it has become "primarily a way in which two adults affirm their emotional commitment to one another." He also argues that while marriage formerly was an institution that "buttresses" kinship and other bonds, today it is for many people "a deep expression of the modern individual's ability to transcend all of those ties in an exercise of radical autonomy."

These are remarkable formulations. They capture, in almost haiku form, the essential vocabulary for deinstitutionalizing marriage. Marriage is society's way of recognizing a private commitment. Marriage is society's way of affirming a person's personal integrity. Marriage is a private bond between two people. Marriage in the old days was about children and buttressing kinship and social bonds, but no longer. Marriage today is more about transcending bonds and being radically autonomous. These ideas add up to an almost perfect expression of "The Full Stacey," a call for the complete deinstitutionalization of marriage.

77 Thomas B. Stoddard, "Why Gay People Should Seek the Right to Marry," in *We Are Everywhere: A Historical Sourcebook of Gay and Lesbian Politics,* ed. Mark Blasius and Shane Phelan (New York: Routledge, 1997), p. 754, first published in *Out/Look,* 1989.

78 Ibid., p. 757.

79 *What Next for the Marriage Movement?* (New York: Institute for American Values, 2004), p. 5. This statement was signed by more than 140 U.S. marriage leaders. In a statement released in 2000, signed by 113 leaders, we said: "We come together to pledge that in this decade we will turn the tide on marriage and reduce divorce and unmarried childbearing, so that each year more children will grow up protected by their own two happily married parents, and so that each year more adults' marriage dreams will come true." See *The Marriage Movement: A Statement of Principles* (New York: Institute for American Values, 2000), p. 4.

80 *Marriage in America: A Report to the Nation,* pp. 5, 13.

81 Margaret Gullette, "The New Case for Marriage," *American Prospect,* March 1, 2004, p. 48.

82 Ibid., p. 49. Gloria Steinem, for decades an implacable critic of marriage, made a similar argument in an interview. See "The Gay Rights Movement, Settled Down," *New York Times,* February 29, 2004.

[83] Richard D. Mohr, *A More Perfect Union: Why Straight America Must Stand Up for Gay Rights* (Boston: Beacon Press, 1994), p. 40.

[84] Ibid., pp. 41, 49–50, 52.

[85] Ibid., p. 48.

[86] Andrew Sullivan, "State of the Union," *New Republic*, May 8, 2000, p. 22.

[87] Andrew Sullivan, "Unveiled," *New Republic*, August 13, 2001, p. 6. When Andrew in this article taunts his opponents by saying that if "you want to return straight marriage to the 1950s, go ahead," but "until you do," there can be no valid objection to gay marriage, exactly what is he promising? And admitting? When he sets up as his litmus test a "return to the 1950s," he is apparently referring mainly to rates of divorce and unwed childbearing, which indeed were much lower in the 1950s. So, if family fragmentation rates in the future were to return to earlier levels, would Andrew change his mind on gay marriage? But U.S. divorce rates are *already* modestly declining, while rates of unwed childbearing have roughly held steady from the mid 1990s through at least the early 2000s. How much more good news would it take—how close to the old rates would we have to be—in order for Andrew to reconsider his position?

[88] Donald Sensing, "Save Marriage? It's Too Late," *Wall Street Journal*, March 15, 2004.

[89] Andrew Sullivan, "The Daily Dish," *AndrewSullivan.com*, posted March 17, 2004. Andrew makes this point again, at length, in "We Are All Sodomites Now," *New Republic*, March 26, 2003.

[90] Sullivan, *Virtually Normal*, p. 179. See also Sullivan, "Here Comes the Groom: The Conservative Case for Gay Marriage," *New Republic*, August 28, 2003; and Sullivan, "The Conservative Case for Gay Marriage," *Time*, June 30, 2003.

[91] For sources, see endnotes 11–16 for this book's Introduction.

[92] *What Next for the Marriage Movement?* pp. 5, 9–11; *Can Government Strengthen Marriage? Evidence from the Social Sciences* (New York: Institute for American Values, 2004); *The Marriage Movement: A Statement of Principles*, pp. 13–19.

[93] Andrew J. Cherlin, "The Deinstitutionalization of American Marriage," *Journal of Marriage and the Family* 66 (November 2004), p. 850.

[94] Norval D. Glenn, "The Struggle for Same-Sex Marriage," *Society* 41, no. 6 (September–October 2004), p. 26.

[95] Peter L. Berger and Thomas Luckmann, *The Social Construction of Reality: A Treatise in the Sociology of Knowledge* (Garden City, N.Y.: Anchor Books, 1967), p. 58. For important analyses of the meaning

and problem of institutions in human societies, see also Peter L. Berger and Hansfried Kellner, "Arnold Gehlen and the Theory of Institutions," *Social Research* 32, no. 1 (Spring 1965), pp. 110–15; Zijderfeld, *The Abstract Society*; and Mary Douglas, *How Institutions Think* (Syracuse, N.Y.: Syracuse University Press, 1986). For a brilliant analysis of marriage as a meaning-making institution, see Peter Berger and Hansfried Kellner, "Marriage and the Construction of Reality," *Diogenes* 46 (Summer 1964), pp. 1–24.

96 Anthony Giddens, *Modernity and Self-Identity: Self and Society in the Late Modern Age* (Stanford, Calif.: Stanford University Press, 1991), p. 6.

97 Anthony Giddens, *The Transformation of Intimacy: Sexuality, Love and Eroticism in Modern Societies* (Stanford, Calif.: Stanford University Press, 1992), p. 58.

98 Ibid., pp. 137, 3.

Chapter 7 ▪ Goods in Conflict

1 Andrew Sullivan, "Why the 'M' Word Matters to Me," *Time*, February 16, 2004.

2 Derrick Z. Jackson, "Echoes of Racism in Gay Marriage Ban," *Boston Globe*, April 2, 2004.

3 Colbert I. King, "Marriage in the March of Time," *Washington Post*, February 12, 2005.

4 Gail Mathabane, "Gays Face Same Battle Interracial Couples Fought," *USA Today*, January 25, 2004.

5 C. W. Nevius, "Time Favors Gay-Marriage Proponents," *San Francisco Chronicle*, September 10, 2005.

6 Justice Doris Ling-Cohan, opinion in *Hernandez et al. v. City of New York*, Supreme Court of the State of New York (February 4, 2005), pp. 45, 3.

7 Steven Swayne, "A Similar Sort of War," *The Dartmouth*, November 4, 2004, reprinted online as "Mile to Go for Marriage" by the Independent Gay Forum.

8 Quoted in Jessica Greenfield, "Radical Right Ignores Courts on Marriage Rights, Attempts to Write Discrimination into U.S. Constitution," *National NOW Times*, Winter 2003/2004.

9 See *Loving v. Virginia*, 388 U.S. 1 (Washington, D.C.: June 12, 1967). The Court's central conclusion is that states may no longer "prevent marriages between persons solely on the basis of racial classifications." Although it is common today for proponents of same-sex marriage to invoke *Loving v. Virginia* as supposed evidence that the Court, in 1967, was already at least implicitly arguing that any person

has the right to marry any other person, the justices in *Loving v. Virginia* in fact said or implied no such thing. The Court's single and vitally important conclusion, stated repeatedly throughout the opinion, is that the right to marry may not be restricted by the state solely on the basis of the *race* of the persons seeking to marry.

10 James A. Brundage, *Law, Sex, and Christian Society in Medieval Europe* (Chicago: University of Chicago Press, 1987), pp. 69–70, 75, 110–12, 150, 214.

11 Commission on Children at Risk, *Hardwired to Connect: The New Scientific Case for Authoritative Communities* (New York: Institute for American Values, 2003), pp. 39–40. See also John Witte Jr., "Between Sanctity and Depravity: Human Dignity in Protestant Perspective," in *In Defense of Human Dignity: Essays for Our Times*, ed. Robert P. Kraynak and Glenn Tinder (Notre Dame, Ind.: University of Notre Dame Press, 2003), pp. 119–37.

12 Michael Ignatieff, *The Rights Revolution* (Toronto: Anansi, 2000), p. 2. See also Ignatieff, "Human Rights," in *Human Rights in Political Transition: Gettysburg to Bosnia*, ed. Carla Hesse and Robert Post (New York: Zone Books, 1999), p. 313.

13 See *Charter of the Rights of the Family* (Washington, D.C.: United States Catholic Conference, 1983); Charles J. Reid Jr., *Power over the Body, Equality in the Family: Rights and Domestic Relations in Medieval Canon Law* (Grand Rapids, Mich.: William B. Eerdmans, 2004), esp. pp. 25–68; and Reid, "Toward an Understanding of Medieval Universal Rights: The Marital Rights of Non-Christians in Early Scholastic and Canonistic Writings," *Ava Maria Law Review* 3, no. 1 (Spring 2005), pp. 95–122.

14 See Margaret Somerville, Testimony, Legislative Committee on Bill C-38, 38th Parliament, 1st Session (Ottawa: Parliament of Canada, June 2, 2005), pp. 1535–40. I also benefited in this regard from Somerville's speech on "Unlinking Child-Parent Biological Bonds" at a conference on "Illuminating Marriage" held on May 18–20, 2005, in Kananaskis, Canada, and sponsored by the Montreal-based Institute for the Study of Marriage, Law and Culture.

15 Mary Ann Glendon, *A World Made New* (New York: Random House, 2001), pp. xviii, 174.

16 We could easily add a seventh idea—marriage is between a woman and a man—to our list of ideas about marriage contained in Article 16. After all, every other human right in the Declaration is described in the first instance as belonging to "all" or to "everyone." Article 16 is the *only* article that announces a human right by referring to "men

and women." The only possible reason, it seems to me, is that the drafters of the Declaration are saying that the right to marry is specifically connected, in ways that other basic rights are not, to human beings' sexual embodiment as "men and women." So if the right under discussion is the right to own property (Article 17) or the right to rest and leisure (Article 24), the word "everyone" works fine. But regarding the right to marry and to found a family, it makes sense to say "men and women," since that particular right, and that one alone, is inextricably bound up with sexual embodiment. Why else would the drafters have chosen to break, in this once instance alone, with the established pattern of saying "all" or "everyone"?

Several years ago, petitioners from New Zealand brought a case seeking recognition of same-sex marriage to the U.N. Human Rights Commission. They argued that the right to marry contained in the U.N. International Covenant on Civil and Political Rights—the legally binding rights instrument based directly on the Universal Declaration—contains within it the right of same-sex couples to marry. (Article 23 of that International Covenant states: "The family is the natural and fundamental group unit of society and is entitled to protection by society and the State." And: "The right of men and women of marriageable age to marry and to found a family shall be recognized.") The U.N. Human Rights Committee, in rejecting the New Zealand complaint in 2002, interpreted the right to marry as defined in the Universal Declaration basically the same way that I am interpreting it and, in its ruling, specifically cited as determinative the "men and women" phrasing in the Declaration's Article 16 and in Article 23 of the International Covenant. See Human Rights Committee, Communication no. 902/1999: New Zealand, CCPR/C/75/D/902/1999 (Geneva: Office of the United Nations High Commissioner for Human Rights, July 30, 2002), esp. 4.3–4.4, 8.2. (One of the petitioners' main supporting assertions (see section 3.3) is that "procreation does not lie at the heart of marriage.")

So we could certainly add "marriage is woman-man" to our list, but such an exercise seems redundant and even, in one sense, misleading. For there is no need to parse or debate the drafters' exact intended meaning of the phrase "men and women." Nor is there any reason to pretend, against all evidence, that the drafters of the Universal Declaration were somehow seeking to alert us about gay marriage. The entire concept of gay marriage was nonexistent for them, just as it was nonexistent for everyone in the world who participated in formulating and adopting the Universal Declaration.

[17] Somerville, Testimony, 1535–40.

[18] Robert E. Goss, "Queering Procreative Privilege: Coming Out as Families," in *Our Families, Our Values: Snapshots of Queer Kinship*, ed. Robert E. Goss and Amy Adams Squire Strongheart (Binghamton, N.J.: Harrington Park Press, 1997), p. 19.

[19] Kath Weston, *Families We Choose: Lesbians, Gays, Kinship* (New York: Columbia University Press, 1991).

[20] Jeffrey Weeks, Brian Heaphy, and Catherine Donovan, *Same Sex Intimacies: Families of Choice and Other Life Experiments* (London: Routledge, 1991), pp. 179, 17.

[21] Mary Bernstein, "Gender Transgressions and Queer Family Law," in *Queer Families, Queer Politics: Challenging Culture and State*, ed. Mary Bernstein and Renate Reimann (New York: Columbia University Press, 2001), pp. 432–33.

In *Reinventing the Family*, Laura Benkov is similarly pleased that the creation of "new family forms and definitions" based on same-sex parenting couples and on personal choice as the sole determinant of kinship will constitute "a force for social change." Exactly what kind of social change? Consider the case of collaborative reproduction making use of sperm donation. Benkov approvingly declares: "To be inseminated as a single straight woman or lesbian is to boldly acknowledge that the resulting child has no father and that women can parent without input from men beyond the single contribution of genetic material." *That* kind of social change. For Benkov, anonymous donor insemination that guarantees fatherlessness for a child means primarily that we should learn to "speak openly" to that child about "another way that people come into the world."

Is it a good idea for the parenting couple to know the identity of their sperm donor? If they do know the donor, or choose to learn his identity, should the child have a relationship with the donor, or not? It all depends on what the grownups prefer:

> Deciding who will be part of one's family is, of course, a highly personal endeavor. The decision regarding a known or unknown donor is partly a decision about what kind of intimate relationships to create. Some are comfortable sharing parenting with people outside a romantic relationship, while others find this a complicated and unrewarding situation.

In a 289-page book about parenting, it does not occur to Benkov even once to discuss—*it never occurs to her even to ask*—whether children need and deserve fathers. Free adult choice in kinship and complete "self-definition" in family life are for her the two all-important ideas—both of which, in her view, require us as a society to "discard a determination of which family structure is 'best' in favor of finding ways to make all the different structures work." See Laura Benkov, *Reinventing the Family: The Emerging Story of Lesbian and Gay Parents* (New York: Crown Publishers, 1994), pp. 145, 117, 119, 126–27, 242.

22 Cheshire C. Calhoun, "Family's Outlaws: Rethinking the Connections between Feminism, Lesbianism, and the Family," in *Feminism and Families*, ed. Hilde Lindemann Nelson (New York: Routledge, 1997), p. 147. For Calhoun, too, the master word is *choice*. She writes (p. 143):

> Choice increasingly appears to be the principle determining family composition: choice to single-parent, choice of fictive kin, choice to combine nuclear families (in extended kin networks, in remarriage, or in divorce-extended families), choice of semen donors or contract birth-givers, choice to dissolve marital bonds, choice of who will function as a parent in children's lives (in spite of the law's failure to acknowledge the parental status of many functional parents).

For Calhoun, choice itself (as compared with any particular good that is chosen) is not only the highest value, but also the priority that dictates all other priorities. In the process, certain words lose their meaning entirely. For example, notice that "parent" for Calhoun means, literally and entirely, whatever the involved adults around a child choose to say that it means.

23 Scott Moore, "Emmett Has Two Mommies," *Portland Mercury*, April 6–12, 2006.

24 David L. Chambers, "What If? The Legal Consequences of Marriage and the Legal Needs of Lesbian and Gay Male Couples," in *Queer Families, Queer Politics*, ed. Bernstein and Reimann, p. 316.

25 Julien S. Murphy, "Should Lesbians Count as Infertile Couples? Antilesbian Discrimination in Assisted Reproduction," in *Queer Families, Queer Politics*, ed. Bernstein and Reimann, p. 197.

In Britain in April 2006, a panel of judges removed two young children from the custody of their lesbian mother and granted primary custody instead to the mother's ex-lover. There was no evidence or accusation of abuse or neglect, only a disagreement between the adults over parenting the children. The partner relationship between the two women ended in 2002, when one of the children was a newborn and the other a toddler. Shortly after the breakup, the mother and the ex-lover each found a new partner.

The head of the panel of judges said: "We have moved into a world where norms that seemed safe 20 or more years ago no longer run." Today a family "may be created by mutual agreement and with much careful planning. Both partners seek the experience of child-bearing and child-rearing in one capacity or another." The judge therefore asks: "Who is the natural parent?" And answers that "the natural parent may be a non-biological parent who, by virtue of long-settled care, has become the child's psychological parent."

In other words, every imaginable dimension of parenthood, including "the experience of child-bearing," is something that is determined by "mutual agreement" of the adult parties involved, preferably accompanied by "much careful planning." In answering the question "Who is a parent?" do biological ties matter? They do not. Do the norms of the institution of marriage matter? Not in the slightest. Does *anything* matter other than the private agreements of the rights-bearing adults? No. (Unless. of course, the parties come to disagree, in which event we will certainly need judges!) As a result, we see again that the word "parent" essentially comes to mean whatever the adults involved say it means.

But that's not the only word that loses its meaning. The triumph of subjective constructionism over physiological fact is so complete that we apparently must also invert the meaning of "natural." Until a moment ago, the word "natural," when used in the context of parenthood, meant "in accordance with or determined by nature" and "begotten as distinguished from adopted." But now—you heard it here first!—"natural" means "psychological."

See Frances Gibb, "Mother Loses Her Children to Former Lesbian Partner," *Times* (London), April 10, 2006; Clare Dyer, "Court Rules Mother Must Give Children to Lesbian Ex-Partner," *Guardian*, April 7, 2006.

In the United States, two recent state supreme court decisions—one in California in August 2005 and one in Washington in November 2005—similarly found that mothers' lesbian partners are in fact parents of the children in question. The justices of the California Supreme Court wrote: "We perceive no reason why both parents of a child cannot be women." The headline of the *Seattle Times* got to the heart of the matter: "Court redefines parenthood." See Adam Liptak, "California Ruling Expands Same-Sex Parental Rights," *New York Times*, August 23, 2005; Lornet Turnball, "Court Redefines Parenthood," *Seattle Times*, November 4, 2005.

26 Ignatieff, *The Rights Revolution*, p. 86.

[27] Fenton Johnson, "Wedded to an Illusion," *Harper's Magazine*, November 1996, p. 50.

[28] The idea that, as the philosopher Isaiah Berlin succinctly put it, "not all good things are compatible" is at the very center of liberal thought. For liberals, the basic distinction is between monism, or the view that all goods revolve around and stem from one master good, one permanent and complete solution, and what William Galston and other liberal theorists call value pluralism, or liberal pluralism, which is the view that the diversity of human goods cannot be measured according to one master standard, or fully rank-ordered, and therefore important human goods can and often do conflict with one another. Sometimes our choice is between good and bad. But often enough in free societies, our choice is between good and good.

Consequently, one of the surest ways to misunderstand the concept of human rights is to imagine that *any* right—take your pick—is absolute, or that the diverse human goods that we call "rights" are, or can ever be, in full harmony with one another. Indeed, viewing human rights in this decidedly illiberal way ends up violating a basic norm or presupposition of human rights discourse itself, and in doing so, threatens to drive the entire conversation to a dead end. Unless we concede that rights exist only in community with other rights, that rights can conflict with one another, and therefore that every right must necessarily contain, *as a part of the right itself*, certain limitations and boundaries, the very notion of rights eventually loses all meaning.

These considerations should give pause to liberals—and I count myself as a liberal—who believe that the reformulated right to marry and found a family is a liberal idea. It isn't. The claim that *I have the right to form whatever family I choose* is fundamentally illiberal. It is an absolute claim, recognizing virtually no boundary, limitation, or social dimension. It rejects the possibility that valid competing concerns—other goods, different from the good of adult free choice—might be at stake. As a result, the new claim strikes me as a clear case of philosophical monism blatantly seeking to override liberal pluralism.

See Isaiah Berlin, "Two Conceptions of Liberty," in *Four Essays on Liberty* (Oxford, U.K.: Oxford University Press, 1969), p. 167 and passim; William A. Galston, *Liberal Pluralism: The Implications of Value Pluralism for Political Theory and Practice* (Cambridge, U.K.: Cambridge University Press, 2002), pp. 4–7 and passim; also Mary Ann Glendon, *Rights Talk: The Impoverishment of Political Discourse* (New York: Free Press, 1991).

[29] In 2001, about 62 percent of all U.S. children under age 18 lived with their biological mother and father. (About 60 percent lived with their two biological *married* parents.) But that is a snapshot—one moment in time. Most scholars agree that, if we look overall at the years of childhood from birth through age 17, *at least* half of all U.S. children today are spending at least a significant portion of their childhoods living apart from one or both of their two natural parents. See Rose M. Kreider and Jason Fields, *Living Arrangements of Children: 2001,* Current Population Reports P70-104 (Washington, D.C.: U.S. Census Bureau, July 2005), Table 1; David T. Ellwood and Christopher Jencks, "The Spread of Single-Parent Families in the United States since 1960," in *The Future of the Family,* ed. Daniel P. Moynihan, Timothy M. Smeedling, and Lee Rainwater (New York: Russell Sage Foundation, 2004), pp. 32–33; David Popenoe, *War over the Family* (New Brunswick, N.J.: Transaction Publishers, 2005), pp. 23–24, 207.

[30] Patrick Heuveline, Jeffrey M. Timberlake, and Frank F. Furstenberg Jr., "Shifting Childrearing to Single Mothers: Results from 17 Western Countries," *Population and Development Review* 29, no. 1 (March 2003), p. 48.

[31] Peggy Orenstein, "The Other Mother," *New York Times Magazine,* July 25, 2004.

[32] I am grateful to Maggie Gallagher for making this point to me.

[33] See Elizabeth Marquardt, *Between Two Worlds: The Inner Lives of Children of Divorce* (New York: Crown Publishers, 2005); Judith Wallerstein, Julia Lewis, and Sandra Blakeslee, *The Unexpected Legacy of Divorce: A 25 Year Landmark Study* (New York: Hyperion, 2000); Paul R. Amato and Alan Booth, *A Generation at Risk: Growing Up in an Era of Family Upheaval* (Cambridge, Mass.: Harvard University Press, 1997); Sara McLanahan and Gary Sandefur, *Growing Up with a Single Parent: What Hurts, What Helps* (Cambridge, Mass.: Harvard University Press, 1994); David Popenoe, *Disturbing the Nest: Family Change and Decline in Modern Societies* (New York: Aldine de Gruyter, 1988).

[34] Pat Conroy, "Divorce," *Altanta,* November 1978, p. 43.

[35] Heuveline, Timberlake, and Furstenberg, "Shifting Childrearing to Single Mothers," pp. 55–63; W. Bradford Wilcox et al., *Why Marriage Matters, Second Edition: Twenty-six Conclusions from the Social Sciences* (New York: Institute for American Values, 2005), pp. 12–14.

[36] John A. Roberts, *Children of Choice: Freedom and the New Reproductive Technologies* (Princeton, N.J.: Princeton University Press, 1994), pp. 119–48.

[37] Mark Henderson, "'No Father Needed' under Shakeup of UK Fertility Rules," *Times* (London), July 12, 2006.

[38] New Zealand Law Commission, *New Issues in Legal Parenthood*, Report 88 (Wellington, New Zealand, April 2005), pp. 2, 66, 120.

Have you heard the term "bothies"? A bothie is a child who is understood to have four parents—two gay fathers and two lesbian mothers. According to the *Bay Area Reporter*, "Some of those families began as four-way agreements. In other situations, romantic relationships began after the children were born to co-parents, and the biological parents were able to add legal protections for their lovers through contracts and court rulings." See Zak Szymanski, "Duffy Enters New Arena—Parenthood," *Bay Area Reporter* 36, no. 14 (April 6, 2006).

Laura Benkov tells the story of eight-year-old Danielle, who, when asked about her parents, says, "I have two moms and two dads." Benkov describes the two mothers, Adria (the birth mother) and Marilyn, and the two fathers, Barry (the biological father) and Michael, as involved in "a complicated dynamic":

> In many ways Adria and Barry developed a primary intimate relationship, one that had to be balanced with their respective partner relationships. It was the beginning of what was to be their particular sort of family—not a uniform, single entity but more like concentric circles, with four overlapping intimate adult relationships.

Benkov, *Reinventing the Family*, pp. 112, 137–38.

Sometimes these arrangements don't last very long. In New Zealand in 2004, one bothie, a two-year-old boy, became the object of an angry court battle between the two "boths": on one side, a gay male couple, one of whom was the sperm donor, and on the other side, a lesbian couple, one of whom gave physical birth to the child. The couples stopped getting along. Everyone got a lawyer. The case was resolved when a court in Auckland amazingly ruled that the little boy has *three* legal parents—the man who donated sperm, the mother who gave birth, *and* the mother's lover. Three is of course a lot, but it's still one less than a bothie. See Peter Hacker, "Toddler Gets Three Gay Parents, Court Rules," *365Gay.com*, posted April 18, 2004.

Elizabeth Marquardt, my colleague at the Institute for American Values, is herself a child of divorce and has spent nearly a decade studying the experiences of children of divorce. Whenever she hears terms such as "collaborative reproduction," or hears about three, four or more adults who say they have agreed to co-parent a child, she reminds me that it seems hard enough these days for just *two* adults to stay together as loving co-parents. But three? Four? More? How much more complex, fragile and vulnerable to breakup are such arrangements likely to be? Elizabeth says: "When they discuss these ideas so optimistically, they seem, in their mind's eye, to see all of these diverse adults entering the child's life. I see them leaving."

39 Calhoun, "Family's Outlaws," p. 143.

40 Alison Harvison Young, "This Child Does Have 2 (or More) Fathers . . . : Step-parents and Support Obligations," *McGill Law Journal* 45 (2000), pp. 108–31.

Young's starting point in this article is the legal obligation of ex-stepparents for child support payments, but she clearly has her eyes on bigger prizes. She wants Canadian law to break open what she calls the "norm of exclusivity"—for each child, two legal and social parents—as thoroughly as possible. She starts out (p. 109) by commenting favorably on

> the relationship that developed between Brian's three ex-wives, who got to know each other through the children of the various marriages (who were half-siblings) who visited back and forth. These networks can be supportive and constructive, especially for the children involved, yet our legal constructs generally fail even to acknowledge their existence.

Young favors laws "recognizing the contributions of various actors who play a role in a child's life," including, she specifically points out, "birth mothers and gestational mothers" who are participants in projects of collaborative reproduction (pp. 109–10). More generally, Young strongly favors a legal approach that "opens the door to the possibility of multiple parents" (p. 127).

In the United States, Nancy D. Polikoff of American University's Washington College of Law favors a similar approach, as suggested by the title of her article: "This Child Does Have Two Mothers." Polikoff's goal is to get rid of "rigid definitions of parenthood." She issues her demand: "Thus, courts should redefine parenthood to include anyone in a functional parental relationship that a legally recognized parent created with the intent that an additional parent-child relationship exist." In other words, if I am a child's parent and I "intend" for some other nearby caregiver also to be the child's parent, then that other person *is* the child's parent! The possibilities here boggle the mind. In this view, parenthood becomes radically elastic and almost entirely subjective. Once "redefined" thus, parenthood would be established essentially the way people establish friendships. If I say you are my friend and you agree, then you are my friend. If I say that you are a parent of my child and you agree, then you are a parent of my child. *And the law will uphold that claim!* And my child simply lives with it. See Nancy D. Polikoff, "This Child Does Have Two Mothers: Redefining Parenthood to Meet the Needs of Children in Lesbian-Mother and Other Nontraditional Families," *Georgetown Law Journal* 78 (1990), pp. 464, 573.

41 The owner of Family Evolutions is Stacey Harris. My colleague Elizabeth Marquardt interviewed her on May 5, 2005. See also Elizabeth Marquardt, "Kids Need a Real Past: Children with Donor Parents Suffer When Those Raising Them Downplay Their Origins," *Chicago Tribune,* May 15, 2005.

42 Sylviane Agacinski, "The Double Origin," in *Parity of the Sexes* (New York: Columbia University Press, 2001), pp. 99–110.

43 Somerville, "Unlinking Child-Parent Biological Bonds." See also Somerville, "Would You Want to Know Who Your Biological Parents Are?" *Toronto Globe and Mail,* September 15, 2004.

44 It may be worth noting that *all* children, including those who are or will become homosexuals, benefit from the principle that every child deserves a mother and a father.

45 See Daniel Patrick Moynihan, "Defining Deviancy Down," *American Scholar* 62, no. 1 (Winter 1993), pp. 17–30.

46 Letters, *USA Today,* February 23, 2004.

47 Jonathan Dobrer, "Marriage Is about More Than Sexuality," *Los Angeles Daily News,* February 27, 2005.

48 Editorial, "An Amendment Would Not Protect Marriage," *Salem (Ore.) Statesman Journal,* July 14, 2004. See also "Court Nullifies Oregon's Gay Marriages," *Los Angeles Times,* April 15, 2005.

49 Norah Vincent, "A Lot of Hooey on Same-Sex Marriage," *Los Angeles Times,* August 9, 2001.

50 Jonathan Rauch, "Power of Two," *New York Times Magazine,* March 7, 2004.

51 Justice Frank Iacobucci, in*Egan v. Canada,* Supreme Court of Canada (1995) 2 S.C.R., 616.

52 Memorandum Opinion and Order on Cross Motions for Summary Judgment, no. 04–2 04964 4 SEA, in *Andersen v. King County,* Superior Court of the State of Washington for King County (Seattle, August 4, 2004), pp. 19–20.

Chapter 8 ▪ Determining Marriage's Future

1 Interview in *Lesbian and Gay Marriage: Public Commitments, Private Ceremonies,* ed. Suzanne Sherman (Philadelphia: Temple University Press, 1992), p. 55.

2 "A Wedding Sermon from a Prison Cell, May 1943," in Dietrich Bonhoeffer, *Letters and Papers from Prison* (New York: Collier, 1972), p. 43.

3 Thomas Hobbes, *Leviathan* (1651; New York: Penguin Books, 1985), p. 186. See also the discussion of Hobbes in Chapter Two of this book, pp. 25–26.

4 Mary Douglas, *How Institutions Think* (Syracuse, N.Y.: Syracuse University Press, 1986), pp. ix, 8.

5 Ibid., p. 55.

6 Ibid.

7 Ibid., pp. 126, 128.

8 Sources:

Percent of Adults Married: Percent of persons age 18 and older who are married. U.S. Bureau of the Census, Current Population Reports, Series P–20, no. 450, *Marital Status and Living Arrangements: March 1990* (1991), p. 17; Series P–20, no. 461, *Marital Status and Living Arrangements: March 1991* (1992), p. 2; U.S. Bureau of the Census, Statistical Abstract of the United States: 2004–2005, Section 1, Population, Table 51, *Marital Status of the Population by Sex, Race, and Hispanic Origin: 1990 to 2003* (2005), p. 49.

Percent of First Marriages Intact: For 1970–1990, percent of ever-married women ages 15–65 still in first marriage. For 2000, percent of ever-married women ages 15–69 still in first marriage. (2001 datum shown for 2000). U.S. Bureau of the Census, Current Population Reports, Series P–20, no. 239, *Marriage, Divorce, and Remarriage by Year of Birth, June 1971* (1972); U.S. Bureau of the Census, June Supplement to the 1980 and 1990 Current Population Surveys, unpublished tabulations; U.S. Bureau of the Census, Current Population Reports, Series P–70, no. 97, *Number, Timing, and Duration of Marriages and Divorces: 2001* (2005), p. 7.

Percent of Births to Married Parents: For 1970, percent of births to married women ages 10–49. For 1980–2000, percent of all births to married mothers. National Center for Health Statistics, Vital Statistics of the United States, *Monthly Vital Statistics Report of Final Natality Statistics* (1970); National Vital Statistics Reports, vol. 52, no. 10, *Births: Final Data for 2002* (2003), p. 10.

Percent of Children Living with Own Married Parents: Percent of children under 18 who live with their two married biological parents. U.S. Bureau of the Census, 1970 Census of the Population, vol. 2, 4B, *Persons by Family Characteristics* (1973), Tables 1 and 8 and unpublished tabulations; Current Population Reports, Series P–20, no. 365, *Marital Status and Living Arrangements: March 1980* (1981); Current

Population Reports, Series P–20, *Marriage, Divorce, and Remarriage in the 1990s* (1992), pp. 11–12; Current Population Reports, Series P–70, no. 104, *Living Arrangements of Children: 2001* (2005), p. 3.

Percent of Children Living with Two Married Parents: Percent of children under age 18 who live with two married parents, regardless of whether the parents are biological or not. U.S. Bureau of the Census, Current Population Reports, Series P–20, no. 450, *Marital Status and Living Arrangements: March 1990* (1991), p. 5; Census 2000 Special Reports, no. 14, *Children and the Households They Live In: 2001* (2004), p. 15.

This index is based on a family strength index that I proposed and principally developed for a 1993 report that I co-authored: See National Commission on America's Urban Families, *Families First* (Washington, D.C.: U.S. Government Printing Office, 1993), p. 63. Regarding the further development of the index, I am grateful to my Institute for American Values colleague Alex Roberts for research assistance.

[9] Norval D. Glenn, *Courtship and Marital Choice: Why They Are Important and What We Need to Learn about Them,* Council on Families Working Paper no. 70 (New York: Institute for American Values, 1999), pp. 14, 33; David Popenoe and Barbara Dafoe Whitehead, *The State of Our Unions 2005* (Piscataway, N.J.: The National Marriage Project of Rutgers University, July 2005), pp. 16–18.

[10] Popenoe and Whitehead, *The State of Our Unions 2005.*

[11] Matthew D. Bramlett and William D. Mosher, *Cohabitation, Marriage, Divorce, and Remarriage in the United States,* National Center for Health Statistics, Vital and Health Statisitcs, Series 23, no. 22 (Washington, D.C.: U.S. Government Printing Office, July 2002), Tables 21, 41; Ross M. Kreider, *Number, Timing, and Duration of Marriages and Divorces: 2001,* U.S. Census Bureau, Current Population Reports P70–97 (Washington, D.C.: U.S. Government Printing Office, February 2005), Table 3.

[12] This body of research has been discussed throughout this book and was summarized in 2005 by an interdisciplinary (and politically and philosophically diverse) team of family scholars. See W. Bradford Wilcox et al., *Why Marriage Matters: Twenty-six Conclusions from the Social Sciences* (New York: Institute for American Values, 2005). In his poem "In Memory of W. B. Yeats," W. H. Auden writes: "What instruments we have agree / The day of his death was a dark cold day."

[13] Wilcox et al., *Why Marriage Matters,* pp. 14, 22, 29, 32; Paul R. Amato, "The Impact of Family Formation Change on the Cognitive, Social,

and Emotional Well-Being of the Next Generation," *The Future of Children* 15, no. 2 (Fall 2005), pp. 80–81; Paul R. Amato and Alan Booth, *A Generation at Risk: Growing Up in an Era of Family Upheaval* (Cambridge, Mass.: Harvard University Press, 1997), pp. 159, 175, 201–2; Frank F. Furstenberg Jr., "History and Current Status of Divorce in the United States," *The Future of Children* 4, no. 1 (Spring 1994), p. 37; James H. Bray et al., *Longitudinal Changes in Stepfamilies: Impact on Children's Adjustment* (Washington, D.C.: American Psychological Association, August 1992).

14 An estimated 35.7 percent of all U.S. births were to unmarried women in 2004. See Brady E. Hamilton et al., *Preliminary Births for 2004*, Health E-Stats (Hyattsville, Md.: National Center for Health Statistics, October 28, 2005), Table 1.

15 Joshua R. Goldstein, "The Leveling of Divorce in the United States," *Demography* 36, no. 3 (August 1999), pp. 409–14; Popenoe and Whitehead, *The State of Our Unions: 2005*, p. 19. David Blankenhorn, "Knowing Full Well," *Propositions* 9 (New York: Institute for American Values, Summer 2000), pp. 4–5.

16 Donald Sensing, "Save Marriage? It's Too Late," *Wall Street Journal*, March 15, 2004; Andrew Sullivan, "The Daily Dish," *AndrewSullivan.com*, posted March 17, 2004; Sullivan, "We Are All Sodomites Now," *New Republic*, March 26, 2003. I discuss these two articles in Chapter Six, under marriage idea number 15 ("Marriage has become much weaker—and that's a reason for gay marriage.").

17 *The Marriage Movement: A Statement of Principles* (New York: Institute for American Values, 2000); *What Next for the Marriage Movement?* (New York: Institute for American Values, 2004).

18 International Social Survey Programme, *Family and Changing Gender Roles III: 2002*, Codebook, ZA Study 3880 (Cologne: Zentralarchiv für Empirische Sozialforschung, September 2004), pp. 26–27.

19 Ibid., pp. 30–31.

20 Maybe the problem with this question is the word "can." Of course it is *possible* for one parent alone to raise a child just as well as, or better than, two parents together—just as it is possible for a person with one arm to become a professional baseball player (that has actually happened!), or for one bricklayer to lay as many bricks in an hour as two bricklayers working together. Such highly unusual things *can* happen. But surely that is not the main issue that the questioners were exploring. They did not want to know whether, in the opinion of the respondent, it is theoretically possible for a certain thing to happen. Instead, they wanted to know whether, in the opinion of the respondent, a

certain thing *usually* or *commonly* happens—whether, all else being equal, a certain thing *tends* to happen more often than not.

Attention ISSP question team: Please reconsider the wording of this important question! How about something like this: To what extent do you agree or disagree that "One parent usually brings up a child as well as two parents together." I'd predict that this small change in wording would produce *major* changes in the distribution of the resulting answers.

By way of contrast, consider a finding from a survey of a nationally representative sample of U.S. adults conducted by Norval Glenn of the University of Texas in late 2003 and early 2004 and published in 2005 by the National Fatherhood Initiative. About 89 percent of respondents agreed (with 36 percent agreeing strongly) that "All things being equal, it is better for children to be raised in a household that has a married mother and father." See Norval D. Glenn, *With This Ring . . . : A National Survey on Marriage in America* (Gaithersburg, Md.: National Fatherhood Initiative, 2005), p. 30.

21 International Social Survey Programme, *Family and Changing Gender Roles III: 2002*, pp. 32–33.

22 Ibid., pp. 34, 35.

23 Ibid., pp. 38–39. In the 2002 ISSP survey, the former East Germany and the former West Germany were polled separately.

24 Glenn, *With This Ring*, p. 29.

25 International Social Survey Programme, *Family and Changing Gender Roles II: 1994*, Codebook, ZA Study 2620 (Cologne: Zentralarchiv für Empirische Sozialforschung, March 1997), p. 19.

26 Glenn, *With This Ring*, p. 30.

27 The 2005 survey by Norval Glenn for the National Fatherhood Initiative actully puts this figure higher than two-thirds; this survey finds that about 74 percent of U.S. adults, or roughly three of every four, agree (and 26 percent disagree) that "Couples who have children together ought to be married." See Glenn, *With This Ring*, p. 29.

28 See n. 20 above.

29 Stanley Kurtz has recently ignited an intense debate about whether and to what degree same-sex marriage is contributing to an alleged weakening of marriage in Scandinavia. See Stanley Kurtz, "The End of Marriage in Scandinavia," *Weekly Standard*, February 2, 2004; Kurtz, "Slipping toward Scandinavia," *National Review Online*, February 2, 2004; Kurtz, "Unhealthy Half Truths," *National Review Online*, May 25, 2004; Kurtz, "Going Dutch?" *Weekly Standard*, May 31, 2004; Kurtz, "No Explanation," *National Review Online*, June 4, 2004; Kurtz, "Dutch

Debate," *National Review Online*, July 21, 2004; Kurtz, "Here Come the Brides," *Weekly Standard*, December 26, 2005; Kurtz, "Fanatical Swedish Feminists," *National Review Online*, February 22, 2006; Kurtz, "Standing Out," *National Review Online*, February 23, 2006; Kurtz, "No Nordic Bliss," *National Review Online*, February 28, 2006; M. V. Lee Badgett, "Will Providing Marriage Rights to Same-Sex Couples Undermine Heterosexual Marriage?" Discussion Paper, Council on Contemporary Families, New York, July 2004; William N. Eskridge, Darren R. Spedale, and Hans Ytterberg, "Nordic Bliss? Scandinavian Registered Partnerships and the Same-Sex Marriage Debate," *Issues in Legal Scholarship*, Article 4, Symposium on Single-Sex Marriage, Berkeley Electronic Press, 2004.

30 Urie Bronfenbrenner, "Discovering What Families Do," in David Blankenhorn, Steven Bayme, and Jean Bethke Elshtain, *Rebuilding the Nest: A New Commitment to the American Family* (Milwaukee: Family Service America, 1990), p. 34.

31 Source for Tables 2–6: International Social Survey Programme, *Family and Changing Gender Roles III: 2002* (see n. 18 above).

These tables suffer from several limitations, of which two seem most important. First, the number of countries surveyed is limited to 34, and this group of 34 is not representative of the nations of the world. Second, among those of the 34 countries currently recognizing same-sex marriage or same-sex civil unions either nationally or in one or more localities, these tables and the accompanying analysis do not take into account how these legal reforms were adopted—for example, either legislatively, in which case significant public support for the reform might logically be presumed, or judicially, in which case significant public support cannot be presumed.

For his valuable work in preparing Tables 2–6, I am grateful to my colleague Alex Roberts. I am also grateful to Norval Glenn for his advice and assistance.

32 Data from 1996.

33 Data from 1997.

34 Data from 1996.

35 Data from 1995.

36 Andrew J. Cherlin, "The Deinstitutionalization of American Marriage," *Journal of Marriage and the Family* 66 (November 2004), pp. 857–58.

37 Stephanie Coontz, "For Better, For Worse: Marriage Means Something Different Now," *Washington Post*, May 1, 2005. Discussing a number of trends contributing to the deinstitutionalization of marriage, Coontz

writes: "We may personally like or dislike these changes. We may wish to keep some and get rid of others. But there is a certain inevitability to almost all of them."

[38] Data from 1997.

[39] Data from 1997.

[40] Data from 1996.

[41] Data from 1996.

[42] Data from 2003.

[43] Data from 2003.

[44] Data from 1996.

[45] Source: Recent waves of the World Values Surveys (available at www.worldvaluessurvey.com). Unless otherwise noted, country data presented in Tables 7–11 are from wave four, 1999–2001.

[46] Stephanie Coontz, *The Way We Never Were: American Families and the Nostalgia Trap* (New York: Basic Books, 1992); Coontz, *The Way We Really Are: Coming to Terms with America's Changing Families* (New York: Basic Books, 1997); Coontz, *Marriage, a History: From Obedience to Intimacy, or How Love Conquered Marriage* (New York: Viking, 2005). See also Coontz, *The Social Origins of Private Life* (New York: Verso, 1988).

[47] Coontz, "For Better, For Worse."

[48] Blankenhorn, "Knowing Full Well"; Goldstein, "The Leveling of Divorce in the United States."

[49] Coontz, "For Better, For Worse."

[50] Adam Thomas and Isabel Sawhill, "For Love *and* Money? The Impact of Family Structure on Family Income," *The Future of Children* 15, no. 2 (Fall 2005), p. 65.

[51] Isabel V. Sawhill, "The Behavioral Aspects of Poverty," *Public Interest*, no. 153 (Fall 2003), p. 86.

[52] "Effect of Family Structure on Child Poverty and Income Inequality," *The Urban Institute Policy and Research Report* (Summer–Fall 1996), reporting on Robert I. Lerman, "The Impact of Changing U.S. Family Structure on Child Poverty and Income Inequality," *Economica* 63, no. 250 (1996), pp. S119–139.

Norval Glenn of the University of Texas writes: "The proposition that the increase in single parenthood has contributed substantially to family poverty is supported by evidence from a variety of kinds of studies, including sophisticated causal modeling. This evidence is about as nearly conclusive as the support for any social science evidence ever is." Norval D. Glenn, letter to the editor, *New York Times*, November 6, 1997 (edited version published November 11).

[53] Robert I. Lerman, "Married and Unmarried Parenthood and Economic Well-Being: A Dynamic Analysis of a Recent Cohort," Urban Institute Report, Washington, D.C., 2002; Lerman, "Impacts of Marital Status and Parental Presence on the Material Hardship of Families with Children," Urban Institute Report, Washington, D.C., 2002. Regarding the methodological issues of controls and selection effects specifically in relationship to this issue, see Commission on Children at Risk, *Hardwired to Connect: The New Scientific Case for Authoritative Communities* (New York: Institute for American Values, 2003), pp. 42, 46, 64 (n. 166), 66 (n. 182).

[54] Paul R. Amato, "The Impact of Family Formation Change on the Cognitive, Social, and Emotional Well-Being of the Next Generation," *The Future of Children* 15, no. 2 (Fall 2005), p. 89.

[55] Vaclav Havel, *Disturbing the Peace* (New York: Vintage Books, 1991), p. 181.

[56] *What Next for the Marriage Movement?* (New York: Institute for American Values, 2004).

Appendix

[1] F. J. Cole, *Early Theories of Sexual Generation* (Oxford, U.K.: Oxford University Press, 1930), pp. 37–38.

[2] Ibid., p. 53.

[3] Ibid., pp. 201–2, 207–8.

[4] For instance, see Gerda Lerner, *The Creation of Patriarchy* (New York: Oxford University Press, 1986), pp. 125–31; Carol Delaney, *The Seed and the Soil: Gender and Cosmology in Turkish Village Society* (Berkeley: University of California Press, 1991); and Nancy Tuana, "The Weaker Seed: The Sexist Bias of Reproductive Theory," *Hypatia* 3, no. 1 (1988), pp. 35–59.

[5] See Torben Monberg, "Fathers Were Not Genitors," *Man*, n.s. 10, no. 1 (March 1975), pp. 34–40.

[6] See David B. Eyde, "Sexuality and Garden Ritual in the Trobriands and Tikopia: Tudava Meets the Atua I Kafika," *Mankind* 14, no. 1 (August 1983), pp. 66–67.

[7] See Brenda Johnson Clay, *Pinikindu: Maternal Nurture, Paternal Substance* (Chicago: University of Chicago Press, 1977), p. 31.

[8] See Erik G. Schwimmer, *Man*, n.s. 4, no. 1 (March 1969), pp. 132–33.

[9] See M. J. Meggitt, *The Lineage System of the Mae-Enga of New Guinea* (Edinburgh: Oliver & Boyd, 1965), pp. 163–65, 168, 180, 217. See also, more generally, R. M. Glasse and M. J. Meggitt, eds., *Pigs, Pearlshells, and Women: Marriage in the New Guinea Highlands* (Englewood Cliffs, N.J.: Prentice-Hall, 1969).

[10] See Fitz John Porter Poole, "Symbols of Substance: Bimin-Kuskusmin Models of Procreation, Death, and Personhood," *Mankind* 14, no. 3 (April 1984), pp. 191–216, quotation at 194.

[11] See E. R. Leach, *Political Systems of Highland Burma: A Study of Kachin Social Structure* (Cambridge, Mass.: Harvard University Press, 1954), pp. 73–75, 166; and Leach, *Rethinking Anthropology* (London: Athlone Press, 1961), pp. 14, 18.

[12] See "Heredity and Gestation as the Azande See Them" (1932), in E. E. Evans-Pritchard, *Social Anthropology and Other Essays* (New York: Free Press of Glencoe, 1962), pp. 243, 247–48.

[13] See Hilda Kuper, "Kinship among the Swazi," in *African Systems of Kinship and Marriage*, ed. A. R. Radcliffe-Brown and Daryll Forde (London: Oxford University Press, 1950), pp. 88–89. More generally, regarding so-called "ghost marriages," through which a deceased man who was childless during his lifetime is viewed as the legal father of a child born to a living couple, see *Notes and Queries on Anthropology*, 6th ed. (London: Routledge & Keegan Paul, 1951), pp. 118–19.

[14] See David M. Schneider, "Introduction: The Distinctive Features of Matrilineal Descent Groups," in *Matrilineal Kinship*, ed. David M. Schneider and Kathleen Gough (Berkeley: University of California Press, 1961), pp. 1–29.

[15] See Nancy E. Levine and Joan B. Silk, "When Polyandry Fails," *Current Anthropology* 38, no. 3 (June 1997), pp. 375–98; L. R. Hiatt, "Polyandry in Sri Lanka: A Test Case for Parental Investment Theory," *Man*, n.s. 15, no. 4 (December 1980), pp. 583–602; Melvyn C. Goldstein, "When Brothers Share a Wife," *Natural History* 3 (1987), pp. 39–48; Goldstein, "Pahari and Tibetan Polyandry Revisited," *Ethnology* 17, no. 3 (July 1978), pp. 325–37; Goldstein, "Stratification, Polyandry, and Family Structure in Central Tibet," *Southwest Journal of Anthropology* 27, no. 1 (Spring 1971), pp. 64–74; Bronislaw Malinowski, *Sex, Culture, and Myth* (New York: Harcourt, Brace & World, 1962), pp. 30–31; Prince Peter of Greece and Denmark, "Polyandry and the Kinship Group," *Man* 55 (December 1955), pp. 179–81. For an example of the (even rarer) case of a society practicing nonfraternal polyandry, see Keith F. Ottersbein, "Marquesan Polyandry," *Marriage and Family Living* 25, no. 2 (May 1963), pp. 155–59.

[16] Drucilla Cornell, "Fatherhood and Its Discontents: Men, Patriarchy, and Freedom," in *Lost Fathers: The Politics of Fatherlessness in America*, ed. Cynthia Daniels (New York: St. Martin's Press, 1998), p. 199; and Cornell, "The Public Supports of Love," in *Just Marriage*, ed. Mary

Lyndon Shanley (New York: Oxford University Press, 2004), pp. 84–85.

[17] See Elizabeth F. Emens, "Just Monogamy?" in *Just Marriage*, ed. Shanley, p. 79. See also Emens, "Monogamy's Law: Compulsory Monogamy and Polyamory's Existence," *Review of Law and Social Change* 29, no. 2 (2004), pp. 287–376. The *Review of Law and Social Change*, published by New York University, is the same journal in which appeared, ten years earlier (1994), Evan Wolfson's seminal article on gay marriage, "Crossing the Threshold."

[18] See "Whole Lotta Love: Polyamorists Go beyond Monogamy," *Milwaukee Journal Sentinel*, September 13, 2004; Jennifer Vanasco, "Are We Not Polyamorists?" *Southern Voice*, April 29, 2005; Daphne Merkin, "Boy Meets Girl, Then More Girls," *Slate*, posted March 10, 2006; "Study Finds Persistent Religious Inequality," *National Catholic Reporter*, May 6, 2005; Andrew Herrman, "Hers, Hers, His and Hers," *Chicago Sun-Times*, April 2, 2006; Stanley Kurtz, "Dissolving Marriage," *National Review Online*, February 3, 2006; and Kurtz, "Here Come the Brides," *Weekly Standard*, December 26, 2005.

[19] E. R. Leach, *Rethinking Anthropology* (London: Athlone Press, 1961).

[20] See Robin Fox, *Kinship and Marriage: An Anthropological Perspective* (Baltimore: Penguin Books, 1967), pp. 10, 27.

[21] See Rodney Needham, *Remarks and Inventions: Skeptical Essays about Kinship* (London: Tavistock Publications, 1974), pp. 39–42.

[22] See Linda Stone, "Introduction: Theoretical Implications of New Directions in Anthropological Kinship," in *New Directions in Anthropological Kinship*, ed. Stone (Lanham, Md.: Rowman & Littlefield, 2001), pp. 2, 8; Nigel Rapport and Joanna Overing, *Social and Cultural Anthropology: The Key Concepts* (London: Routledge, 2000), p. 217. For a fascinating insider's look at the state of mid-twentieth-century social anthropology, especially in Britain, with its strong focus on marriage and kinship, see a highly critical article by George Murdock and a spirited response by Raymond Firth: George Peter Murdock, "British Social Anthropology," *American Anthropologist*, n.s. 53, no. 4 (October–December 1951), pp. 465–73; and Raymond Firth, "Contemporary British Social Anthropology," same issue, pp. 474–89. See also E. E. Evans-Pritchard, "Social Anthropology," in *Social Anthropology and Other Essays* (New York: Free Press of Glencoe, 1962), pp. 1–191. Another valuable exposition and critique of mid-twentieth-century British social anthropology, which includes an extended discussion of Malinowski's role and influence, is I. C. Jarvie, *The Revolution in Anthropology* (Chicago: Henry Regnery Co., 1969).

[23] For a survey of this recent intellectual history, see Michael G. Peletz, "Kinship Studies in Late Twentieth-Century Anthropology," *Annual Review of Anthropology* 24 (1995), pp. 343–72. Perhaps the single most important contribution to the transformation of ideas that I am describing is David M. Schneider, *A Critique of the Study of Kinship* (Ann Arbor: University of Michigan Press, 1984).

[24] For an overview of sociologists' treatment of marriage in recent decades, see Barbara Dafoe Whitehead, *The Experts' Story of Marriage,* Working Paper 14 (New York: Institute for American Values, 1992); Dan Cere, *The Experts' Story of Courtship* (New York: Institute for American Values, 2000); David Blankenhorn, "The Shift: 1987–1997," *Propositions 1* (Spring 1998), pp. 4–6; and Blankenhorn, "The Shift (cont.)," *Propositions 3* (Winter 1999), pp. 4–8. Regarding the beginning of a comeback for kinship studies and marriage in the field of anthropology—one largely led by feminist scholars—see Linda Stone, *Kinship and Gender: An Introduction* (Boulder, Col.: Westview Press, 1997); and Stone, *New Directions in Anthropological Kinship* (Lanham, Md.: Rowman & Littlefield, 2001).

Index